With Angel's Wings

by Stephanie A. Collins

Second Edition, March 2016
First Edition, October 2013

Edited by Donna J. Erickson

Cover Design: Nick Trahan
www.studiowalljump.com

Cover Design Concept: Sue Petersen
www.sspetersen.com

Format: Charlie Davis, Northfield, MA
www.DavisImages.com

Printed in the United States of America

ISBN 978-0-578-17975-9
Library of Congress Control Number: 2013945932

Dedication

This is dedicated to my Pierre Jon Luke, my Muy Macho, my McHaggis...my hon. Words can't express the depths of my gratitude for your presence in my life. You amaze me every day. You make me a better person. You have gifted me with a life of laughter and inspired my faith in love. You've made this book possible; you've made me possible. Everyone should be as lucky and have someone as wonderful as you in his or her life. Thank you, hon. I love you.

Acknowledgements

Thank you to Aunt Cathy, who taught me not only how to write well, but also that writing can be enjoyable. Thank you to Doug Gray for telling me time and again (when I was a child), "Just tell me the time, Stephanie. I don't need to know how the watch was made."

I humbly offer a huge thanks to Donna Erickson for reminding me of that as an adult. Donna, your editing makes me so much more proud of this story, which I needed to share. Your wise guidance, through the editing and publishing process, has been invaluable. Thank you for taking a chance with me as a new author. I was so fortunate for the opportunity to be taken under the wing of A Flair For Writing–Publishing Services. Thank you to production manager/head illustrator, Charlie Davis, and designer, Sue Petersen. I very much appreciate your contributions to the design and production of this book.

A heartfelt thank you also goes out to Nick Trahan for the creation of our beautiful cover, wonderful website, and fabulous Facebook page. Thank you to Jane Weber, Fay Houde, Abbie Richerzhagen, Rich Collins, and Ramina Dehkhoda-Steele for your encouragement and words of advice throughout the writing process.

Finally, I'd like to thank every (renamed) character in this book--yes, every character. You all played a role in leading me to this wonderful life I now share with my beautiful family and dear friends. I would not want to change any part of it, due to the fear of altering the miraculous end product. Thank you all.

Table of Contents

Prologue

When I was carrying my first child, experienced parents never hesitated to offer their advice and predictions. For instance, I repeatedly heard that once the baby came, I should expect much less time to myself. That seemed reasonable. However, weeks after my daughter was born, I could be found balled up on my bed, crying in a state of panic, due to the realization that less time to myself didn't mean fewer occasions to paint my nails as I had originally interpreted. It meant not being able to pee when I had to.

I became angry with those who had offered their words of wisdom in the form of advice. They hadn't prepared me at all! I soon forgave them when I recognized that a non-parent couldn't fully understand what it means to be a parent. Then I was suddenly responsible for two children with special needs and was immediately ushered into yet another world that I had not been prepared for. I was fascinated, petrified, proud, ashamed, angry, and remorseful. As I was swept into a whirlwind of conflicting sensations, they left me scrambling to hold on for the emotional journey.

For therapeutic purposes, I began writing about my experiences. In time, I decided to share my journey. I consider it my way of paying it forward, in regard to all of the wonderful people who helped me through some very turbulent times. My hope is that writing with my heart on my sleeve will perhaps offer some help, hope, or, at least, some peace of mind to someone else who finds him or herself in similar circumstances.

Although fictional names technically make this a work of fiction, this is actually a true story. It is my story. These events took place in the mid 1990s. An epilogue is available at www.withangelswings.net—along with pictures that correlate with each of the chapters, a few deleted scenes, some bonus features, and an Ask The Author forum. I hope you enjoy my labor of love.

Chapter I

Negotiations & Love Songs

Sixteen-year-old Laura was feeling rather bored while skating at a chilly Remick Park rink in her small, relatively new hometown of Littleton, New Hampshire. On that particular Saturday evening in January, she was nearly ready to head back home when she met fourteen-year-old Kevin. She was generally annoyed with him, but having nothing else to do and still feeling somewhat like an outsider, she didn't turn him away when he continually skated over to her. He boasted about his abilities as a hockey player and raced some other boys around the rink, as if to validate his claims. His impressive skating and nice butt almost made up for the fact that he was ridiculously mouthy and tenacious.

Laura knew she should skate away—his young age, alone, was bad enough. After all, she was struggling on the social food chain, and hanging out with an annoying freshman wouldn't help at all. However, she still skated with him...and accepted his calls... and went to watch his hockey games. Little did Kevin know at the time, but some key allies made his quest for Laura's attention considerably easier that fateful first night on the ice. The existence of her chaotic home life, low self-esteem, and (most powerful of all) her loneliness were all issues in Kevin's favor.

Laura's love life had officially begun, but it certainly wasn't the love life she had envisioned for herself. She never felt quite the way she imagined she would, but feeling unworthy of experiencing

1

anything better, she attempted to make the best of it. She figured if she just worked hard enough on her relationship with Kevin, everything would be fine.

All too soon the couple graduated to the next level of involvement. Sadly, the experience clearly illustrated that the love, romance, and emotion, which every girl hopes to associate with her first sexual encounter, was lacking.

"Okay, if it will shut you up, then *yes*, you *can*, but if you get me pregnant, you're _dead_," Laura had said with an exasperated sigh.

Kevin had quickly and excitedly assured her. "Of course not; I know what I'm doing." That forty-five-second encounter certainly did not shut him up. In fact, that sexual occurrence was merely the beginning of a nine-year, bittersweet chapter of their lives.

Laura and Kevin were married on January first in the living room of Laura's grandmother, who happened to be a justice of the peace. Kevin was nineteen and training in Tennessee as a marine. Laura was twenty, and enrolled as a third-year psychology major at Plymouth State College. Residing 1,200 miles apart wasn't ideal, but Kevin was attracted to the higher pay offered to married marines, and Laura was attracted to the romantic notion of marrying her high-school sweetheart, making her the only married person in her dorm.

In June, after Kevin had finished training, the couple planned a second, more formal wedding ceremony. That celebration took place at Laura's family camp on Neal's Pond in Lunenburg, Vermont. The day was gorgeous, the food was delicious, and she loved spending time with friends and family. Everything was just as Laura had dreamed a wedding day should be—with the glaring exception of Kevin getting completely wasted and passing out on their wedding night.

Within days they were driving west to Kevin's new station in Tustin, California, and they were fighting within three states. By the time they had reached Pennsylvania, Kevin had blown up. "It's all your fault! You manipulated me into marrying you. You're the older, more mature one; you should have known that we shouldn't have gotten married!" he yelled. At that point, Laura knew she should have turned back and headed home, but she feared admitting her mistake to everyone she had just faced at the wedding. She also feared being alone and the permanent scar of *divorced* in her records. She vowed to do whatever was necessary to make the marriage work.

The reality of the marital workload consumed Laura. During the early honeymoon months of their stay in California, divorce had been discussed a disturbing number of times (often very loudly). Living within the same time zone put a definite strain on the relationship. Laura still feared facing the family with news of her failed marriage. Kevin feared the cost of divorce. In addition, Laura's father, Steve, had provided some words of advice on her wedding day: "If you ever think about throwing in the towel on the marriage," he said, "give it six more months, and see if things improve with time." Steve's guidance and the couple's fears held the marriage together by the thinnest of threads.

A festive holiday season offered Laura hope that a happier marriage was within reach. However, just days after the New Year, she discovered she was pregnant. That news changed everything; the subject of having children had been one of the most contentious for the couple. Laura wanted nothing more than to start a family, but Kevin's position appeared more conflicted. He didn't like, didn't have the patience for, and didn't want anything to do with having kids, but he never used protection. Laura chose to focus on his actions, not his words. Subsequently, her dream— and his nightmare—had come true.

Within hours of Laura receiving the news, Kevin arrived home for lunch. As he entered their small apartment, he was sputtering some complaints about the military. Laura tried to wait patiently, but she couldn't seem to wipe the smile off her face or tone down the glow in her cheeks. When he finally finished, she said, "Well, I have some news."

"You're pregnant, aren't you?" he asked, his voice filled with tension and bitterness.

Ignoring his tone, Laura was unable to contain her overflowing excitement any longer. "HOW did you KNOW?"

"You just looked like you were going to say that...MAN, I can't believe it," Kevin said, slowly shaking his head. He sighed heavily and leaned against the doorframe—definitely not excited.

Laura confronted him. "You want me to abort, don't you?"

"I'm not going to say anything," he said. Then he turned, and with an abrupt slam of the door, he left for work.

Laura felt she needed to demonstrate that her pregnancy and the birth of a child would not be the inconvenience he was envisioning. She was desperate to prevent Kevin from rushing into getting a vasectomy. But her attempts were proving to be much more difficult than she had anticipated.

The pregnancy was not problem-free. Laura had to fight through morning sickness and learn to accept stretch marks. Even worse, for the final three months of her pregnancy, the upper portion of her large intestines was pinched, causing excruciating pain. Most distressing, however, were Kevin's complaints that Laura was no longer attractive to him because she was pregnant. This belief further diminished a sex life that had already left him unsatisfied.

Kevin began spending a lot of time with a woman who lived in their apartment complex, saying he "could *really* talk to her," that she "understood him," and she was "helping him" come to terms with the impending birth. Laura knew he was probably cheating on her, but a part of her actually felt thankful. That realization reduced some of the pressure to have sex and...at least he hadn't left her.

• •

Emily Alexandra was born on September ninth, weighing in at 8 lb, 2 oz and measuring 21¾ inches. Laura was in love. However, Emily was unfortunately determined to exhibit every frustrating element regarding life with an infant. She hated the car seat and screamed the entire way home from the hospital. She had her days and nights mixed up. When she was awake, she was HUNGRY, so she'd nurse for five minutes but then pull away. Ten minutes later, she was HUNGRY again. Kevin wasn't amused by any of this. Panicked by his frustration, Laura flew back to New Hampshire with Emily for a two-week visit. But running away didn't solve any problems. By then, Emily had become colicky. Upon their return to California, she was sleeping a little better, but she was screaming nearly all of her waking moments. Kevin had just been somewhat perturbed with parenthood before Laura had left. He was downright disgusted with it once they returned.

Laura was not immune to frustrations either and had plunged from feeling in love to feeling distraught. She cherished her daughter at a level she had never known was possible, but the constant crying was driving her to her breaking point. At times she wanted to throw that loud, ungrateful, constantly complaining little being across the room. She felt incredibly guilty about the dark thoughts she was having. Luckily, the colic finally subsided about two months after it had begun. Unluckily, a new challenge replaced it–chronic ear infections. During her first year, Emily averaged two infections per month. Laura eventually requested inserting tubes in her ears, but Emily's pediatrician kept holding off. Watching her baby girl endure such pain was maddening, while knowing the minor surgical procedure could easily solve the problem.

Meanwhile, Kevin was due to head out to sea for six months, so Laura returned to New Hampshire while he was away. She first stayed at Steve's house in Littleton, but Steve's third wife, Janet, and her two kids, Daniel (eighteen) and Wendy (nine) had arrived at the same time. After a few months of too little space and too much chaos, Laura gladly accepted an offer from friends of the family, Tom and Susan, for temporary lodging at their home in Belmont, New Hampshire.

Tom and Susan served as a wonderful example of a couple who knew how to make a marriage work. Laura hungered to learn all of their tricks. Despite taking note of a few key ingredients, such as communication and a sense of humor, Laura struggled to translate lessons learned from Tom and Susan into success for her own marriage. She was frustrated to discover, for the first time in their relationship, that distance didn't solve all strife.

Laura was stressed with challenges she had never faced before, and she resented Kevin for not being there—neither physically nor emotionally—to help her.

Laura returned to Plymouth State College to finish the required course work for her psychology degree. The large class load she had taken on was made all the more grueling by the additional demands of simultaneously solo-parenting a toddler. Emily wasn't making that easy on Laura, either. Ear infections continued regularly, she had developed asthma and an allergy to penicillin, and had even spent four days hospitalized for pneumonia after her first birthday.

The couple reunited after nearly a year of separation, and Laura worried about the trip back west. Emily required a lot of patience, and Kevin admittedly had none. *What will he do when she screams and protests at bedtime? How will he react when she won't pick up her toys? What will he say when she insists on an answer after posing a question clearly asked in a language other than English? Emily's a whole different person now at one-and-a-half than she was at eight months when we left California,* Laura thought. As much as Laura wanted Kevin and Emily to have a good relationship, she struggled to believe it could happen.

Living without Kevin for such a long time helped Laura gain more independence. She dreaded going back to the arguments and compromises associated with being together; the situation had been hard enough while apart. She felt a sense of emptiness when she thought of her husband, but ultimately she decided to try reconciling again, for Emily's sake.

Almost immediately, Laura regretted her decision to return to California. In their marriage of thirty months, they had only spent fourteen months living together, twelve of them categorized as the "six-month trial periods" Laura's father had prescribed. After only one week back together, they decided a third trial period was necessary.

Laura began visiting a counselor weekly. She certainly didn't want to have Emily become the child of divorced parents—

without first attempting to do everything possible to avoid it from happening. The counseling proved helpful to Laura, but it didn't do much for the marriage. She was about to give up on it when Kevin shocked her by suggesting they try to have another baby. A voice within screamed at Laura, warning her that his idea was wrong on every level. She knew Kevin didn't *really* want another child; he just wanted the sex that was involved. But her voice of reason was drowned out, as Laura's head began swimming with visions of a new baby in her arms and Emily, a proud big sister, standing nearby. She was filled with excitement at the thought of her family (a loose interpretation of the word) becoming a family of four.

Chapter II

A New Beginning

Laura felt pleasantly surprised and relieved, as she began to notice her marriage pulling together. Midway through her pregnancy, she was preparing for her trip back to New Hampshire with Emily. At the same time, Kevin would be returning to sea, yet the sense of relief that usually accompanied their separations was absent. At this point, they lived a relatively comfortable life on base, which she would actually miss.

After her fourth wedding anniversary, Laura headed back east with Emily that June. They stayed with Laura's grandparents at the family camp in Vermont. Laura could not have felt more at ease during those last two months of her pregnancy. Along with the thrill of a new baby kicking and rolling around inside of her, Emily was entertaining her with her own excitement from experiencing the wonders of life at the lake. And Laura's grandparents were there to comfort her and keep her grounded. She also had occasional visits to look forward to—from her sister, Jennifer, and her new stepbrother, Daniel.

Life was good. Laura spent many evenings lazily sitting on the edge of the dock with her feet dangling in the water, soaking up the setting sun as its rays painted a sparkling portrait on the lake. Emily was often splashing nearby in search of unsuspecting minnows. Laura looked forward to the occasional night of falling asleep to the hypnotic beat of rain on the tin roof, and she loved waking up to the inspiring call of the loons. In the morning, she would look out of the window to a perfect mirror blanketed by a fine mist where the rippling waters of the lake had been the night before. During the evenings, long card games and dominoes were played at the dining room table with her grandmother and guests who visited, while cool breezes drifted through the screened door off the porch. Laura realized she was a lucky, lucky woman.

When Laura got the final call from Kevin, telling her he was about to board the ship, her mood immediately changed. After months of feeling happy and confident about her approaching parental challenges, her world suddenly crashed. She panicked. If something were to go wrong, Kevin couldn't hop on a plane to be there. Laura felt as if she couldn't breathe, or even stand. Six months of single parenting was far more than she could handle. Laura sat on her grandmother's bed and tried to pull herself together. *Okay,* she thought, *I can do this. Stop bellyaching and just do it. You're a big girl; you put yourself in this situation— deal with it.*

After feeling she was in better control, she headed upstairs to put away some laundry. Daniel and his girlfriend, Kelly, were playing a board game nearby. Unexpectedly, Laura's emotional state weakened, and she broke down. Kelly scooted downstairs, understandably appearing uncomfortable. Laura was disappointed in herself for putting Daniel in a position where he would feel compelled to console her. He had the sweetest, purest, and most innocent heart she had ever come across. Therefore, she knew he'd want to say or do something to make her feel better, but there wasn't anything that could help. She was scared, and she had to get over it on her own. Besides, Daniel was twenty, in college, and like a ten-year-old trapped in a six-foot tall body. What could he possibly know about her situation?

Daniel seemed to read Laura's thoughts. He hugged her and said, "It's okay," as he stroked her back. All Laura needed was permission to let it out, and that's exactly what Daniel had given her. Within minutes she calmed down, and they were able to sit and talk about it.

Laura and Daniel had clicked from the time they had met three years earlier. Weeks after they had met, Daniel had returned to his new home (Laura's dad's house) after work and found Laura sitting silently on the couch. She had been having a horrible day and was wondering how she would survive the rest of it. Other family members had passed through the room, unaware of her inner struggle.

Upon entering the room, Daniel had stopped short. He said, "Are you okay?" Trying desperately not to cry, Laura had shaken her head no. Daniel had had a deeply concerned look on his face. He said, "Go. Do whatever you need to feel better. Don't worry about anything here. Come back when you feel up to it. Don't worry about Em; I'll take care of her. Just go for a drive, or a walk, or something. Take some time for yourself."

Time alone had been exactly what Laura had needed. She hadn't realized it, but somehow, Daniel had. This time, Daniel told Laura how strong she was, and if anyone could succeed at single parenting, she would be the one. Laura didn't believe him and objected with a "what do you know; you're just a kid" attitude. But he didn't allow that to discourage him and answered her doubting remarks with actual examples to back up his claims. Hearing his sincere encouragement lifted Laura's spirits. Once again Daniel had peered into her heart and responded to her needs perfectly. He then reminded her that soon he would be back at college (he was beginning his second year as an art major at Plymouth State), but his dorm was only a short drive away and he'd be back every weekend, if she needed him to help her. He wrapped up their chat. "And Jennifer is still in the area, too. She'll be available to help from time to time. You know, whenever her social life slows down." They shared a good chuckle afterwards; Laura's sister had a social life that *never* slowed down.

• •

About a week before Laura's due date, her mom, Carol, left her home in Kentucky and flew in to help Laura. With the exception of a summer here or there, Laura and her mother had lived apart since she was fourteen. Laura was happy to see her, and the visit was particularly special because her mom had missed Emily's birth.

Hannah Grace was born that summer on August 22, weighing only 5 lb, 10 oz, and measuring 19½ inches. As most mothers would say, the births of her children were the most memorable and significant events of Laura's life. While Emily's birth would always remain in her memory as a wonderful, life-altering experience, the images had "weathered" over time. Some details had slipped away, and some trivialities had changed shape or meaning, making the experience a little more romantic or charming. That particular day, however, the 22 of August—when Emily was nearing three years old, when Laura had recently turned twenty-five, and Kevin was on a ship off the coast of Saudi Arabia—Hannah Grace had entered their lives. The day was such a turning point, such a major event, and such a momentous occasion that the happenings of that day were permanently etched into Laura's memory in abject crystal clarity. August 22 was the first day of the rest of her life.

The day had started off nicely enough—on the warm side, but still pleasant. Laura was past her due date by one day and was actually hoping labor wouldn't start until the next day, Kevin's birthday. When labor began that afternoon, she assumed it would continue through midnight; she had endured a relatively long labor with Emily and expected the same, once again.

At about 8:30 that evening, Laura entered the delivery room and changed into her hospital gown. An initial examination found she was 3 to 4 cm dilated. Her labor with Emily had continued from the 3 to 4 cm dilation point for another fifteen hours, so Laura settled in for the long haul. She made a call to her Aunt Nancy (whom she had lived with during many of her teenage years) and asked her to come to the hospital. In an attempt to speed things along, Laura decided to go for a walk at around 9:15 p.m. But when she tried to sit up in bed, she felt an incredible urge to push. Laura was confused; this wasn't supposed to be happening yet. To the amazement of everyone in the room, an exam revealed that Laura was fully dilated. Her nurse ran to call the doctor while Laura panted through contractions, as her mom and aunt were both coaching her not to push yet.

The doctor arrived, performed a quick exam, and broke Laura's water. A major contraction was the result, and Laura yelled out. Her mom, aunt, and doctor were all in her face, telling her to calm down, to focus, and to breathe. They warned her this would take awhile, and she needed to conserve her energy. Meanwhile, the nurse returned. She yelled, "Doctor, Doctor, look—we're crowning! We're crowning!" With disbelief, he moved down to take a look. With not even enough time to put gloves on, he reached out and caught Hannah as she arrived at 9:40 p.m.

The nurse carried Hannah over to an Isolette to clean her off and weigh her while the doctor prepared to examine Laura and deliver the placenta. Nancy was busy talking on the phone, and Carol toggled between the beds of her daughter and new granddaughter.

Laura was tired and in considerable pain, but the worst part, at that point, was waiting for the nurse to bring Hannah back, which was taking forever. Hannah's nurse appeared to be awfully rough with her. She kept flicking at Hannah's feet and shaking her legs. Then she began suctioning Hannah's airway. If she had shoved that bulb syringe down Hannah's throat any further, it seemed it would have appeared out of Hannah's other end.

The doctor casually asked Hannah's nurse how they (she and Hannah) were doing. The nurse didn't seem pleased, reporting that Hannah's feet weren't "pinking up" as they should and that she was "flopsy-wopsy" and "juicy." Laura wanted to jump out of bed and run over to her baby girl. She probably would have tried, if she hadn't been actively delivering the placenta. The doctor, however, didn't seem concerned with the nurse's report, muttering something about the cord around the baby's neck. Laura nervously asked him to explain. He assured her that she didn't have to worry; the cord had been around Hannah's neck when she was delivered, but it hadn't been tight and he had been able to slip it off easily.

Okay, Laura thought, desperately trying to remain calm. *But that doesn't explain why she still doesn't have good color.*

Next the doctor and nurse commented on how unusually large the placenta was, intensifying the odd feeling Laura had had since the birth. She had rationalized that her nervousness stemmed from the shock of delivering so quickly and the lack of an epidural to relax her. But soon she was sensing a lot of anxious "vibes" from Hannah's nurse. Something wasn't right.

Laura began to keep a close eye on the Isolette. Hannah was still being suctioned. That was something Laura was familiar with; Emily had been born with mild meconium aspiration. Whenever this occurs, the meconium must be completely removed from the lungs, as soon after birth as possible, due to its toxicity. Laura figured the same thing must have happened. Hannah was receiving oxygen, though, and Laura had no explanation for that.

Finally, after the doctor had conferred with Hannah's nurse in the corner for a few minutes, they returned Hannah to Laura's arms. They explained that Hannah was just a bit "stunned" after the speedy delivery. That explanation didn't seem right, but Laura looked down at Hannah and thought, *How could anything be wrong? She looks just like her sister; she's fine.*

By midnight, all guests and hospital personnel had finally left the room. Laura continued trying to shake her uncomfortable feeling. The nurse had reported Hannah's weight at only 5 pounds, 10 ounces. But the doctor had said he didn't consider Hannah to be a low-birth-weight baby, since Laura was in no particular risk group (she didn't smoke, drink, or use drugs). *What? Either you're low-birth-weight or you're not, right? Emily was 8 pounds, 2 ounces. Why is Hannah so much smaller? I don't know—maybe he's right. Maybe she's just small.*

Laura snuggled Hannah closer. Throughout the first night, Hannah seemed to have a difficult time keeping warm. Her hands and feet kept turning blue, and she was distressed when her blankets were unwrapped. The nurse had put a heat lamp over Hannah's bassinette, but Laura had rolled the heat lamp closer and put Hannah in bed with her. She felt Hannah needed *Mommy* warmth.

"Good night, sweetheart," she whispered before kissing Hannah on the forehead. "Sweet dreams..."

The highlight of the next day was a call from Kevin. The American Red Cross had contacted him with the news of Hannah's birth, and he was permitted to call from the ship. On that day, which was

Kevin's birthday, Laura happily shared that his newest daughter looked just like her big sister and that both girls were doing great. Laura felt herself actually missing Kevin and she wished he could have been there. At last she felt as if they were truly a family. To have them anywhere but together seemed like such a waste of a sacred time.

Three days later, Kevin called from land. By then Laura was back home, settling in to her new life with two children. Not long after her second conversation with Kevin, however, Laura's happy glow was completely doused by fatigue. She was growing increasingly frustrated. Hannah slept—a lot, which, oddly, added to Laura's exhaustion. She couldn't sleep due to pain. She had experienced cramping after Emily's birth, but she felt that this pain deserved a stronger, more sadistic title. She would double over, lie still, cry, or try to breathe through it. Whatever she did brought no relief, and she was certain these pains felt worse than her labor contractions. Tylenol didn't even touch the pain. Laura's only saving grace was Carol's continued help.

Laura had heard tales of parents' eight-hour slumbers and leisurely afternoon naps, as she stumbled around like a zombie with a screaming Emily, but something seemed amiss. Hannah was sleeping *all* the time. Laura hated to wake a sleeping baby, but she often tried to wake Hannah for a feeding, as the pressure in Laura's chest felt strong enough to launch the space shuttle. When Hannah awoke, she was clearly hungry. She'd latch on, but almost immediately pull away. Feedings reminded Laura of the carnival game that has you shoot the water pistol into the clown's mouth to blow up the balloon on top of its head. Then, after their little song and dance of a feeding attempt, Hannah would promptly go back to sleep, leaving Laura to suffer through the "cramps from hell," which the short nursing attempt had induced.

Because of Hannah's small size, Laura worried about the feeding problems and whether the tiny amounts of breast milk were enough to sustain her. Emily had taken a few days to get the knack of eating, but at eight pounds she had had a little room for error. Unlike Emily, Hannah was extremely small.

"*This* little thing is the baby?" asked Daniel when he first saw her. "I could fit her in my back pocket!"

Laura fretted. *Hannah's tiny, and she's still having trouble staying warm. Her hands and feet keep turning blue whenever her blanket's unwrapped. This is only August. What will we do in January? She needs to put on some weight.*

Hydration was also a concern. By the sixth day at home, Laura called the pediatrician, Dr. Michaels. He said a minimum of five to six meals per day was acceptable. Laura concluded if a force-feeding consisting of mere drops could be counted as a feeding, then Hannah was getting the bare minimum. He told Laura to call, day or night, with any further concerns; otherwise he'd see them during their scheduled visit in a week and a half.

The next day, a nurse from the hospital arrived for a one-week home visit. She apparently thought Hannah was doing well. Friends and family members also brushed off any concerns Laura voiced. The general consensus was that Hannah was simply a small baby, and she would take a bit longer than Emily to make progress. Nobody seemed to understand how Laura felt, from day one, that something was wrong.

Well, thought Laura, *the doctor, the nurse, and the whole family seem to agree that everything is fine. Things can't be that bad, then, right?*

That weekend the family gathered at camp to celebrate Emily's upcoming birthday. Laura was certainly not in a festive mood. Hannah's good quality had disintegrated. She was still sleeping a lot, but she would awaken quite often and had become very fussy. She acted hungry, yet refused to eat. Laura had tried everything–breastfeeding in every plausible position, pumping milk, and using a variety of different nipples on the bottle. She tried formula–heating it and cooling it–but nothing worked.

Supportive family members continued to assure her that all was well, but Laura could not stop fretting. *Why do I feel so wrong if everything is right? Why didn't I feel this way when Emily was born? I had been nervous, tired, and frustrated, but it never felt like this.*

15

At one point during the party, Nancy came inside from the porch with Hannah in her arms. She had attempted a bottle-feeding, so Laura and Carol could each take a break, since the two women were visibly exhausted.

"I got an ounce into her, but Laura, her feet are pretty blue," said Nancy.

Laura sighed. "Yeah, that's the other thing she keeps doing. She gets cold really easily. You have to bundle her up really well." *Is it me? Laura wondered. I haven't gotten Hannah to eat a whole ounce in a single sitting yet. Am I doing everything wrong? Am I just going out of my mind? Is this what postpartum depression feels like? Why does everything feel so wrong!*

Laura went into the bathroom to pull herself together. When she came out, Nancy was laying down a sleeping Hannah. Laura stood there and looked at her baby, feeling as if she were looking at something she knew nothing about. She felt lost and couldn't hold back the tears. Nancy put her arm around Laura. "Ah, it'll be okay, Laura. You'll get through this."

That evening, Laura told Carol she was calling Dr. Michaels in the morning—even if the call would be for nothing. Carol agreed that something seemed amiss and told Laura to follow her intuition. The next day was Labor Day, and Hannah was thirteen days old. For those entire thirteen days, Laura had silenced her intuition. But she could no longer ignore the little voice that had been crying out from inside of her.

Chapter III

Sweet Denial

The night before Laura had called Dr. Michaels, Hannah had an increasingly difficult time trying to get comfortable. That morning Laura waited until after eight o'clock to call. The idea of calling on a holiday seemed rude enough, and she didn't want to make it worse by phoning at an ungodly hour.

While talking on the phone, Laura struggled to form and communicate coherent thoughts that would penetrate the sleep-deprived fog she was in. Dr. Michaels seemed to get the message, and he wanted Laura to bring Hannah into his office in a half hour.

Laura had no energy and little time to shower. She quickly dressed herself and the baby, telling Carol she hoped to be back in about an hour to help clean up after breakfast. On the way to the doctor's office, Laura wondered what he would say—maybe some problem with digestion requiring a special formula. She was afraid he would tell her what everyone else had been saying—that she was overreacting and her baby was fine.

The office was quiet when she walked in, but Hannah broke the silence with one of her crying spells. She had recently begun crying that way almost anytime she was awake. Even when asleep, she looked like she was crying because tears would be streaming down the right side of her face. Laura hadn't worried much about that, since her eye didn't look infected, and tears, at least, suggested that Hannah was hydrated.

Hannah weighed in at 5½ pounds. She should have surpassed her birth weight by then, so they weren't off to a great start. Next the doctor inquired about her fussing. Laura explained that Hannah's crying never equaled an all-out wail, but lately, she had been fussing constantly. Her cries were rather quiet, as if she didn't have the energy for anything more strenuous.

Dr. Michaels got out his stethoscope and proceeded with the exam. He listened to Hannah's heart. "Uh-oh..." he said.

What do you mean, "Uh-oh?" There's no "uh-oh" at this point in the exam. This is just a formality before we get down to the real problem—her stomach and why she won't eat!

The doctor continued. "We've got a problem here," he said. "I'm hearing a substantial murmur."

Feeling somewhat like a bad parent for not thinking, *Oh God, my poor baby!*, or *No!*, or *What? You must be mistaken!*, Laura found herself oddly relieved. She continued feeling tense and fearful, but she was glad the doctor had an answer. *Oh, so there is an explanation. See? I knew it was something. Now...what's a murmur? I know I've heard the term before...*

Not wanting to appear panicked (or, worse yet, ignorant), Laura remained quiet. She assumed by the doctor's tone that the situation was serious enough to warrant a detailed explanation.

Still listening with the stethoscope, Dr. Michaels explained that Hannah probably had a hole in her heart. Instead of a "lub-dub...lub-dub," he was hearing a "whoosh-whoosh...whoosh-whoosh." After a few more minutes, he handed the stethoscope to Laura. She was afraid she wouldn't be able to pick up the subtle differences, but as soon she placed the stethoscope on Hannah's chest, Laura was sure the heartbeat didn't sound normal. Stunned and confused, she tried to focus as Dr. Michaels reassured her. Although this was a serious problem, he explained that it occurred quite often, and corrective surgery was often performed on infants this size. He also reminded her that they were lucky to live in New Hampshire.

"Children's Hospital in Boston is right down the road," he

said, "and they have some of the best heart specialists in the world who handle problems like this—and much worse—all the time."

Next, Dr. Michaels wanted to know about Hannah's breathing. "How would you describe it?" he asked.

"Well..." Laura was searching for the right words. "Her breaths are...choppy."

They took a moment to observe Hannah. After a few quick, shallow breaths, her breathing slowed, and even stopped, for a few seconds. Then she took a deep breath, followed by some rapid, shallow ones.

"Yep, you're right." Dr. Michaels confirmed his observations as he wrote on the chart. "They're choppy. What about her color?"

Laura was thankful for the prompt. "Oh, yeah. I wanted to mention that. She seems to get cold easily. Her hands and feet get blue sometimes."

"Dark blue-purple or more of a dusty gray?"

"Uh...a dark, dusty blue, I guess—oh, like that." Laura pointed to Hannah's foot.

"Oh, yeah," he said. He was writing more notes on the chart.

Dr. Michaels quickly sent them next door to Littleton Regional Hospital's Emergency Room with orders for an EKG, chest x-ray, and blood-oxygen levels. He said he'd meet them there shortly. Laura felt numb, as she and Hannah headed to the ER. *This isn't real. This isn't how today was supposed to go!*

The ER wasn't busy, so the tests didn't take long. The shocking results came quickly. The technician could hardly believe the EKG results, and the chest x-ray showed considerable fluid in the lungs. Plus, Hannah's blood-oxygen saturation was in the mid 80s when it should have been 100%—or at least, in the mid-to-high 90s. The news caught Laura off guard by such an extent that she didn't know where to direct the worry consuming her. She began obsessing about the fact that she hadn't showered.

I'm obviously going to be here for awhile today, she thought, *and I'm not even showered...*

Dr. Michaels soon arrived and reviewed the test results. He didn't like what he observed, but he wasn't surprised. While standing in the middle of the ER bay, he began stroking his beard and studying Hannah, who was half asleep on the stretcher.

"Well, I'm...I'm *reasonably* confident that she'll be okay over the next hour or two...I think..." He sighed after a long pause and continued. "I don't think we need the helicopter...I think I'll just send for an ambulance."

Hold on! What? Back up! Did he just say "for the next hour or two!" What happened to "This is a serious situation, but it happens all the time and can be corrected with no problem?" Laura's mind raced, desperately trying to absorb the doctor's words. She had pictured them making an appointment for Hannah to see a specialist the next day. She had pictured going home and having plenty of time to pack bags and so forth. Instead, things were happening too fast. She began to panic. *Oh, God. What's happening? Wait...wait...what's...oh, God...what's going on!*

Dr. Michaels ordered an ambulance to transport Hannah to Dartmouth-Hitchcock Medical Center's [DHMC] intensive care nursery [ICN] in Hanover. *Intensive care. That term doesn't sound right. Intensive care is a place for elders fresh out of surgery, or right after a heart attack, or people rescued from car accidents. Hannah just attended a birthday party yesterday! A few days ago, a nurse said she was doing fine! She doesn't need intensive care...oh...wait...if we're going there, we might not be home tonight. I'd better call Mom.*

Minutes later, Dr. Michaels joined Laura, as she waited beside Hannah's stretcher. After watching Hannah sleep for a few moments, he let out a heavy sigh. "They want us to get an IV into her, so she'll be ready for transport. This is gonna be quite a trick."

Laura uttered a determined sigh, herself. If an IV were needed, then she would help Dr. Michaels make the procedure as quick and painless as possible. Dr. Michaels picked up Hannah's limbs, one by one, examining for potential veins. He wasn't thrilled with what he found. He rolled over a spotlight to provide a better view. The area on top of her right wrist was a possibility, but not very promising. He decided to try.

Hannah lay quietly while Dr. Michaels wrapped a rubber band around her tiny arm as a tourniquet. She remained asleep while the needle pierced her skin and barely roused, as Dr. Michaels moved the needle in, out, up, down, and around, in an attempt to penetrate the vein. Laura stroked Hannah's forehead, whispering words of encouragement. As Dr. Michaels had feared, his first IV attempt failed, so he moved on to the next best vein, at the top of her left foot. Nothing. Hannah began whimpering, and Laura wished she could take the needle for her baby girl.

After the third attempt, Laura asked, "Are we having trouble because she's small, or is it that she's dehydrated?"

"This kid has no veins to begin with, and those that she has are small and thick-walled. Even when I find one, the needle's just slipping off to the side. On top of that, I'd call her moderately dehydrated, so that certainly doesn't help matters." He then muttered to himself, as he fumbled with the light to get a better look at her left hand. "Boy, what I wouldn't do for umbilical access right now. That'd be easy—just pop a line right in."

"Umbilical access?" asked Laura.

"Yeah, when a baby is born and the cord is cut, for a while, you can use that site for IV access. That's usually the first IV site for preemies. Okay, well, I'm not finding anything here. We're gonna have to move up to her head." He removed the rubber band from her arm and grabbed a larger one to go around Hannah's head. "The veins in a baby's head are close enough to the surface, so when you can't get a line in anywhere else, you can sometimes find one there."

"It isn't normal for her to be so relaxed while you're doing all of this to her, is it?" Laura asked.

Dr. Michaels answered in a very definite tone. "No."

Laura scolded herself. *Of course not. Emily would have been clinging to the ceiling by now and waking up comatose patients on the third floor. Why does Hannah's constant fatigue seem so odd now, but I was so oblivious to it at home? She didn't eat, and I thought she was just stubborn. Her hands and feet were blue, for crying out loud, and I thought she was just cold. What kind of idiot am I? I have another kid; I'm not new at this. I shouldn't have been so blind to such obvious signs of trouble. Now she's dehydrated and really weak. I should have brought her in sooner. I should have known...*

Dr. Michaels interrupted Laura's thoughts. "I think I might have one here. Can you hand me some more of those alcohol wipes over there?"

By then Carol had arrived—after leaving Emily with Steve and Janet—and Laura was relieved to see her. The site Dr. Michaels thought he had found was yet another disappointment. The most frustrating tries involved gaining access to a vein, but when he tried to push in a little fluid, it would "blow," and they were back to square one. Once they started searching for another site on her head, Hannah woke up and began to fuss. Laura was finding it harder to watch the multiple needle pokes on her helpless little girl. Feeling woozy, she didn't know how much longer she could continue helping Dr. Michaels, but she didn't want to leave Hannah's side. *So I'm a little faint and nauseous—big deal. Hannah's going through a lot worse, and if I'm asking her to be strong and get through this, the least I can do is get past my measly discomfort.*

He tried getting a line in Hannah's head a few times, but frustration grew with each failure. Finally, after more than an hour of IV attempts, the ambulance arrived. Dr. Michaels was visibly relieved to see them. He had just about given up, anyway.

Laura tried to remain hopeful. *Maybe when they see how impossible it is to get an IV placed, they'll wait until they get to the hospital. Maybe they can give her fluids to help pump up her veins, so they'll be easier targets. Maybe they can put her under anesthesia and somehow put an IV in surgically. Oh yeah, you need an IV for fluids and surgery. Duh...man, this sucks. Hannah shouldn't have to put up with this torture. After tolerating an hour of poking, she at least deserves a restful ride to Hanover.*

No such luck. The transport team didn't want to go anywhere or do anything without a line in. Laura understood the decision was in Hannah's best interest, but she could hardly contain her frustration. She welcomed the short break when Dr. Michaels updated the team.

The three people in the team from Dartmouth-Hitchcock Medical Center were from the intensive care nursery, itself, and they quickly took over the task of IV placement. Finally, after another thirty to forty-five minutes of attempts, they successfully got a line in, on the right side of Hannah's head. They bandaged and taped it up as securely as possible. Then, holding their collective breaths, they loaded Hannah into the incubator for transport.

Laura was upset when she learned she wasn't allowed to ride in the ambulance with Hannah, due to insurance liability. Not wanting to waste valuable time arguing, she simply agreed and ran to her car, hoping she would be able to stay close to the ambulance. Her mind raced as fast as the car while speeding down I-91 to Hanover. *Is Hannah hungry? She hasn't eaten all day, but I guess that's no different from any other day. Plus, now she has the IV. What's the intensive care nursery going to be like? How long will she have to be there? What am I going to do when Mom has to go back home to Kentucky? Oh, crap! She's due to fly home tomorrow! How is Em doing? I wish I had been able to tell her goodbye. God, what am I going to do with her? Where am I going to stay while Hannah's in the hospital—at a hotel? But she's going to be in the intensive care unit. They probably don't let parents stay there, much less siblings. But what are you supposed to do when you breastfeed? I can't be driving back and forth from a hotel every twenty minutes.*

Inside her head, Laura's thoughts began spinning faster and faster until she could no longer concentrate on anything. Sensing Laura's tension, Carol tried to strike up a conversation.

She shook her head as she spoke. "I just can't believe all of this," said Carol.

"Yeah, Hannah could have died last night."

Carol sighed heavily. "I know. I was thinking that, too. What would we have *done*?"

Laura replied angrily, through gritted teeth. "I don't know, but I'd like to know how that visiting nurse could have thought Hannah was perfectly healthy."

"*Really.* Just think; what would have happened if you hadn't called the doctor today? What if you had waited for the well-baby checkup on Wednesday?"

Both women shook their heads in disbelief, and Laura returned her focus to the back doors of the ambulance in front of them.

Once they arrived at the hospital, the women ran into the emergency room—but discovered there had been no need to rush. Dr. O'Connor, the pediatric cardiologist, was examining Hannah and performing an echocardiogram [an ultrasound of her heart] in the intensive care nursery. A nurse told Laura and Carol that the doctor would be available to consult with them in about an hour. Laura was fuming inside. *No, no, no. You don't seem to understand. I'm the mother. What do you mean I have to wait to see my daughter! Isn't it my right as a parent to be with her!* Feeling exhausted, confused, frustrated and worried, they waited for Dr. O'Connor's update.

Finally, at about 4:00 p.m., the doctor met them in the ICN parents' lounge. After a brief introduction, he began to explain Hannah's medical condition. With a sigh, he handed Laura a booklet entitled, "If Your Child Has A Congenital Heart Defect." *Okay, so Dr. Michaels was right. Hannah has a hole in her heart. Just get on with what you have to tell us, and let me go see her!*

Dr. O'Connor first offered a quick overview of the normal workings of the heart, tracing the flow of blood from a picture in the booklet. "Low-oxygen blood from the body goes to the heart's right side. Then it's pumped to the lungs. In the lungs, it releases carbon dioxide and picks up oxygen. Then the oxygen-rich blood is pumped back into the heart's left side. From there, it goes to the aorta and out to the body."

Yeah, I remember this stuff from biology class. Get on with it.

With another sigh, Dr. O'Connor turned the page to a different diagram of the heart. "In the echo, I found that Hannah has an atrial septal defect (ASD)." He drew a circle on the diagram to represent a hole in Hannah's heart. "With a hole here, much of the oxygen-rich blood from the heart's left side leaks back into the right side. Then it's pumped back to the lungs, even though it's already been oxygenated."

Okay, that's what I expected. She needs surgery, so let's set a date and get going.

"Now, Hannah also has a good-sized hole here, which is called a ventricular septal defect (VSD). Because of this hole, a lot of the oxygen-rich blood from the heart's left side is forced through the hole to over here—to the right side." Dr. O'Connor pointed out the area on the diagram. "Then it's pumped back to the lungs, even though it's already been refreshed with oxygen. With these two holes, most of the blood that's already been to the lungs is returning there, and blood that needs to go to the lungs isn't making it. Therefore, Hannah's heart is having to work extra hard to pump and re-pump the blood, and her lungs are having to work extra hard to deal with the returning blood."

Two holes—okay, more than I expected, but if they can fix one hole, they can fix two. I'm sold on the surgery. Let's get on with it. I want to see Hannah.

Dr. O'Connor turned back to the inside of the book's front cover and wrote:

Plumbing:

 1. Large atrial septal defect

   (Large hole between the upper chambers)

 2. Large ventricular septal defect

   (Large hole between the lower chambers)

Dr. O'Connor turned to yet another heart diagram and began to draw. "This, here, is the aorta. It's the main artery that carries blood from the heart to the body. Hannah has a coarctation. It's pinched or narrowed...right about here. This is our biggest concern for Hannah right now. It creates a few problems. Number one, it means that blood isn't getting to the rest of her body like it should. Number two: blood pressure is increased above the constriction. Her heart is having to work extra hard to get blood to her body, and the increased pressure is placing that much more stress on her heart."

Laura finally offered some words beyond the "um-hum... yeah...right...oh, okay...oh, I see..." that she had been mumbling in between the doctor's drawings and explanations. "This is unbelievable. It's no small wonder why her poor little heart hasn't given out before now. I don't understand. Why does she have all of these problems with her heart?"

The doctor began fidgeting in his seat. "Well, we'll get more into why in a moment. First, there's more." He half smiled at Laura, apologetically.

Laura's mind raced once again. *Oh my God! My baby has been a ticking time bomb! When we were home, she could have died in my arms at any moment. What the hell was that visiting nurse's problem! How could she have overlooked three heart defects! What the hell was my problem! I should have called Dr. Michaels earlier. Maybe it wouldn't have been so bad at that point. This is too much. The Marine Corps had better let Kevin come home for this. We may have a serious problem here.*

With wide eyes, Laura and Carol shot each other a glance, as they realized at the same time what the doctor had just said. "Wait, there's more?" they asked in unison.

"Yes, but this ends up 'complementing' the other defects." He went back to his drawing. "This is the pulmonary valve here. It opens to let blood flow from the right ventricle to the lungs. Hannah's is narrowed, which would normally make the right ventricle pump harder to get blood past the blockage. With this hole over here, though, it's...kinda working for her. But then there's this, over here." He began drawing again. "Umm...every baby is born with a ductus arteriosus. It's an open passageway between the two major blood vessels (the pulmonary artery and the aorta). The pulmonary artery carries venous blood from the heart's right side to the lungs. Then it picks up a fresh supply of oxygen. The aorta carries the oxygen-rich blood from the left side of the heart to the rest of the body. Normally, the passageway between these two arteries closes within a few hours after birth. If it doesn't, some blood that should have gone through the aorta–and on to nourish the body–goes back to the lungs. Hannah's didn't close. This is a common problem for premature babies, but it's fairly rare in full-term babies like Hannah."

Wow, this guy has had a lot of coffee today. I think I'm getting a contact high from his breath. Darn, I wish I had paid closer attention in biology class. If I had known I'd eventually be tested like this, I would have taken better notes. I wonder how much of this Mom understands.

Once again, Dr. O'Connor turned back to the book's front cover and continued with his list.

3. *Coarctation of aorta*

(Narrowed aorta)

4. *Patant ductus arteriosus*

(Fetal blood vessel between lung artery and aorta)

He stopped writing temporarily and spoke through another apologetic half smile. "Hannah also has a narrowed tricuspid valve. Um...it's not mentioned in this book. I don't think it will present much of a problem for her, but, to be honest, it's really rare, and I'm not sure what it will mean for her. I can't remember the last time I saw one, much less remember what it might mean. Again, though, I don't think it will be that significant a defect." He continued with his writing. "So we have..."

5. *Abnormal "narrowed" tricuspid valve of unclear*

but *probably* *mild degree*

6. *Mild pulmonary valve stenosis*

(Pulmonary valve "narrowing")

Probably will not be a problem

Okay, I'm gonna puke if he goes on much longer. I've never smelled coffee-breath so strong. I wonder what time he started drinking the stuff. Come on, Laura, focus...focus... Nope, it's too much. I hope Mom is getting this all in, 'cause he lost me a while ago. He should have just told us that Hannah's heart is like a piece of swiss cheese. I can't believe this.

"Now, I picked up on one more thing during the echo..."

Both women attempted to lighten the mood. "Oh, just one more thing?" said Laura.

"And that's it?" said Carol.

"All of these things I've mentioned, so far, have been plumbing problems. They can be repaired surgically. I also picked up on an electrical disturbance. Hannah has some extra beats, up in the atrium. It could mean nothing for her, or her heart could begin beating erratically, and we would have to correct that electrically. We'll be monitoring her, of course." He continued to write:

Electrical:

7. Extra upper-chamber heartbeats

(Atrial preemptive beats)

Okay, my brain is mush. I want to go see Hannah. It'll make sense to me later.

"Now, all of this explains her constant fatigue, right?" Carol asked.

"Yes. The typical heart rate for a baby this size is 120 to 140 beats per minute. Hannah's heart is running in the 175 to 185 range. Her body's working pretty hard all the time to keep her heart beating, so she's going to be pretty tired."

Carol quizzed further. "And what about her refusing to eat?"

Thank God for Mom; these are good questions that I should be asking—would be asking—if I weren't brain-dead.

"Well, the typical respiration rate for a baby Hannah's size is twenty to forty breaths per minute. Again, Hannah is working extra hard because of the extra flow into her lungs. Her breath rate is more like eighty to ninety. Trying to eat would be like trying to drink a glass of milk through a straw while running a marathon. It's just easier to starve."

Laura felt as if she were trying to find her way out of a terrible fog. "So, what's the plan now?"

"Right now we have her on a drug called digoxin, which helps the heart to beat stronger. We've also started her on some Lasix, a diuretic. That will help Hannah rid her lungs of the excess fluid you saw in the x-rays back at the ER. And we've begun feeding her via nasogastric or 'NG' tube—a tube running from her nose to her stomach, to try to get her weight up a bit and get her a little stronger for surgery. We're also working on trying to answer an earlier question of yours—why. Heart defects are relatively rare. About eight in every 1,000 babies are born with one. Obviously, babies with seven heart defects are extremely uncommon. Unfortunately, we don't know what the cause is behind most congenital heart-defect cases. For Hannah, we hope to find an answer. Dr. Brennan, a geneticist, will be visiting Hannah sometime within the next few days to take a look at her and draw a little blood."

"When can we operate?" Laura asked. She was hoping it would be before Carol had to return home the following day.

"It's really hard to say. It depends on how fast we can get some weight on her and how she responds to the drugs. Surgeons can operate on a child this size—and they do—but they don't like to unless they absolutely have to. You're dealing with a heart the size of a walnut, and it's difficult to be accurate when repairing specific valves and vessels. Our plan is to hold off as long as we can by treating her with the medications while we work on fattening her up. The more she weighs, the better her chances of surviving surgery. We'd like to see her up to at least seven pounds. To answer your question, though, I would count on at least a week or two before surgery."

A week or two! How am I going to do this? Mom has to go back to Kentucky tomorrow. What am I going to do with Emily? And seven pounds! Laura laughed out loud, voicing how ridiculously far-fetched seven pounds sounded. But, on a more serious note, she asked him for his honest opinion on Hannah's chances of survival.

"I'm...cautiously optimistic," he said.

The "choppy breathing" Laura had described to Dr. Michaels is known as Cheyne-Stokes respiration. The abnormal pattern of respiration is often related to congestive heart failure, and is frequently demonstrated just prior to death. It served as *one* of the factors Dr. Michaels was considering when attempting to decide between the helicopter and an ambulance, and then became *one* of the factors Dr. O'Connor was considering when attempting to answer Laura's last question.

Without thinking about Dr. O'Connor's response–and therefore, completely missing the gravity of his "cautious optimism"–Laura's eyes passed over his watch as he spoke. She saw it was past 6:00 p.m. "Is it alright to go see her now?" she asked.

"Of course." He began shuffling his paperwork back together.

"Thank you very much for taking the time to explain all of this to us," Carol said.

Laura was ashamed of herself for not thinking to thank him on her own. "Yes, thank you very much–oh, wait. Would you mind doing me a favor, if you have a moment?"

"What do you need?"

"My husband is in the Marine Corps, and he's out at sea right now. In order to get word to him, we need to go through the American Red Cross at this number here. Unfortunately, I can't make the call myself. They need a doctor to verify we're actually in the hospital and that there's really a problem. I'm hoping they'll allow him to come home, if you call. Would you mind?"

"Not at all. I should certainly hope they'll send him home."

"Thank you very much, Dr. O'Connor. And...not that I'm trying to get away with something that I shouldn't or anything but... well, they won't let him come back unless it's really something life-threatening...so don't, you know, don't...sugarcoat anything. Give them the worst-case scenario type of stuff."

Dr. O'Connor realized how little of what he had said had sunk in. He paused, looking at Laura. He spoke, with both pity and frustration in his voice. "Don't worry. It's worst case enough, just with the bare facts." Then he turned to leave.

Oh...I...oh...

Chapter IV

Redefining Time

An incredible sense of relief swept over Laura when she finally arrived at Hannah's Isolette. Hannah appeared the same as when Laura had last seen her. Thankfully she still had her IV. She also had a heart-shaped sticker on her chest with a wire leading to the Isolette for monitoring and controlling her temperature. Three more stickers on her chest with wires led to a large monitor screen close to her Isolette. These probes tracked her heart and respiration rates.

Hannah wore a tiny, white blood-pressure cuff on her arm and a Band-Aid-type sticker on her hand that glowed red. They, too, had wires that led up to her monitor. Laura's least favorite new addition was the small white NG tube that Dr. O'Connor had spoken about. It would provide much-needed help with feedings, but it looked rather uncomfortable. Overall, Laura thought she'd be much more overwhelmed or frightened by the equipment, but once she learned what the various wires and tubes were for, they didn't really bother her.

Hannah's nurse helped Laura get situated in the glider rocker that was next to the Isolette. She stressed that everything attached to Hannah could be easily reattached or replaced—except the IV. They'd all have to be really careful with that. Trying to rock Hannah with all of the new equipment was awkward and nerve-racking at first but Laura soon got the hang of it. As she rocked her baby, she felt the stress of the day melting away.

Carol stayed a bit longer before heading back to Littleton to get Emily and find out about changing her flight date. Laura rocked Hannah as long as she could, until 10:30 p.m. The unit coordinator had gotten Laura a room at a Ronald McDonald-type place called David's House. It was walking distance from the hospital, and the doors locked at 11:00 p.m. She'd be able to come and go as she pleased, as soon as she had a key, but for that first night, she ran the risk of getting locked out. She hated the idea of not sleeping next to Hannah, but the nurse had given her a pager and promised to contact her if any issue were to arise. With the pager in hand, Laura summoned up the strength to leave. A smiling volunteer soon welcomed her into the absolutely gorgeous David's House just before eleven o'clock. She made her way to her room (the "Duck Room") and promptly passed out, exhausted.

Laura abruptly awoke at 7:00 a.m. the next morning and immediately called over to the hospital, in case the pager had malfunctioned. Once assured that everything was fine with Hannah, Laura indulged in a long-overdue shower. Refreshed by the sleep and shower, she returned to the ICN feeling rather upbeat. However, she was quickly disappointed when told she was, yet again, not able to see Hannah. The doctors were making their rounds, and parents were not permitted inside the open room at that time, due to patient confidentiality.

Once she had permission to enter, Laura rushed through the gowning-up process and settled onto the rocker with Hannah. The nurse reminded Laura to expect the sound of beeps and whistles and not to worry about it. She explained that it usually means a baby has wiggled around and jostled his or her leads (the little stickers with the wires leading to the monitor). She also suggested that Laura ignore Hannah's monitor, because she'd make herself crazy, if she watched the numbers jump up and down all day.

But Laura couldn't keep her eyes off of Hannah's monitor. Once she figured out what each number meant (one indicated Hannah's heart rate, another was her oxygen saturation, the third her respirations), she found them strangely calming. They may not have been in the normal range, but at least she could plainly see that Hannah's heart was still beating, and she was still breathing. Plus, watching the numbers helped to pass the time.

Of course, the best way to pass the time was "people watching." On the way in, Laura had noticed the tiny preemie named Jason in the crib next to Hannah's Isolette. She began watching for his mother, hoping they could chat, since they were probably going to be neighbors for a while. She wondered about the other babies around her, too. Were they all preemies like little Jason, or were others sick like Hannah? Maybe one of them had heart problems. Laura looked forward to meeting the other mothers.

She was surprised at the minimal number of parents she saw, as the hours passed. She figured they were working and assumed she would see them during the weekend. She continued to cuddle with Hannah. Dr. O'Connor had said his goal was to help Hannah put on some weight, so Laura devoted herself to making sure Hannah didn't burn any unnecessary calories. She was working hard enough to simply breathe and pump blood, and she didn't need to work any harder by crying.

Since rocking her baby had become her main purpose in life, Laura had plenty of time to think. Her thoughts ran wild. *Why did this happen? How long will it last? When will we get back to the life we've put on hold since yesterday? Is insurance going to cover all of this—or some of this? What will Kevin think? How is my absence from Emily, for a week or more, going to affect her? Is anyone remembering to read her a bedtime story? Is anyone gently explaining what is going on? Should I call her, or will that just remind her that I'm not there? Did she brush her teeth this morning? Will Hannah's surgery leave a bad scar? Will it be unsightly when she wears her prom dress someday? How much of this will she remember? Will she hate doctors and hospitals after this? Do I have bills at home that need to be paid? Did I put that load of laundry in the dryer before I left the house?*

Laura quickly found that concentrating on the happenings around her was less stressful than focusing on her own situation, which appeared to make her thoughts spin out of control. After all, control was the issue here. Laura was a woman who was used to being in control. She was the girl who had started planning for retirement before she finished college. She was the one who knew on Monday what they would have for dinner on Friday. Lack of control scared her more than anything else.

Having enjoyed a few weeks of being in complete control, regarding matters related to both girls, she found herself feeling as if she were copiloting—or perhaps just riding in the back seat. Even though she trusted Carol to give Emily the best possible care, *she* wanted to be there for her little girl. She was incredibly thankful for Hannah's doctors and trusted them, but *she* wanted to decide what was best for Hannah. She appreciated the expertise of Hannah's nurses, but *she* wanted to determine how and when to carry out the doctors' orders.

Laura was also finding it difficult to settle into a routine. In order to produce breast milk, she had to eat regular meals, keep hydrated, and get plenty of sleep. By spending as much time as possible in the rocker with Hannah, Laura was not having any luck with a structured schedule. In fact, during the third day at the hospital, Laura resolved to quit pumping altogether. She felt horrible about her decision, because she had nursed Emily for a year and was a huge believer in the overwhelming benefits of breast milk for babies. By quitting, she felt as if she were cheating Hannah out of those benefits. After all, Hannah was struggling with the two issues breast milk is best known for helping: nutrition and immunity. Laura knew producing milk under such stressful circumstances would be difficult for anyone, but accepting the idea felt as if she were accepting defeat.

Even with the extra time she gained once she quit pumping milk, Laura felt as if her time with Hannah was regularly cut short. She was constantly stepping aside for an invariable stream of specialists who needed information about Hannah. The geneticist stopped by a few times, spending considerable time asking about the health of family members on both sides. He performed a complete exam, noting even the smallest dimples on Hannah's ears. Laura knew nothing about genetic disorders and wondered what kind of information ear dimples could possibly give him.

A social worker paid a visit, as well. Understanding why the woman was there, Laura did her best to provide her with the information she needed, while attempting to be as honest as possible with both the social worker and herself. She assured the woman that she and Hannah's father had a strong marriage and were ready to face this challenge—both emotionally and financially. Her words seemed to pacify the professional, and she was soon on her way to another family.

The social worker's departure left an opening for a pediatric ophthalmologist (eye specialist) to step in for an exam. Hannah's eyes appeared to be healthy, but two minor issues were identified. She had blocked tear ducts, which explained the constant tearing of her right eye, and she also had "incomplete eyelid closure"– most likely due to shallow orbits. The doctor explained that both issues would probably self-correct with time.

Mostly, a steady stream of nurses, interns, residents, and the like routinely checked on Hannah's vital signs, got blood samples, weighed diapers for an output measurement, administered tube feedings and/or medications, took x-rays, checked her EKG strips, etc. The person Laura was always anxious to see was Dr. O'Connor. She marveled at his incredible expertise, decisive leadership, and his commitment to Hannah's care. He was the man she felt most connected to, and, of course, he was their ticket home. Their lives hung on his words–his observations, predictions, and decisions.

Occasionally, Laura would notice a family member walking toward the Isolette. She had mixed feelings about family visits. Although she was always glad to see them, she felt pressured to keep everyone calm, updated, encouraged, and entertained–an exhausting routine. The job was an especially trying one when family members seemed to resist Laura's positive vibes. During one visit in particular, Laura's stepmother, Janet, had walked in and almost immediately began to weep. Laura found herself mildly annoyed and oddly panicked. *I don't get it. What is she crying about? There's nothing to cry about here. Hannah's in the right place, and the doctors are making her better. This is a good thing. Why doesn't she see that?* Janet's emotional reaction became a direct attack on Laura's heightened level of denial, and Laura didn't like how that felt, at all.

Despite Laura's best efforts to stubbornly cling to that denial, which protected her from the brunt of the fear and sorrow she faced, glimpses of reality were fighting their way into her consciousness with ever-increasing ferocity. She worked hard at maintaining a calm, cool exterior, because she wanted to be strong for Hannah—and also because crying would validate the gravity of the circumstances they were in. Laura was not yet fully ready to accept the severity of Hannah's health problems.

In addition, she was concerned about the onlooking nurses. Laura didn't want to appear as a weak individual who couldn't handle pressure. She felt the nurses might try to "protect her" by limiting her involvement, if they believed she couldn't handle it.

Adding to all of Laura's concerns were her worries that Kevin's arrival would drive her over the edge and open the emotional floodgates. Falling apart would be the worst thing she could do, because Kevin didn't do well with hospitals, sickness, or newborns. He was going to face a difficult enough time as it was, without having a wife going through an emotional meltdown, too. Laura realized she needed to remain strong.

The rest of the time (when she wasn't preoccupied with the presence of staff or visitors) was a waiting game. Ultimately, she was waiting for Hannah to gain weight, have surgery, and return home. Prior to that, she was waiting for Kevin. He was sailing off the coast of Saudi Arabia when Hannah had been admitted and was expected to come home in about a week.

Waiting was especially difficult, since the whole concept of time was quickly becoming unrecognizable. Time was no longer about getting up when the alarm went off, making sure dinner was on the table by six o'clock, planning a family activity for Saturday, and remembering next Tuesday's hair appointment. For Laura, time was now measured in kilos and grams. Unlike time measured in minutes and seconds, she was frustrated that kilos and grams couldn't be counted on.

The purpose of Hannah's hospitalization was for her to gain weight, and Laura's life revolved around that issue. Instead of catching the morning news or checking out the weather forecast, Laura's mornings centered on Hannah's weight report. Unfortunately, those reports showed that the scales were headed in the wrong direction. No matter how painstakingly hard the medical team worked, the grams kept melting away. Even though they were dripping Hannah's feedings (to prevent spitting up or stomach upset), changing diapers the moment they were moist (to keep her as stress-free as possible)—along with Laura rocking her in the glider, allowing Hannah to sleep soundly in her arms— Hannah's weight did not improve. Laura would be depressed about a weight drop of ten grams one day, excited about a two-gram gain the next, but devastated by a twenty-five gram loss the day after that. Hannah's admitting weight had been 2.5 kilos (5.5 pounds). During the first twenty-four hours, she had lost quite a bit of weight due to the initial doses of Lasix, which got rid of her extra water weight. But after being on a strict feeding schedule for a few days, her weight had dropped even further to 2.42 kilos (5.34 pounds).

At this rate, we'll be here forever. How will she ever have surgery, if she keeps losing weight? Dr. O'Connor said we'd be here a week or two. He probably assumed she would be gaining weight during that time. How long will we have to stay here now? How the heck am I supposed to make any plans? What if the military calls Kevin right back? What if they consider this a non-emergency situation, because we're holding off on surgery? What will I do with Em, if Kevin can't stay? God, even if Kevin can stay, how will he do, alone with Emily? They've never spent time alone together. Plus they've been apart for quite some time now. What if Em doesn't take well to him when he gets back? What's the deal with insurance? Is this going to land us in debt for the rest of our lives? What if Hannah keeps losing weight? She's more than two weeks old now, and she still hasn't even gotten back to her birth weight. ...Deep breath, Laura. Focus on the here and now. Think of something else. What's going on with the baby around the corner?

Laura had been watching the monitor of a nearby baby when she noticed the heart rate had jumped to the mid-200s. She knew the leads often had little or no reception, but that would result in low numbers (or no numbers at all) on the monitor, not an increased heart rate. Laura's mind raced, trying to solve the mystery. An enraged baby may have explained the higher heart rate, but the baby wasn't crying. The warning bells were ringing, but nobody seemed worried. The only alarm that got any attention in the ICN was the one from the oxygen saturation monitor. Finally, a nurse walked by, and Laura asked about it as calmly as she could.

"Should that heart rate be up like that?"

The nurse studied the monitor for a moment, as if she needed a little extra time to process the information, and then backed away. "No...no it shouldn't!"

Before Laura could even process what was happening, a mob of white coats zipped past her toward the nearby Isolette.

Laura heard one of the nurses pleading with the child. "Come on now; don't do this!"

Doctors began yelling out orders for equipment and tests. Laura continued to rock Hannah, but slowly, every muscle in Laura's body began to seize up as the reality of the situation consumed her. Just five feet away, a baby could be dying. *Oh, God...this is... this is _real_. No, no, no...it can't be...it must just be...oh God...this is it...this is what happens here...what if it happens to Hannah? What if it's her turn next? Nooooo...this doesn't _happen_...it just doesn't happen...*

Wide-eyed and pale, Laura continued rocking Hannah. That afternoon, the rose-colored glasses that denial had so generously provided were being ripped away by the reality of the intensive care nursery. She now understood that she had grossly underestimated the situation they were in, as this big slap of reality quickly cleared her false sense of security.

A few minutes later, Laura knew the baby had made it through the episode, and the nurses were back to work. Laura never found out exactly what had happened. Throughout the rest of the shift, the nurses jokingly reprimanded the tiny baby boy for scaring them and, worse yet, creating more paperwork. Those were the only indications that something had gone wrong. Otherwise, Laura never would have guessed that anything out of the ordinary had happened. She then realized the situation hadn't been anything out of the ordinary. For the nurses, the incident simply depicted life as usual in the ICN.

That night Carol picked up Laura to go to dinner, since she would be flying home to Kentucky the next morning. Laura found it hard to "switch gears" and focus on spending time with her mother, because the events of the afternoon kept flashing into her mind. At the restaurant she would occasionally hear beeps and alarms from the kitchen that sounded remarkably like those in the ICN. She would tense up in her seat, reminded of what could be happening in her absence. Laura tried to mask her discomfort. Carol already felt horrible about leaving, and Laura certainly didn't want to make her feel any worse.

After a difficult goodbye, Carol headed south. When Laura went to bed, she felt so alone. The rest of the family was scattered. Emily was an impossible one-and-a-half hours away, Kevin was somewhere in Europe, and Hannah was close by but inaccessible until the doctors finished with their morning rounds. She had tried calling Daniel before going to bed, thinking maybe he could work his magic by knowing exactly what to say, and she'd feel better. Unfortunately, a new school year had begun at his college, and he hadn't been available the few times she had called. Laura left another message with Daniel's roommate and finally succumbed to sleep.

The next morning started the same as every other morning in the four-day stretch that was beginning to feel like a lifetime. Laura began relying on an alarm clock because of her increasing difficulty with waking up in the morning. The sleepless nights she had endured back home, in addition to the four- to six-hour nights at David's House, were beginning to take their toll. Laura was actually getting the bulk of her sleep in the ICN. She would cuddle with Hannah in the rocker, Hannah would drift off, Laura would close her eyes, and when she opened them again, she would find that somehow an hour had slipped by.

As Hannah began to drift off again, a few hours after such a nap, Laura placed her in the Isolette, so she could take a lunch break. She tidied up the area around their "new little home" and was about to head to the cafeteria when Hannah awoke screaming. Laura couldn't understand what was bothering her. As she stood near the Isolette, pondering the situation, she suddenly realized that a crowd of white coats had gathered around Hannah. She didn't know what was happening, but her view of her baby was becoming completely obscured by those white coats. Confused,

Laura glanced up at Hannah's monitor, instantly devastated by the readings—heart rate...235...240...

No...no...not today, Hannah, not today! I'm not ready for this, sweetie! Please...pleeeeaaassee...oh, God...what happened? What...What's happening? This can't really be happening. It's not your turn, Hannah. It's not your turn! Daddy hasn't even met you yet. You haven't met your daddy. Kevin's due in tomorrow... why today? Come on, baby, come on...please—oh Goooodddddd, noooooo...

Laura stumbled over to the phone hanging on the wall next to Hannah's Isolette and dialed with shaking fingers.

"Hi, Dad? Uh...something's going on with...with Hannah, and uh...it um...it's not looking so good." *Stay out of their way, Laura. That's it; stay on the phone, and stay out of the doctors' way...let them work...don't cry...there's nothing to cry about...stay calm, Laura, come on...*

Laura was doing her best to stay under control, but she was painting a fairly grim picture. Steve knew he couldn't alleviate Laura's pain by simply saying, "Don't worry, Laura. Everything will be all right." All he could do was wait on the phone with her.

In the meantime, a doctor was using an esophageal pacemaker on Hannah. She had developed a tachyarrhythmia due to an atrial flutter. In other words, the problem with extra atrial beats, which Dr. O'Connor had mentioned a few days earlier, had manifested, causing Hannah's heart to beat out of rhythm and out of control. The treating physician first tried using a medication called adenosine to get her back into a normal sinus rhythm, but it failed. He then fed a tube down her throat and into her esophagus. When activated, it would deliver an electrical charge to her heart and hopefully "jump-start" the normal rhythm. At last, it worked! Hannah's heart rate returned to normal, and she soon fell asleep, utterly exhausted.

Laura hung up the phone and returned to the Isolette. She didn't want to disturb Hannah, so she pulled over a stool and sat with her for the remainder of the afternoon. As time passed, each successful minute felt like a triumph. Kevin was expected to return to Boston at two o'clock the following afternoon. Nancy planned to pick him up and drive him to the hospital. The hours dragged. Meanwhile, another scary incident took place with Hannah—not as dramatic as the episode the day before. She had similar symptoms but no arrhythmia, which meant she had extra atrial beats, but this time, they didn't trigger her heart beating out of rhythm. The wait for Kevin's arrival became even more intense. The thought that he could miss out on meeting Hannah by a matter of hours—or even minutes—was nearly too much to handle.

Actually, while part of Laura was desperate for Kevin to arrive, she mostly felt nervous about seeing him again. With the nurses mulling around, she experienced an unspoken pressure to welcome him in an endearing way. She assumed since they all knew her story, they probably thought being apart was sadly romantic, and a beautiful reunion would soon take place. Of course, they didn't know their reunions usually involved no more enthusiasm than a peck on the cheek. At the same time, she was worried she'd make a complete spectacle of herself, if she were to let go of all the emotion she had been holding in for the past few days.

Laura also thought about the issue of private time at David's House. After Laura had moved her belongings from the "Duck Room" to the "Dog Room," (which had a double bed), the realization occurred to her that she had "wifely duties" once again. She wasn't ready for that. She knew they would have to work hard to keep their marriage strong through this crisis, but she couldn't handle the thought of intimacy while her little girl was clinging to life.

Still lost in thought, Laura suddenly realized that Kevin was walking toward her. Without thinking, she walked up to him and hugged him with all her might. That type of gesture had rarely felt natural before, but it was all she could imagine doing at the time. With their embrace, she felt a great release, but she didn't break down, as she had feared. When they pulled away, she led Kevin to Hannah's Isolette. "Come on. Come meet your daughter."

Kevin did very well, considering Hannah's heartbreaking appearance. She had mysteriously broken out in a rash and was still worn out from the events of the past twenty-four hours. While sleeping soundly, her tiny body had an eerie appearance of lifelessness, especially since her eyes weren't completely shut, due to her shallow orbits. Because of Hannah's close calls, the crash cart had been positioned next to her Isolette, adding further to the overwhelming feel of medical technology. In addition, her head was shaved in patches—the remnants of past IV sites and failed attempts. The skin on her cheeks was broken down, due to the tape used for the NG tube. The back of her hands and heels were purple and were covered in cuts and bruises from further IV attempts and multiple blood draws.

Regardless of her obvious physical maladies, Hannah looked absolutely beautiful to Laura. She wanted Kevin to see that beauty, too, so she quickly began explaining the purpose of every piece of equipment. Laura hoped he would feel more comfortable that way and less intimidated by the surroundings. Although she had given the little speech numerous times to other family members, this time she realized how much she was attempting to calm her own fears, as well.

Laura and Kevin headed to David's House at about 9:00 p.m. Laura felt uneasy about leaving Hannah before midnight, but Kevin had grown more uncomfortable with the ICN, and Laura could no longer divert his attention away from the negativity of the situation. At David's House, Kevin was clearly disappointed that Laura wasn't feeling ready for intimacy yet, but he said he understood. Instead, they attempted to address some of the more difficult issues they faced.

"So, do they have any answers yet about why this happened?" asked Kevin.

"No. The geneticist is supposed to be getting back to me within the next few days."

"Do they have any *ideas*? I mean, come on...seven fuckin' heart defects! You don't just have that many for no reason."

"Well, actually, they say that, in most cases, they never know why."

"That's fucked up. So, do you think they'll find anything?"

"I don't know...I mean, what *could* they find? It's not like she has Down syndrome or anything. Other than the heart defects, she's fine. But we'll find out pretty soon. I wonder how Em's doing tonight. Today's her third birthday. I hate that we can't be with her. Our family is finally all in the same state, and we can't even be together to celebrate the day with her."

"I know. Well, she won't know the difference, and I'll be seeing her tomorrow. What I'm worried about is how much this is gonna cost us...how much insurance is gonna pay. This is gonna be *expensive.*"

"I've thought about that, too," said Laura. "I heard somewhere that a bed in the ICN is like six hundred dollars a day. That's without the meds and x-rays and echoes and stuff–never mind the surgery down in Boston."

Kevin swore bitterly at the thought of the growing expense.

"I looked at one of the last insurance statements, and it said something about two thousand dollars. I'm not sure if that's a deductible or if that's what they'll cover. And if it's what they'll cover, I don't know if it's per family member or for the whole family. I haven't had a chance to call them. The way I see it is, it's nothing I'm gonna worry about right now. I have enough to worry about for the time being. If it's a two-thousand-dollar deductible, well, that's no fun, but we have that much money available, and it could be a lot worse. If all they'll cover is two thousand dollars, well, what can they do? We don't have a house or anything that they can take away from us."

"I'll check into it with the recruiter. So I have two weeks of leave, and if things aren't resolved at that point, I'll go on humanitarian duty–working for the local recruiting station."

"Well, hopefully, Hannah's surgery will be done in two weeks, but the way things are going with her weight, I'm not so sure. If you have to work, what are we going to do with Em?"

"Well, we'll cross that bridge when we come to it."

"Yeah, I guess. Now, do you remember Emily's routine? You've never had to take care of her for more than a few hours on your own."

Kevin spoke in a dismissive tone. "Oh, we'll be just fine."

"I know...I know...but, you know how she needs routine in her life."

"She doesn't need routine; it's you who needs routine. We'll be just fine."

"Kevin, she's been through a lot. It's hard enough on her that I'm not around. We've never been apart like this. She needs to be able to hold onto something constant in her life."

"Well, she'll have her dad, and we'll get by fine."

"Okay...goodnight then..." *Oh man...this'll go downhill fast. He's wrong. Emily* does *need consistency. Without it, she's okay until something goes wrong, and then she has a total meltdown— and I can't imagine him reacting well to that. I don't know... maybe it'll all work out. What am I saying? They don't stand a chance! Well, it's not like I have any choice. What else can I do—leave Kevin here with Hannah? He was ready to leave her at nine tonight. He can't stay here! Well, it's his first night back— best not to argue right now.*

As Laura walked Kevin to the car on her way to the ICN the next morning, she felt compelled to say more. "Kevin, look, no matter what happens with Hannah, no matter what the geneticist says, this is gonna be hard on us. We've struggled before, but I'm happy with where we are now. We need to make a conscious effort to keep working on our marriage, so that we don't get lost in this storm."

"Laura, I think we're adult enough to put the marriage aside for a little while and concentrate on getting Hannah better. This is her time."

After a quick hug, he got into the car and was on his way to Littleton. Laura headed to the ICN, fearing for the future of their marriage and knowing that setting it aside wasn't the best plan–especially since Hannah's recovery was apt to be a long haul. However, hearing him speak in Hannah's defense was encouraging.

Laura's grandparents visited later that day. Although Laura enjoyed seeing them, she felt that her little sales pitch, (which implied, "see; this isn't so bad") was losing its momentum as she attempted to explain the purpose of each piece of equipment.

Then her grandmother surprised her by bringing up a subject she hadn't even thought about. "Laura, do you have a burial plot?"

She felt completely confused by the question. "Uh...noooo," she said.

"Well, your grandfather and I bought plots years ago in the cemetery where your great-grandfather is buried. If anything should...um...happen...you can use one of those plots."

"Oh, thank you, Grammy. That would really help–I guess."

"Hopefully you won't need it, but if you do, it's there for you."

An uncomfortable silence, which seemed to be included with every family visit, followed. Laura had come to dread this awkward quiet that desperately needed to be filled with words she always seemed to lack. Laura also felt growing trepidation for the ways in which family members would attempt to comfort her. While she could certainly recognize their attempts as loving gestures, the words often sounded downright odd to her. Just before leaving, Laura's grandfather gave her a hug.

He said, "Well, at least it didn't happen to Emily...you know... someone you're attached to."

When her grandparents left, Laura had a lot to mull over. *Burial plots...wow...no wonder people are crying when they come in here. They're thinking about burial plots–and not getting too attached. This whole episode has gotten me very attached to Hannah. Heck, I was attached to her even before this. Does Grandpa mean I shouldn't be attached to her? Should I be preparing myself for her death? Noooo...well...I guess I should...I mean...look at the past few days. But the funeral would be for the death of me, as much as it would be for her. What if my family can't understand? What if they can't see how I possibly could have become so attached to my little girl? I guess I'd have to be as strong at the funeral as I've been here and wait until later to mourn. What am I saying? There isn't going to be a funeral. Hannah will make it through this just fine. They just don't understand all that's going on because they're not here every day. Well, I guess it's good to keep in mind anything as a possibility—considering the past few days.*

Soon after Laura's grandparents left, Dr. Brennan, the geneticist, approached her.

Laura gladly welcomed the intrusion, hoping he could help alleviate her gloomy thoughts.

"Any news yet?" she asked.

"Nothing concrete, but I do have a theory." He leaned against the Isolette. "I noticed the shape of Hannah's mouth, these dimples on her ears and elbows, her small size, and other subtle characteristics. She reminds me of another patient of mine who was born with a slight defect on about the sixteenth band of the "p" arm of his fourth chromosome. The preliminary results are supportive of my theory, but we won't know for sure what's going on until the test results come back. They should be in on Monday. I'll be by, as soon as I get them. At that point, we can chat more about what it all means."

"Soooo...the heart defects could be due to a problem with her genes?"

"Yes."

"So this is something that Kevin or I passed on to her?"

"Probably not; most often, genetic defects are just a fluke occurrence. But again, we'll know much more when the results come in. Until then, try not to stress over this or worry about it. We'll discuss it later when we have more information to go on."

"Okay. Thank you, Dr. Brennan."

"You're welcome. Have a good afternoon."

Right...a good afternoon...sure. My world, as I know it, has disappeared, and my current world is falling apart around me, but I'll be sure to have a freakin' great afternoon. I should call Kevin. No, we don't know anything for sure yet, and he's doing well with all of this, so far. I don't want to stress him out for possibly no reason.

With her head spinning, her heart racing, and feeling as if she were going to throw up, Laura left the ICN to sort out her thoughts. She tried visiting the parents' lounge, then the cafeteria, but she couldn't get her mind to stop racing. Finally, she found a phone and called Daniel. After close to a dozen unsuccessful attempts during the past few days, Daniel answered the phone.

As always, Laura was instantly soothed by his voice, but to her dismay, and for the first time ever, she didn't walk away from the conversation with her stepbrother feeling satisfied. She still felt a certain distance, like she had been feeling with the rest of the family—that uncomfortable silence lingering in the background, even as they spoke. *Why don't I feel like I thought I would? What is it that I'm looking for? The whole family is being so supportive, and I'm feeling like something's missing. Even with Kevin, it's good to have him home, but I still feel like...ah...I don't know. Maybe I'm being unfair. I just had a nice conversation with Daniel. I have no right to walk away from it feeling like Daniel, or anyone else in the family, somehow isn't there for me. I don't want to be unfair, but I just don't want to feel this way anymore. I don't want sympathy. I don't want prayers. I want Hannah to get better. I don't want throwing up, weight loss, blood draws, and inconsolable crying spells. I don't want IV attempts, little shaved spots all over her head, and tubes jammed down her throat. I don't want to think about funeral arrangements and burial plots. I want my baby home in her crib. I just want to be with both of my little girls.*

Laura wanted to return to Hannah, but she realized she had to calm down first. She didn't want Hannah to sense her anxiety, and she also didn't want the nurses to see how upset she was or attempt to talk to her. Her thoughts weren't coherent enough to be talking to anyone. She headed for the hospital chapel. The area was dimly lit and quiet, and Laura was thankful that no other people were there. She sat down, feeling rather intimidated by her surroundings. She had attended church regularly during her childhood, but many years had passed since she had last gone. *What am I doing here? I don't belong here. I'm too ticked off at God to pray right now.*

She felt like she was being dragged along for a ride at a dizzying pace, and as she clung on for dear life, her sanity was slipping out of her grasp. *I hate this! I HATE this!* She wanted to cry and let it out, but the tears wouldn't come. She wanted to scream at the top of her lungs, but she didn't want anyone else to hear. She pounded her legs with her fists. *Everyone talks about the miracles that take place in the ICN, but all I see is suffering.* Her mind flashed back to the scene where needles were jabbing into Hannah's flesh over and over again. *The other mothers and I swap stories about torturous procedures and brushes with death like moms on the outside chat about teething.* Laura envisioned the wall of white coats blocking her from her baby. *Our children are living out the dark side of the miracles that people ooh and aah about.* Laura's mind tortured her with the image of Hannah's tiny bruised and battered body—black and blue, sliced, raw, and bleeding. *When's the suffering going to end, so Hannah's miracle can begin— huh, God? When have we had enough? Does Hannah have to die first? Will that end it? What did she ever do to deserve this? UGGHHH!* Laura's inner voice quieted, as if silently sobbing in a far corner of her mind.

A second voice existed in Laura's head, one that had grown increasingly familiar during their stay at the hospital—the voice of a critical, demanding parent that demeaned Laura and barked out orders. The second voice spoke up, loud and clear. *Oh, enough of this. Laura! Hannah will be fine. It's getting late. Hannah is probably crying, and you know the nurses aren't gonna have time to calm her down. Now just quit your bitchin', and get yourself back to the ICN where you belong.*

Chapter V

Lonely Days

Laura was anxious to hear the awaited news from Dr. Brennan on Monday and grew disappointed as the day wore on with no sign of the doctor. That evening, Dr. O'Connor appeared with an update. He wasn't happy. Hannah's heart and respiratory rates were continuing to climb steadily. Her temperature was in the 38–39.4°C (100.4–102.9°F) range, and her white-blood-cell count was up. Yet no one had been able to find a source of infection. She was somewhat dehydrated, but without IV access, there was little he could do to remedy that problem. NG tube feedings continued but, unfortunately, Hannah had developed some diarrhea–bad news, since she was already dry and her weight was down to 2.4 kilos (5.28 pounds).

"I've contacted the doctors in Boston. We've done all we can do here, and what we're doing obviously isn't working. Hannah will be transferred to Children's Hospital tomorrow afternoon. She needs surgery. We just can't get her stabilized until we get some of these plumbing issues addressed. Her downhill progress over the past few days clearly demonstrates that."

Laura controlled the urge to make an exasperated sigh and an obnoxious roll of her eyes. She had thought immediate surgery would be best for Hannah from their very first day at the hospital. Dr. O'Connor was finally seeing that need, too.

"So tomorrow she'll be getting the open-heart surgery?" she asked.

"No. When she gets there, the surgeons will evaluate her case and decide what surgery to do and when to do it. I'm hoping that they'll opt for the open-heart; I think she really needs it, but they may decide to go with a bypass procedure and just address the coarc (the problem with the aorta) and maybe the PDA. With her weight loss and general decline over the past week, they may feel she isn't strong enough for the open-heart. With corrective surgery to the aorta and PDA, the theory is Hannah would be able to stabilize enough to gain some weight. Then, when she's older and stronger, we'll be able to look at doing the open-heart."

Laura hoped Hannah would have the full open-heart surgery done at Children's Hospital. She figured Hannah would be more likely to get better if the most extensive procedure was performed—sooner, rather than later. She desperately wanted to put this nightmare behind them.

"So tomorrow, huh?"

"Yes, at two o'clock."

"Thank you, Dr. O'Connor."

Laura rocked Hannah with a wealth of new things to think over. *So, I need to check out of David's House. I'd better get packed up, before I go to bed. I wonder where I'll stay when I get to Boston. I hope Dr. Brennan will have his report ready before we leave. Wow, this is going faster than I thought. Hannah's been here a week, we'll be at Children's Hospital tomorrow, the surgery will probably be scheduled for Wednesday, we'll stay for a few more days for recovery, and then we'll be on our way home. How much longer will Kevin be home? Will they send him back to the ship, or will we be going back to California early? Will his time on the ship count, or will he have to head right back out to sea for another six months? Boy, I can't even imagine moving back to California. If Hannah still needs open-heart surgery, we'd have to have it done out there, but they say Boston Children's has one of the best pediatric cardiology departments in the world. I don't want to take her out west until everything is done. Kevin will have to go ahead of us. But, then what'll I do with Emily, if things don't go well with Hannah? Laura sighed deeply. Deal with today, Laura. Just get through today.*

Laura arrived in the ICN the next morning, only to learn that Hannah hadn't improved overnight. Her weight had dropped to 2.34 kilos (5.15 pounds), and her feedings had been stopped due to severe diarrhea. Her diaper had been left open, because she had a diaper rash with areas that were cracked and bleeding– definitely time to change the game plan.

Laura was determined to spend as much time as possible holding her baby, because she didn't know what would happen when they got to Boston. Just after rounds, she struggled to get settled into their chair–a much more difficult task since Hannah's diaper had been left open. She was soon interrupted by one of the nurses and was asked to join her in the Koala Room. Dr. Brennan would be there with the results of Hannah's blood tests.

The Koala Room was offered to parents the night before a baby was discharged. For at least one night parents were completely responsible for their child's care while having the security of knowing the ICN staff was outside their door. When it wasn't in use for discharge, the room served as a more confidential setting for parent conferences.

Laura was worried that the more private setting could mean the doctor had bad news. She situated Hannah in her Isolette, kissed her forehead, and followed the nurse. Once they were all seated in the Koala Room, Dr. Brennan spoke.

"How's Hannah doing this morning?"

"Not great, but they're transferring us to Boston, so things should get better soon," said Laura.

"Yes, I heard you two would be leaving. Best of luck to you."

"Thank you."

"Okay, well, we've found the cause of Hannah's heart trouble. My original theory was confirmed. Hannah has a rare genetic disorder called Wolf-Hirschhorn syndrome."

Wolf-Hirschhorn...eww. Of course she couldn't have something feminine sounding like "Kimberly-Rose syndrome. Wolf-Hirschhorn syndrome. It sounds soooo...rough.

"The "shorthand" name for it is four-p-minus. As I began to explain the other day, it's a slight deletion in genetic information on the fourth chromosome. The information involved is on the "p," or petite arm of that chromosome, and, of course, because we're talking about missing information we have "minus" in the name. Not much is known about it; it's pretty rare, but I do have some information here for you."

Rare...that's not bad, right? She's just unique. "When you say rare, like...how rare?"

"There are about 150 documented cases in the U.S. right now. There's likely more, but until recently, the technology wasn't available to correctly diagnose, so older children were likely to be misdiagnosed. And, unfortunately, the literature is based on these cases from the 60s and 70s when only the worst cases were detectable. Remember that when you read it. Every parent will tell you that the stuff in those books is worst-case stuff—not your child. A syndrome is simply a group of characteristics; not every child shares every characteristic."

"What else does it involve, other than the heart defects?"

"Some of the physical characteristics include cleft lip/cleft palate, which, obviously, Hannah does not have. They tend to have slightly downturned mouths, their noses tend to have a wide base, they often have microcephaly (smaller-than-usual head size), low-set ears..."

Hannah's nose is just like her sister's. Does that mean Emily has it, too? What does he mean by "small head?" Hannah is small all over. "Hannah's head is smaller than it should be?"

"Just slightly."

"'Cause I hadn't noticed that. What about her ears? They're low-set?"

"Again, just slightly. Most people probably wouldn't notice these things on Hannah unless they were looking for them. Now, four-p-minus also includes physical and mental delays, and some can suffer a seizure disorder."

Emily is way behind in speech, but I figured that was from all of the ear infections. The girls look so much alike. Oh, God, what if I caused this? This isn't good...this isn't good. Deep breath, Laura. Stay calm. "So, this is genetic? It's from Kevin or me?"

"Like I said the other day, probably not. Ninety-six percent of the time, it's a fluke. It's just something that happens that no one can explain. However, we'll be interested in getting blood samples from you and your husband, to find out for sure."

The delays—ask about them—but don't sound too stressed out about them. "So, about the delays you mentioned—how much of a delay? Do you mean like 'a little slow in school' delay?"

"It's impossible to say. They all vary in their abilities."

Laura suddenly recalled a conversation she had had with Kevin as teenagers: "Man, I couldn't handle having some freak kid," Kevin had said. Laura had voiced her discomfort about the term "freak" and about a handicap not being the child's fault. Kevin had said, "I don't care. I just couldn't handle that."

Oh, man, what am I gonna do? Hold it together, Laura. You don't want them to think you love Hannah any less. Don't act devastated by any of this. She's still the same baby girl you just kissed on the forehead. "But, uh, since she isn't as affected physically, she won't be as affected developmentally, right?"

"Unfortunately, we have no way of knowing. We'll just have to wait and observe."

Fight it, Laura. Your voice is shaky. Pull it together. Hold it together.

"It's going to be a tough row to hoe, but remember that it won't be as bad as the literature will make it seem. I have contacted the parents of that other patient of mine who has Wolf-Hirschhorn syndrome—Jacob Breckenridge—and they have given me permission to give you their names and number. You can feel free to call them with any questions you might have."

Oh, I can handle tough; look at all that's happened with Em and her struggles—colic, ear infections, asthma, and behavioral issues. "Is Jacob badly affected?"

"Jacob has characteristics that set him apart from other kids, but just a few months ago, I saw them walking away from me down the hall. If I hadn't recognized his mother, I never would have known that was him. He could have been any other boy walking down the hall in a baseball cap. Granted, he looked two or three years younger than he actually is."

"Is that what you mean by physical delays?"

"Right. These kids tend to grow slowly and stay relatively small."

Okay, can this guy be any less specific? "How big will Hannah be?"

"I don't see any reason why, health permitting, she wouldn't be able to grow to five feet."

Well, at least she'll be petite. At least this isn't some disorder where she'll be some six-foot tall, 350-pound giant. "What's the prognosis for kids with Wolf-Hirschhorn syndrome?"

"If they can survive the first three to five years, they generally have a good chance at a relatively long life."

What do you mean "if they can survive" and "relatively long life"? What, exactly, am I looking at here? Get this guy outta here. I'm gonna lose it if I have to keep playing twenty questions. Just leave me alone with the paperwork. I'm sure the answers are there in writing. "By 'relatively long life,' do you mean fifty or sixty years?"

"I don't see why not."

Right, but you have no idea. "Well, I have the information that you've given me. Would you mind giving me some privacy, so I can read this stuff over?"

"Of course not. Here's my card. When you get to Boston, feel free to call me at any time with any questions you might think of. This is a lot to take in, all at once."

Go, go, go. Get out of here—leave. "Thank you, Dr. Brennan."

56

The door closed and Laura was all alone. She shot a sideways glance at the booklets lying next to her. She was afraid to open them. That would make the situation even more real. Instead, Laura wanted to pretend that Dr. Brennan had just announced something of little significance, such as, "Your daughter has blonde hair." She wondered what kind of mother she was by reacting to Hannah's diagnosis differently than she would have to something as benign as hair color. But no amount of wishing was going to lessen the impact of Dr. Brennan's words. The diagnosis was hard to accept. Laura was sad for her baby. She was sad for herself. She was a thousand kinds of sad. She hated herself for feeling that way, but she couldn't help it.

After a few minutes of absently staring out the window, Laura decided to begin her reading with an article written by another mother of a Wolf-Hirschhorn child. From what Dr. Brennan had said about the other literature, Laura wasn't sure if she ever wanted to read it.

I STEAL HEARTS by: Valerie A. Dillavou *

Ever since Justine's birth, I have been told so many negative things. Justine was born with a rare chromosomal abnormality called 4p- or Wolf-Hirschhorn Syndrome. She was supposedly 1 in about 100 in the country who had this syndrome at that time. Since then I have found out that many of the things that I was told about her were either erroneous or rare occurrences...

Okay, this is sounding better.

I have set out to prove the doctors and all of the statistics wrong. Justine is now 4½ years old and is able to do many of the things I was given no hope of her ever doing. She is so full of surprises and always makes me smile...At almost 2 she learned how to sit...Doctors never thought she'd be able to sit up by herself...Justine, who weighs only a little more than 16 pounds...

* Valerie A. Dillavou, originally published as "Beware! I Steal Hearts," *Exceptional Parent Magazine*, July 1991.

Oh, my God...oh, my God...that's...that's what he meant by "delay"? Not being able to sit is not a delay...oh, Christ, what am I going to do? Why didn't he tell me? Oh, God, Kevin's never going to be able to handle this. What am I going to do? What am I going to <u>do</u>!

Laura couldn't finish the article. She wanted to cry. She wanted to roll up in a corner and not come up for air until this had all somehow magically passed. Instead, she just sat there, completely numb. The tears did not come. The room was so quiet. She had never felt more alone.

I can't be alone right now. I need someone here. I've gotta have someone here to help me. I need to call Kevin. Are you crazy? You can't call Kevin! If you want to feel a hundred times worse when he freaks out, then you go right ahead and call him. He's already said he can't handle this, and you know that's true. But, who should I call? Everyone's a couple of hours away. You're alone, Laura. You're all alone. **NOOOOO**!

She shook all over and was sweating, but the tears still did not come. *I have to scream. I have to let some of this out, but where? If they hear you carrying on, they'll come in here with a straightjacket, for sure. Call Aunt Nancy. She'll come. Okay, okay, stop shaking, pull yourself together and dial the phone.*

"Hi, Aunt Nancy?" Suddenly the tears came—uncontrollably. "Oh God, Aunt Nancy, I need you...I need you to come here right now...please...please ...oh, I need you right now..."

Slamming the phone down, Laura ran to the private bathroom attached to the Koala Room. She screamed, she shrieked, she wailed, she sobbed. She died inside. Feeling her soul twisting and writhing in pain, she fought back. She slammed herself up against the door and banged her fists on the sink. She pulled her hair, slapped her face, pounded her legs, and then slid slowly to the floor—empty and exhausted.

Why, why, why, why, why, why, why, why, why, why, why, why, why, why, why?

Laura wasn't sure how long she had sat there. Finally, she returned to the Koala Room, afraid that the nurses had heard her and were waiting for her. But the room was empty, and she felt thankful for that. At least her private hell had remained a private one.

Pull it together, Laura. Your little girl needs you in the other room. She's gonna be stuck in the ambulance later. Oh crap, what time is it?

The clock on the wall showed that it was 1:30 p.m. Dr. O'Connor had said they would be leaving for Boston at 2 p.m. Panicked, Laura ran back to the bathroom and splashed cold water on her face, desperate to wipe away any trace of her tears. After a deep breath, she headed back to Hannah's Isolette and was thankful the transfer crew had not arrived yet. Apparently the transfer had been called off. A nurse explained to Laura that Hannah had spiked a fever, and Dr. O'Connor didn't dare chance the long two-hour drive. From one point of view, remaining in the ICN was scary since Dr. O'Connor had said the night before that Hannah's stay there was doing more harm than good. From another point of view, Laura had had enough for one day and preferred to stay put.

In the meantime, Nancy arrived in record time. She was extremely scared. Laura's emotional call had included no details, which left Nancy fearing the worst. They sat in the hallway and discussed the diagnosis, while looking over the information Dr. Brennan had provided. They agreed that the situation might get easier to handle in time.

"Besides, Laura," said Nancy, "there's nothing we can do about it. Whatever happens, we'll get through this together."

Now that she felt some family support, Laura was renewed with hope. Nancy encouraged her to talk to Kevin, assuring her that she might be surprised by his ability to handle the news. When Nancy headed back home, Laura took a deep breath and called him.

Nancy had been right. Laura was *very* pleasantly surprised by Kevin's response to the day's events. Actually, Kevin didn't say much, at all, concerning the matter.

"Well, whatever the future brings, we'll get through it," he said.

Laura feared denial was preventing him from getting the full impact of her words. Nonetheless, his response wasn't the harsh and painful one she had imagined, so she felt thankful for that and decided not to proceed any further.

As Laura had feared, the next few days in the ICN showcased Hannah's deteriorating state. Her latest weight was 2.27 kilos (4.99 pounds). Her feedings were still on hold due to the diarrhea. The plan was to try a central IV line for larger venous access, so she could be fed intravenously. That meant an IV would be going into a big vein, such as her jugular. Unfortunately, trying to place a central line proved to be just as difficult as the peripheral ones. After a failed attempt on her jugular vein, the plan was to try for a femoral line (access would be through the femoral vein, the major vein leading from the leg to the heart), but the doctors were growing increasingly skeptical and very frustrated.

Meanwhile, Laura began to receive phone calls from family members who felt less than supportive. Apparently they wanted to make sure Laura understood she did not have any legal obligation to consent to Hannah's surgery and that she could "let nature take its course." They all assured her that, of course, they would support her decision, either way. However, she got a distinct sense that they leaned toward a decision of no surgery.

Laura called her dad, knowing she would get a straightforward answer about his view on the matter. He understood that, as a parent, she was torn. He recognized that other people were more likely to form snap decisions and opinions when they weren't as emotionally invested.

"But," he said, "it's better to have an uncomfortable situation now rather than a whole fucking tragedy for *everyone* later."

Right...they "support me either way." Well, you asked for that one, Laura.

Feeling overwhelmed and distraught, Laura called Kevin. She felt that *both* of Hannah's parents needed to contribute to this particular decision.

Kevin said, "I'll leave that decision to you. *You're* the one emotionally involved." That hurt Laura more than her dad's words ever could.

Meanwhile, Laura was even disappointed with the thoughts running through her own mind. When other babies would leave the hospital, she would feel jealous and bitter. She didn't even want to look at the families as they headed out the door. *Laura! Cut this out. Listen to yourself! You're jealous that someone else has had the "privilege" of having a baby who had to stay in the hospital for three months? Do you hear what you're saying? But they get to go home, knowing this is all over for them. This stuff with Hannah is gonna go on for life. They get to think about dance classes and Little League. They get to hope for honor roll. They get to look forward to the prom and maybe even a wedding someday–but we won't for Hannah. That's all gone now. Christ, I don't even know what we have to look forward to.*

By the end of the week, with a femoral line miraculously in place, Hannah was scheduled, once again, to transfer to Boston. This time they were determined to succeed. Dr. O'Connor had intubated her (provided her with a breathing tube) for the trip, because her respiratory rate and work of breathing had further increased. He talked with the surgeons in Boston, and surgery was scheduled for the following day–Monday.

Laura wasn't sure what she expected Boston Children's Hospital to be like, but she wasn't happy with what she found. Rain poured as she entered the massive building and Laura found her mood matched the weather outside. She was so used to Dartmouth-Hitchcock. As soon as she walked through the doors of the big-city hospital, she realized she missed a certain "north-country welcome" she had taken for granted at DHMC.

This place was huge. She immediately felt like...a number and realized she would need to take a more active role in meeting Hannah's personal needs. They were in the cardiac intensive care unit (CICU)—just young patients with cardiac problems—and the sheer number of babies and children there absolutely shocked her.

Laura soon found out how spoiled she had been by the comforts of David's House. Luckily, space was available for her in an old ICU ward that had been partitioned off with curtains and filled with cots for parents of children in the CICU. She had been told that the room usually filled up quickly, and her next best option would be the Ronald McDonald House—across town. No homemade quilts, prepared breakfasts, or loving volunteers could be found here. She had just arrived and she was already homesick.

Later that night, Laura was approached by one of the doctors. He informed her that Hannah's surgery had been bumped to an undisclosed later date, due to an emergency involving a child who had just arrived. Laura was surprised to hear that a case more urgent than Hannah's could exist. On the following day, Monday, a nurse informed Laura that Hannah's surgical team had met and decided to reschedule surgery for Wednesday, and that they would attempt only the bypass procedure and save the open-heart surgery for when Hannah was older and stronger.

With Hannah intubated, rocking her was impossible, but since she was in a medically induced coma, Laura knew Hannah wasn't missing their time together. Laura started walking the halls to pass time. She quickly discovered that a sure-fire cure for self-pity was a walk through the halls of Boston Children's Hospital. The suffering and anguish that radiated around her completely overshadowed her personal woes. Laura would sit and listen intently to the stories other parents poured out to her. The distraction helped, because she didn't have to worry about her own situation when she was focused on their lives. She greedily welcomed the escape. Tuesday night Laura was slapped back into facing the reality of her own situation. She was approached by both the surgeon and the staff geneticist and was quizzed about why she was consenting to surgery. They each very carefully pointed out that surgery was not something they had to do. Being reminded of that fact angered Laura. She explained to the doctors that she never really felt like she had much of a decision to make.

"There's no guarantee that Hannah will have a poor quality of life. While we do know that she'll have physical and mental delays, we have no idea to what extent. There is no evidence that a chance at life would sentence her to a life of pain and suffering. This being said, who am I to decide that she, as an individual, isn't worth the chance of having a long and happy life? Besides, in the small amount of information on Wolf-Hirschhorn syndrome that I have been given, I've read that the one ability every Wolf-Hirschhorn child is reported to have is the ability to smile. I figure, then, that they must have something to smile about. I'd like to give my daughter an opportunity to smile one day, too."

Apparently, Laura's explanation served as a suitable defense for her decision. Hannah's gurney was rolled into the operating room the next morning at 9:00 a.m. sharp. Laura figured the "right" way to approach such an event meant having some sort of a spiritual moment with her daughter before she was wheeled off. She imagined herself becoming weepy, as Hannah glided down the hall facing an uncertain future. But that didn't happen. Laura was so physically and emotionally drained at that point, and still under the influence of so much denial, that she saw the surgery as little more than a quick, necessary step to help Hannah "get better" and return home to Emily. Dr. O'Connor's worrisome words echoed somewhere in the back of her mind, leaving her somewhat concerned, but she wasn't accepting the full gravity of the situation.

Dr. Hillard performed the surgery, and a few hours later, Laura, Kevin, and Nancy saw him walking toward them. The surgery had been a success. Dr. Hillard had corrected the aorta and the PDA (fetal blood vessel). Laura was amazed as he described what had happened in the operating room. This man—who easily stood six feet tall with big, burly hands—had been able to repair a *single vessel* of a heart the size of a walnut. He said that the longest, most difficult, and by far, the most frustrating part of the surgery was getting an IV in place. Hannah had lost her femoral line a day or two earlier. He ended up having to do a cut-down—a procedure during which they cut into the skin, expose the vein, pierce it, and stitch around the site once the line is in. Laura almost wished the cut-down procedure hadn't been described to her, because the mental picture was far too disturbing. She tried to dismiss the image from her mind and just focus her attention on the fact that Hannah was now okay.

A few hours later, Hannah was back in the CICU and was ready for visitors. The nurses had warned Laura that she was likely to find Hannah's appearance disturbing. She had told her to expect many more tubes and wires than she previously had and that Hannah would be bloated and puffy all over, due to excess fluid.

Hannah appeared pale and felt extremely cold, but other than that, her appearance was not terribly different than before the surgery. She had a bandage covering an IV site on her right wrist, which presumably was the cut-down site. There was clear evidence of other IV attempts on her scalp and all four limbs. New tubes protruded from her chest for drainage around the surgical site and she had a catheter, draining and measuring urine output. Laura didn't pull down the blankets to inspect the surgical area more closely because Hannah was so cold, and she didn't want to hurt or disturb her.

Soon Nancy and Kevin left. Laura appreciated that they had been there for the surgery, but she was relieved to see them go. She still felt as if she had to entertain her family whenever they appeared, and that always left her feeling exhausted.

Laura was surprised the staff moved them from the CICU to the cardiac floor (where rooms for the less critical cardiac patients were located) just two days after the surgery. At first she was excited, because she assumed they might be going home soon—perhaps that weekend. But, within a day, she was calling Dr. O'Connor, begging to be transferred back to Dartmouth-Hitchcock for an opportunity to finish the recovery there. She told Dr. O'Connor she was willing to sign an agreement stating he and his staff would not be held responsible for anything that might happen during the trip if he were to let them come back. He apologized, but explained that Hannah could not be transferred until she was more stable.

Laura hated the cardiac floor. She felt as if she had become a prisoner in Hannah's room. The room wasn't even in view of the nurses' station. Since Hannah was unable to push the call button to get help, someone had to be with her at all times. Laura didn't even feel comfortable running to the cafeteria. Her frustrations boiled over one afternoon when a new nurse came on duty to get vital signs. Just when the nurse had arrived, Laura noticed Hannah was showing some signs of heart failure. She was sweaty (diaphoretic, as she had learned to call it), her respiratory and heart rates were elevated, and worst of all, her lips were blue. Laura worried that this setback would send them back to the CICU. She wasn't overly worried, though, because she assumed the nurse would know what to do.

The nurse casually worked her way through the assessment, striking up a conversation of small talk as she proceeded, which Laura interpreted as the nurse's attempt to keep Laura calm. When the pulse oximeter produced a reading in the high 80s (which should have been 100%, or at least in the 90s), the nurse finally asked about Hannah's color.

"So she's always blue like this?"

Laura raised her voice. "NO!"

She wondered if the nurse had even listened to the report from the previous nurse or had bothered to look at Hannah's chart. Cyanosis (blue color) definitely was no longer normal for Hannah. Laura's mind raced with "what if" questions, specifically wondering what would have happened if she had gone to the cafeteria to grab some lunch. She feared the nurse might have come and gone without questioning her findings or following up on them. Laura was practically vibrating with the desire to leave Children's Hospital after that.

Laura was confused by Dr. O'Connor's words. She questioned why Hannah had been stable enough to move out of the CICU to the cardiac floor but was not stable enough for the transfer. She reasoned that Hannah had to be more stable following the surgery than she had been for the last ambulance trip.

However, the latest findings clearly showed Hannah was less stable than they'd like. She was still having bouts of heart failure, and her weight was horribly low at 2.24 kilos (4.94 pounds). When she changed Hannah's diapers, Laura had to lift Hannah carefully from the hips, because her tailbone appeared dangerously close to poking through her skin. Hannah had no weight left to lose. Skin and bone were all that remained. Laura figured since they were going to stay in Boston for a while, Emily should join them for a visit. With a private room, they didn't have to worry about her disturbing other sick children. Laura called Kevin to plan a stay for the weekend.

"No," he said. "That's a three-hour drive, Laura."

"Right, but Em has gotten much better about being in the car, and it'll be worth it when she gets here. I mean...we haven't seen each other in almost three weeks now."

"No. It's too much of a hassle."

Laura hung up the phone, devastated. *I can't see my little girl? I can't believe he won't let me see Em. Doesn't he understand how much I miss her? Doesn't he see how this is killing me to be apart from her? No, Laura, and do you know why? Because you didn't tell him. If you want something as much as you want to see Emily, you're gonna have to get yourself a backbone and fight for it. Well I shouldn't have to! He must understand how hard this is. Why doesn't he want to come to see us? Hannah is his daughter, too, and he has hardly seen her at all. Are you kidding? You know he doesn't care about any of this! Well, this would be a perfect opportunity for our whole family to be together finally—but we're not. And for what reason—because it's a hassle?*

The weekend dragged by. Laura sulked in their room, feeling particularly sorry for herself. On Sunday, she called and talked to Daniel again, which helped a lot, lifting and brightening her mood. He suggested that she talk to Kevin, explain how she was feeling, and not rely on the assumption that Kevin would simply understand without an explanation. After that they spoke about nothing in particular. Because of the situation Laura had been thrown into, senseless conversation had become a rarity. Discussions were businesslike with the doctors and nurses, consisted mostly of venting with the other parents, and were usually uncomfortable, awkward updates with family members who called or visited. The talk with Daniel provided her with a much-needed break from all of that while serving as a reminder that she wasn't just "the mother" and nothing more.

By Monday Laura felt she was going to go out of her mind if she didn't get out of that room for at least a few minutes. She created a goal for herself. Since music had seemed very therapeutic for Hannah at DHMC, Laura's new mission was to find a tape recorder. She would head into town in search of music during the times she felt confident that Hannah was asleep for a while. She would go in one direction and walk for a half hour to forty-five minutes and then head back, in case Hannah had woken up. The following day she'd tackle another direction. Since she had no car (Kevin was using their one automobile) and absolutely no idea where she was going, her search turned into an all-week project. Finally, on Thursday, she stumbled upon a Radio Shack, and a record store was located nearby that had a few classical tapes. Laura found the walks surprisingly therapeutic for her. By the week's end, she felt like a new woman. With newfound confidence, she called Kevin and demanded to see Emily. He finally gave in.

That weekend was wonderful. Laura wanted to spend quality time with Emily, so she asked her sister to babysit Hannah while they went out into Boston, but first, she wanted Emily to spend a few minutes with Hannah. Laura explained to her that Hannah had been born with a broken heart, and the reason they had spent so much time away from home was because the doctors need a lot of time to mend a broken heart. Emily asked about the NG tube and the leads, but seemed to easily accept the explanations and appeared generally at ease with her baby sister.

After the brief visit with Hannah, Kevin and Laura took Emily to the Boston Aquarium. Emily loved it, and Laura absolutely loved being with Emily. Laura dreaded saying goodbye at the end of the day and was comforted only by the hope that she would soon be home with Hannah.

The weekend had renewed her waning energy, but the news she received on Monday had her absolutely overjoyed. The doctors felt Hannah was stable enough to head back to DHMC and finish her recovery there. They were scheduled for discharge on Monday, October 3, after eighteen long days in Boston. Laura called Kevin, thrilled to tell him he was going to have to turn around and drive south again. Hannah spiked another fever, but this time, the departure was only delayed by a day.

Laura didn't dislike the people at Boston Children's Hospital. After all, they had saved her daughter's life, and she would recommend that hospital to any parent of a child in need of surgery. She left the building, feeling inspired by the other parents she had met. *Yes, I have a sick child. Yes, it sucks being stuck in the hospital, watching my baby girl go through hell. But don't let that pull you down. Yeah, you never thought this would happen to you, but don't get lost in the "Why me?" Stand up. Don't let the situation consume you. Do what you need to do to get through it—because you can get through it. Look at what you've already accomplished—what you never thought you'd be able to get through. Go home and fight this, Laura. This is the last mile. You'll be home soon. You can do this.* Wanting to leave Boston toward the end wasn't as much about being unhappy with where she was, as it was about being anxious to move on.

Chapter VI

Running on Empty

With a renewed sense of energy, Laura vowed to devote equal time (or as equal as she could manage, at least) to both of her daughters. She felt quite confident about leaving Hannah with the ICN nurses. Although she would have preferred to stay at the hospital, Laura realized that giving Hannah all of her attention and leaving none for Emily wasn't fair. In some ways, she was afraid of going home to Emily, mainly due to concerns about the workload she was facing. Laura knew how much energy she had typically devoted to Emily's care before Hannah's birth, and she knew the amount of energy she now had. The two energy levels did not match up in any way. Laura feared the most trivial parenting chores—brushing hair, picking out clothes, picking up toys, answering 1,001 "why" questions, planning and preparing nutritious meals, reading bedtime stories, potty training, and so on. She wondered where she would ever find the energy to face all of it, especially when coupled with daily trips to the hospital.

Worse yet, Laura feared that parenting Emily would be even more difficult because she expected Emily to be a physical and emotional mess, due to their extended separation and Emily's time in Kevin's care. Laura had little confidence in Kevin's parenting. With the underlying anger she had from her recent struggle just to see Emily, she was ready to pounce on any of Kevin's parental shortcomings—especially anything that would make her job as a mother more challenging.

Determined to make her new plan work, Laura formulated a daily schedule. She would try to get Emily to Rosie, the sitter, by 8:00 a.m., which would enable her to arrive at the hospital by around 9:30 a.m., when rounds usually ended. Then she'd stay at the hospital until 5:00 p.m., pick Emily up at around 6:30 p.m., get dinner thrown together, do a little housework, spend the night at home, and then head out the next morning the same way. Laura wished she could eliminate the three-hour daily commute needed for the plan, which she saw as a waste of time that neither of the girls would benefit from, but, otherwise, she thought the schedule would work well.

Dropping Emily off at Rosie's house soon became one of Laura's least favorite parts of the day. After being apart from her for so long, Laura hated saying goodbye to Emily, and the farewells seemed to get more difficult with each passing day. Laura found that Emily's increased separation anxiety served as an all-too-frequent reminder of her absence as a parent, which she saw as a failure on her part. She could only guess the level of psychological damage that Emily suffered due to recent events. After all, Laura had walked out of the house one day, telling Emily that she and her new baby sister would be back from the doctor's office in a few minutes, when, in fact, she returned a month later—without her sister. Laura dwelled on how terrifying that must have felt to a three-year-old. She imagined that transitioning from being an only child to an older sister was hard enough, without having the baby snatch your mother completely away from you—for weeks. Laura believed she had failed her little girl, so the best she could do was to give Emily some extra time when she was having a particularly hard time letting go—and there were all too many mornings when Emily wanted nothing to do with letting go. Unfortunately, whenever Laura was gently trying to help ease Emily through one of these tough transitions, her imagination further punished her with visions of Hannah screaming, at the other end of her long commute, and the nurses too busy to attend to her.

Laura was pleasantly surprised, however, that aside from the increased separation anxiety, Emily wasn't acting as emotionally scarred by the events of the past weeks as she had feared. Potty training remained the biggest challenge with Emily, but that had been an ongoing dilemma; there appeared to be no regression of Emily's progress. Emily had been interested in potty training from the age of eighteen months. Laura somehow thought mastering toilet training usually happened faster, but, at age three, Emily still needed Pull-Ups at night, and Laura always carried a change of clothes with them when they were away from home. Laura would often just dress Emily in Pull-Ups if they planned on being away from home for a significant length of time, knowing otherwise Emily would have an accident. Laura was perplexed and frustrated that Emily couldn't grasp the concept of going to the bathroom whenever she started to feel her bladder getting full. Instead, Emily would wait until she felt the first dribble coming. Then, she'd panic, and her pants would be soaked before she could even say the words "I have to go potty." Laura was becoming an expert on recognizing the "potty dance" and taking immediate action to avoid the impending messy situation. Because there were often only seconds between the dance and the deed, using Pull-Ups in public was simply necessary, especially if Laura wasn't well versed on the location of local restrooms.

Laura felt her only hope for progress with Emily's potty training meant keeping on top of the situation. But having to keep the condition of Emily's bladder and bowels in the back of her mind at all times was exhausting—especially when she felt as if no end was in sight. At times Laura wondered if she'd be sending Emily to her prom with an extra set of clothes.

Constantly having to make excuses to the family for Emily's routine accidents was stressful for Laura, too. When Emily would stay with Steve and Janet, Laura requested that they prompt Emily to try to go to the bathroom every few hours. They agreed, but it was obvious they felt (along with most of the family) that Emily should have already been completely potty trained. They thought the incontinence was simply a behavior issue. Laura could see how they'd come to that conclusion. When Emily was asked if she had to go to the bathroom, she'd be adamant that she didn't have to go, but then she'd often wet or soil herself within minutes. Most people assumed that Emily was simply lying about not having to go. Laura, however, wholeheartedly believed they were dealing with something else—she just didn't know what yet. She desperately wanted to make others understand that this wasn't a discipline issue, but she just didn't have the answers to back up her beliefs.

Meanwhile, Kevin felt the problem was definitely a discipline issue. In his eyes, if you yelled hard and loud enough, the child would surely get the message. Therefore, the stress resulting from Emily's lack of potty training was one of the most taxing issues on their marriage. Kevin and Laura were clearly at odds about toilet-training techniques. Kevin wouldn't make the effort to keep the "potty gauge" in the back of his mind. Consequently, Emily was much more likely to have accidents while in his care. Then he'd become angry—extremely angry—and that would annoy Laura. She felt Kevin had no right to be angry with Emily for not doing something she had clearly and repeatedly demonstrated she could not yet do on her own.

Laura was at a loss on how to argue the point with Kevin if he couldn't see the wrong in his thinking. After all, certain actions were simply beyond Emily's capability. He would have had as much luck if he had yelled at her to do long division. Adding to Laura's frustration, he appeared to have no idea that he could be doing more harm than good when he yelled at his daughter.

To avoid future arguments, Laura's only answer was to strongly encourage Kevin to put Emily in Pull-Ups in her absence. No training would get done, but no damage would be done, either. Unfortunately, that arrangement led to Laura resenting the fact that she was the only parent taking the responsibility of working towards potty-training success. That realization was one of the many reasons why Laura was happy to have Rosie in their lives. As a very experienced sitter, mother, and grandmother, Rosie had been involved with the potty training of many, many babies throughout the years. With that thought in mind, Laura felt she could shift her attention back to Hannah.

• •

Although Laura trusted the nurses in the ICN as much as one possibly could, she couldn't get to the hospital fast enough each morning, and 5:00 p.m. always came much too early. And even though Hannah was in the hospital simply for recovery, the days weren't uneventful. Weight gain remained the biggest challenge.

After being discharged from Boston, during the beginning of October at roughly six weeks old, her weight still hadn't returned to her birth weight of five pounds, ten ounces. That created a major problem. Hannah's life was on hold until she could gain some weight—and the seeming simplicity of the situation was maddening.

Laura never would have imagined the number of problems that could crop up with such an "insignificant" issue as weight gain. She learned a lot more than she thought was available—and more than she ever wanted to know—about the dietary needs of infants.

For instance, breast milk and the baby formula sold in stores are generally twenty calories per ounce. You can increase caloric value of breast milk or formula by adjusting the amount of powder added to the water or breast milk and/or by adding other ingredients like corn oil, corn syrup, MCT oil and/or polycose. Calories should always be increased slowly, because a baby's digestive tract is only designed for twenty-calorie food. If increased too quickly, the baby's delicate system will reject the unnaturally rich formula, resulting in vomiting, and/or diarrhea, which cause further weight loss.

The formulas, themselves, can also cause diarrhea or vomiting for various reasons. A lot of different formulas are available, and many aren't even sold over-the-counter, such as Alimentum and Pregestimil. Hannah ended up taking Pregestimil, after numerous unsuccessful trials on various other formulas.

The toughest lesson Laura learned was that regardless of which formula Hannah consumed, or how slowly calories had been increased, or how many other precautions they took, Hannah could continue to lose weight. Hannah was still experiencing heart failure. Heart failure can cause the digestive tract to fail, because it isn't getting the blood or oxygen supply needed. The situation had turned into a vicious circle for Hannah. She needed to gain weight in order to withstand open-heart surgery and overcome her heart failure. But she couldn't gain weight *because* she was in heart failure. Hence, trying to treat Hannah was like trying to drive a car with a bad engine into an auto-repair shop to be fixed. Her stomach rejected nearly everything—in one direction or the other—and adding more calories to the mix was even harder on her digestive tract, which just worsened the situation.

Hannah's diarrhea continued, which gave her a severe diaper rash. Voiding had become excruciating because of the burning that would ensue on her raw, exposed flesh. Laura became an expert at combining the products available to treat severe diaper rash, in order to achieve the maximum protection, but nothing completely protected Hannah from the pain.

Meanwhile, because of the energy required for the physical task of eating, an NG tube was still a necessity, which did not please Hannah at all. In fact, she became quite adept at pulling out NG tubes, no matter how well they were taped into place on her cheeks. The tape, in turn, was so irritating to her skin that her little cheeks became as raw and bloody as her bottom. However, the tape was an absolute necessity, because an incorrectly placed or slightly dislodged NG tube could lead into the lungs, instead of the stomach, and result in drowning.

Laura had mixed feelings for the NG tube. She was glad that Hannah wasn't wasting energy on eating and that the exact amount of food she was consuming could be easily measured. But Laura also learned that a baby who doesn't suck for an extended length of time could forget how to suck altogether. A baby who doesn't know how to suck may not learn to how to chew, and eventually, may not even have the oral dexterity necessary for speech.

Laura worried that the continued need for the NG tube would jeopardize Hannah's future eating and speaking abilities. She also worried about the constant need to replace the NG tube. Every time Hannah moved her tube and every time a nurse replaced it, the possibility of Hannah drowning remained a genuine risk. Laura also worried about the injuries to Hannah's face due to constant re-taping, and the pain it was causing her baby girl. But she understood that no other option seemed to exist. Hannah was dying. Gaining weight was her only hope of survival. If the NG tube could ultimately help with that goal, Laura would just have to set her concerns aside.

After a week at DHMC, Hannah's condition had still not improved. A group of her doctors approached Laura one morning. One of them explained the situation.

"As you know, we're all pretty frustrated with Hannah's lack of weight gain," he said. "We've been doing just about everything that we can think of, and we're still not really seeing the results we'd like to be seeing at this point."

Yeah, tell me about it. I've been frustrated for weeks now. Nice to see we're all on the same page here. "Yeah, I'm pretty frustrated, too," said Laura. *Frustrated that I can't always be here to change her diaper when needed, so her bottom won't bleed. Frustrated that I can't be here more often to rock her and keep her calm, so all of her calories will be going toward weight gain instead of crying. Frustrated that when I am here, her sister's missing me on the other end.*

The doctor continued. "Well, we've discussed Hannah's case at length, and there's something we think we can try that might help considerably. We feel that it would be beneficial to place a tube, called a gastrostomy tube or a G-tube, directly into her stomach. With that in place, her feedings could go in at a very slow, constant drip, which would help her to absorb them better. That would address the diarrhea issue. And a G-tube is reversible. Should we decide that we don't need or want it in, down the road, it can be removed, leaving just a very small scar in its place—about the size of the current chest-tube scar she has from her surgery. For now, though, it would help her to grow without the risk of so many complications, such as the NG tube being pulled out and skin breakdown from the tape, since we'd obviously be able to get rid of the NG tube."

Get rid of her NG tube? Well, what have we been waiting for! Why didn't we do this a month ago! "Sounds good to me. When can we do it?"

"Although Hannah's condition isn't really improving, we feel that she's stable enough to handle the anesthesia needed for the procedure. We'll consult with Dr. Abigail Nelson, our pediatric gastroenterologist. She's wonderful. Then she'll be by to discuss the details of the procedure with you, and you'll be able to talk about actual dates."

Ooo, with a G-tube, I won't have to learn how to place an NG tube, like some parents around here have to do, in order to go home. Yeah, this could be good. Oops, that's the "wrap-up" tone I just heard. I'd better ask any questions I have now, or they'll be on their way out the door. Crap...questions...think, Laura, think. You know you'll have fifty, the minute they walk away. "Um, so it goes straight into her stomach? Is that painful at all? Or...like... what's involved?"

"Well, it's a surgical procedure, so there will be some discomfort associated with that, but we will, of course, treat Hannah's pain appropriately. However, the tube is placed in an area where there are very few nerve endings, so it doesn't cause the kind of pain that you would imagine."

"And you said that it's reversible?" asked Laura.

"Yes. Kinda like an ear piercing; if the tube is removed for any length of time, the area naturally regenerates and closes back up. And, like I said, scarring is very minimal."

Does that really matter at this point? She already has a chest-tube scar and a big scar going all the way around the side of her ribs from her surgery. Plus, she'll soon have a matching scar going all the way down her chest, and probably a few more chest-tube scars after we finally get her open-heart surgery over with. It's not as if she's looking forward to being an underwear model, anyway, or that she'll ever be seen running on the beach in a bikini. "Well, that sounds good. I guess we should go ahead, then."

The surgery was scheduled for mid-October. Laura didn't have extensive planning to worry about; she just had to make sure Emily had care available, in case any complications were to delay Laura at the hospital that day. She was glad she didn't have to devote time to major planning, because she was swimming in an overabundance of bureaucratic paperwork. And the work involved was becoming a full-time job.

For instance, Champus, Kevin's military insurance company, sent a letter asking for insurance information from another party, apparently assuming some of Hannah's "injuries" were caused by someone else (i.e., in a car accident). Laura wrote a long, detailed letter back, explaining Hannah's diagnosis, her current condition, and possible prognosis. But soon after she mailed that letter, Laura received a duplicate letter from Champus. She ignored it, believing that their correspondence must have just crossed in the mail. Then she got a third, much nastier letter, stating Hannah's benefits would be in jeopardy, if Laura didn't respond immediately.

Curious to understand how her letter could have been deemed insufficient, Laura set out to remedy the situation. After an extensive game of phone tag, Laura finally reached a human Champus representative and pleaded her case. She offered a heartfelt narration of the events preceding Hannah's hospitalization. She then explained about the recent mail correspondence. The woman's response was summed up in just a handful of stunning words.

"You need to return the form with *N/A* written across the front."

"That's it? Couldn't you people tell that it was not applicable by what I had written in my letter of explanation? An explanation, by the way, that you asked for in your form?"

"No. Just write *N/A* across the form and send it in."

Laura couldn't argue with such airtight reasoning. She thanked the woman and hung up, before neatly writing *N/A* across the form and sealing it in the envelope provided. She never heard from them again regarding that matter, but a multitude of other, equally ridiculous requests would come later.

The insurance company wasn't the only organization keeping her busy, either. Since their arrival at the ICN, Laura had been inundated with pamphlets and handouts about various social programs recommended by the nurses and social workers. After reading the first few, Laura felt they were all just a waste of her time. Not only did she feel that she didn't have the time for them, she couldn't even distinguish one program from another. She already knew about Early Intervention, but she wasn't completely sure how it could help Hannah. Laura had always imagined that Early Intervention helped kids with a little speech delay or something similar. Hannah had issues down to the *chromosomal* level. Laura couldn't understand what intervention, early or otherwise, could do for her. When she tried to recall the other programs, they all blurred together—as if they were the same program with a bunch of different names. They included the Bureau of Special Medical Services, Community Services Council, Community Action Program, Community Health and Hospice, Health and Human Services, Partners in Health, Parent-to-Parent, and the list went on and on. Just looking at all of the information had Laura tired out; she certainly didn't have the energy needed to follow up on any of them.

However, the staff had strongly recommended two particular programs. One was called the Katie Beckett Waiver. Laura didn't know what it was all about, but it was some type of Medicaid benefit that everybody went crazy over. She wasn't even sure what Medicaid was—she assumed some sort of children's equivalent of Medicare. Laura wasn't sure how it would help, but everyone was encouraging her to find out. She would have to contact the local Health and Human Services office. The other popular program was part of Social Security, called SSI (Supplemental Security Income). For that one she'd have to get in touch with the local Social Security office. Laura was soon wishing she had known about Hannah's condition halfway through her pregnancy, so she could have gotten a head start on her workload. She was having a hard time cramming it all into an already-packed schedule.

From her first visit to the Health and Human Services office, Laura found out how much of an oxymoron that title is—specifically, Human Services. Everything had to be done on their schedule. Laura had to call for an appointment and just hope she could make whatever appointment time they issued her. Also, when she arrived and didn't know much about the program, she felt she was an even bigger target for abuse.

The intake worker started off, appropriately enough. "How may I help you?"

"Well, my daughter's at Dartmouth in the Intensive Care Nursery. She's been diagnosed with a rare genetic disorder called Wolf-Hirschhorn syndrome, and the nurses and social workers told me I should apply for the...umm...Katie Beckett Waiver."

"You do realize that the child would have to be *severely* handicapped, in order to qualify for this program."

Well, don't sugarcoat it lady, please, certainly don't spare my feelings or anything...bitch. And, incidentally, didn't you hear me? She's in the intensive care nursery. She has a genetic disorder. Do I need to spell it out for you? "Yes, I understand. Hannah may not live past the age of five, and if she does, she may not ever learn how to sit up on her own." *WA-BAM...take that! Okay, bring on the sympathy. Whip out the apology.*

The intake worker replied in a nearly disbelieving, mildly irritated, and thoroughly unimpressed tone. "Uh-huh. Well, here's the form. It will need to be completed, not only by yourself, but the child's doctor, as well."

Laura was stunned. *Whatever you need, you coldhearted wench. Just get me the hell out of this godforsaken place. I've got to get to the hospital, anyway. My "severely handicapped" daughter needs me.* Laura smiled sweetly. "Thank you very much. I'll return them as soon as I can."

"They need to be completed within the next two weeks, or the case will be closed."

Right. Yesterday you didn't even know Hannah existed; now, there's a huge urgency to complete the paperwork. "Thanks again. I'll get these back to you ASAP." *Christ, there's a short novel of paperwork here—like I have nothing better to do these days!* Laura sighed deeply as she left the office.

Infuriated by the appointment, Laura got onto the highway and sped away, feeling appalled by the amount of time she had spent away from the girls—just to be tortured by an insensitive government employee. *Oops...slow down, Laura. You're at ninety-five miles an hour here. Ah, screw it; let the cops stop me. If one dares to arrest me, well...it'll be an excuse to get away from all of this crap. Of course, if the cops don't get me, that clump of trees over there might. That'd be a nice escape, too. God, what are you saying? The girls need you. Who's going to be there for Hannah and nurture Emily if you aren't here? Kevin? Come on! Snap the hell out of it! That woman at the Health and Human Services office was right; there's nothing extraordinary about our situation. So you have a sick kid—get over it! Stop being so dramatic. Besides, you're almost at the hospital, and you don't want the nurses to see you all emotional. Pull yourself together. I don't even know what you're looking for from people, anyway. You're just gonna have to suck it up. Nobody's gonna be able to say or do anything to make it better. It's just gonna be our reality right now. Shake it off. But it's not fair! Hannah deserves better. Before her diagnosis, people looked adoringly at her with concern in their eyes and hope in their hearts for her health and future. Now...even looking at her seems to make them uncomfortable. Now they look at me, instead, like they're thinking, "Oh, I'm so sorry you have this...situation...on your hands." And hidden even further behind those thoughts are the judgments they're passing on me for making the mistake of agreeing to her surgery. Well, if people are responding differently to Hannah now, than they did before her diagnosis, that's just human nature—like it or not. It may not be the pretty side of it, but you can't expect everything to change just because you're the one hurting. And don't get all high and mighty, either; you know that things changed for you when you got the diagnosis too; you're still struggling with it. ...But I still feel so alone. I mean...the one person who should be just as involved as I am is Kevin. Why doesn't it feel like Kevin's in this with me? We should be on the same page, right? Ah, I don't know. Well, go hold your baby, and think about that crap on the way home.*

Although the car ride from her home to the hospital had originally seemed like a terrible waste of time, Laura soon began to see it as her only refuge. But, in reality, her refuge was her death trap. She was driving for an hour and a half at a time, on a nearly deserted highway with hardly any scenery—not much to keep someone awake at the wheel. She was an emotionally unstable and physically overtired woman who was driving erratically every day for weeks–at speeds between eighty and one hundred miles an hour. Laura was feeling less and less understood, less and less like part of society, and less and less human. She was living in an emotional haze and was just going through the motions for the girls. Laura still wasn't able to cry, but driving alone on the deserted roadway gave her an outlet. She could blast some music that would sweep her away to the places in her soul she could no longer access on her own.

The surgery for the G-tube placement went well, and the tube helped substantially. Several days later, the nurses had a "birth-weight celebration" for Hannah and posted a congratulations sign on her crib. Hannah had finally reached that important milestone–at just two days shy of two months old.

"We're thinking that Hannah is starting to turn the corner," said one of the doctors. "What do you think?"

"Yeah, I agree. She's looking better to me every day."

"Well, we think she may be ready for home recovery. How do you feel about that?"

HOME? Holy crap! Take care of Hannah at home? God, can I do that? Sure you can, Laura; don't be ridiculous. Man, just in time. I thought we were going to miss our first holiday at home. Now the girls can go trick-or-treating together like I had imagined. Hannah can wear that little pumpkin outfit that Emily wore on her first Halloween. Whoa! Stay on track here, Laura. Calm down, for Christ's sake. Answer the doctor's question, and don't act like a blubbering idiot. "I'm absolutely ready to give home a try."

"Great. We'll send the discharge planner over to chat with you. One thing that you'll be doing is spending a night in the Koala Room with Hannah to be sure you're comfortable with her care before you actually leave the hospital. You'll be completely on your own, but you'll have nurses and doctors at the other side of the door, should you run into any problems."

"Okay. Sounds fine."

The discharge planner was nervous because home-health nurses were so scarce in the Littleton area. The only available nurses did just weekly home checkups, which was fine with Laura. She felt uncomfortable with the idea of having a stranger in her house for hours at a time, anyway. After a brief discussion, the staff was convinced that Laura would be fine on her own. They began concentrating on her training—infant CPR, feeding schedules, formula recipes, and medication training. Laura was not looking forward to preparing the formula mixture. She could only make small amounts at a time, because it would spoil before she could use it all, if she made too much.

Proper mixing was important, too. Giving Hannah one meal saturated in oil and the next with no oil at all could create problems. After going over the time-consuming mixing process, just thinking about the feeding schedule exhausted Laura. Hannah needed 50 cc (just less than 2 ounces) every two hours and forty minutes. Laura would offer feedings by bottle first, and any not taken orally would be administered by G-tube.

The most important (and intimidating) lesson was about medications. Laura had seen the nurses dispense them plenty of times, but she didn't know exactly what Hannah was getting or how much. She was taking three heart medications—captopril, to keep her blood pressure down; furosemide, to help her eliminate extra fluids, so they wouldn't fill up into her lungs; and digoxin, to keep her heart strong and working rhythmically.

The nurse had emphasized the importance of giving the doses of furosemide and digoxin at the prescribed times. Since Hannah was experiencing heart failure, not administering the medications could either kill her or make her sicker. However, overdosing on either of those medications, especially the digoxin, could certainly kill her, too. In addition, the nurse strongly recommended that Laura keep the medications locked and stored in a high place, because a single bottle of digoxin could kill an adult—which was more than enough to kill Emily, if she ever were to ingest it.

The night in the Koala Room was rougher than Laura had expected. She ended up making an embarrassing medication error. Hannah was okay, and the nursing staff was forgiving, but the incident gave Laura a heightened sense of awareness regarding the dangers of Hannah's medications.

Just before Halloween (precisely fifty days after Laura and Hannah had left), they finally returned home. Laura was nervous, relieved, happy, and tired—mostly tired. Underneath those emotions was a sense of something strange—homesickness. As good as it was to be home, and as nice as it was to be done with the daily commute, being home didn't feel right. Nobody seemed to understand Laura anymore. Nobody seemed to understand what was going on. Laura quickly found herself absolutely drowning in her day-to-day responsibilities; yet Janet asked her why she still had Emily going to Rosie's since Hannah was out of the hospital. Laura was too tired to formulate the necessary words to respond to her stepmother. Family members weren't exactly lining up to help her, because they apparently didn't see the need. But Laura was too overwhelmed and exhausted to think about asking for help (or to even know how to ask for help), so she trudged on the best she could on her own.

She missed the support of the hospital staff, both physically and emotionally. She no longer had the nurses to discuss vital signs with. She didn't have daily updates from doctors to help form her expectations for the next day. She felt as though she didn't have anyone in her world anymore. Despite the convenience of no longer having a commute, Laura even found herself missing the time to herself in the car. She no longer had those three hours each day, during which she could escape from reality. But Laura wasn't about to complain. After all, they were home. She thought people would surely think she was crazy if she were to complain now. Besides, she didn't have the energy to examine her feelings; she was fading too fast.

Days had become tiring blurs that melted together into a long, gray haze. The once-per-week visiting nurse was more of a headache than help. The woman was nice enough, but Hannah obviously scared her to death. She was a geriatric nurse, used to dealing with eighty-five-year-old men recovering from strokes—not two-month-old babies in heart failure. She couldn't answer any of Laura's questions.

The most Laura got from those visits was a little more incentive to get the house cleaned and the dishes done. Household chores were difficult to accomplish. With the addition of Hannah's care, Laura felt as though she had forty-eight hours of work to cram into a twenty-four-hour day. Although housework was low on her list of priorities, Laura fretted that she'd have to call the paramedics on a day when she hadn't been able to get the dishes or the laundry done. She imagined how the "whole world" would then know what a slob she could be.

On the bright side, the crazy pace Laura was keeping turned into an easy way to lose the post-pregnancy weight she had been worried about. In the hospital Laura had been surviving on cran-orange juice and Twizzlers. Once she had arrived back home, she couldn't find time to eat even that "well". She welcomed the loss of weight, but fainting spells and a complete lack of concentration were unfortunate side effects.

With her stress level mounting and her energy reserves dwindling, Laura was having an increasingly difficult time coping. "med-draw time" was becoming more and more of a lure. While drawing up the digoxin, Laura would think, *It would be sooooo easy. Just down this little bottle of liquid, and it would all be over with. I can't even imagine that it would be very painful–just a few minutes of discomfort, and it would all be done. I could rest– no meds to give, no feedings to prepare, no forms to fill out–just rest.*

Then she'd picture the girls without her, and she'd snap out of it. But each morning, that temptation would be waiting for her once again. Soon Laura wasn't even waiting for med-draw time. When she was feeling particularly low or tired, she would look longingly at the kitchen cabinet that held her easy way out. However, the dreamy thoughts of everlasting peace were always followed by a snap back to reality with the contemplation of what life would be like for the girls, if she were gone.

Another demanding aspect of Laura's daily routine involved the required contact with doctors. She usually spoke to Dr. Michaels and/or Dr. O'Connor daily and went to one of their offices about every third day. Although Laura needed to accurately communicate what was happening at home, forming coherent thoughts had become nearly impossible. She ended up writing down everything she did each day for Hannah, so she wouldn't forget or fail to recognize anything important. A typical page from her notebook looked like this:

11/7 ••• Feedings from 10:50 a.m. and on are made with six scoops of formula per Dr. Michaels's order. •••					
Time	**Temp**	**Pulse**	**Resp**	**Feeding**	**Meds**
8:00AM	102.1	170	80		0.5cc fur. 1cc cap. 0.2cc dig. 0.2cc Iron
8:10AM				50, All Orally	
9:30AM					Tylenol
11:50AM	101.2	176	85	50, All Orally	
1:30PM					Tylenol
2:30PM	100.9		103	50, All Orally	
4:00PM	100.4	177	94		0.5cc fur. 1cc cap.
5:10PM				50, 0 Orally	
6:30PM					Tylenol
6:50PM	99.6	173	88	50, 0 Orally	
8:00PM					0.2cc dig. 0.2cc Iron
9:30PM	98.6	155	88	50, 0 Orally	
Vomited twice, once right after eating & once just prior to next feeding					
12:00AM	96.9				0.5cc fur. 1cc cap. Tylenol
12:10AM				50, 0 Orally	
Vomited twice, once right after eating & once just prior to next feeding					
2:50AM	98.2			50, 0 Orally	
5:30AM				50, 0 Orally	

Meanwhile, Laura had essentially done what Kevin had suggested weeks before–put her marriage on hold. Unfortunately, the marriage was a high-maintenance relationship. With little-or-no attention, patience, or energy to devote to it, whatever connection the couple did have, quickly deteriorated. Laura hoped if they were to stay busy enough, they wouldn't notice. Kevin seemed busy with his recruiting position in Berlin, New

Hampshire, which included a hefty commute of an hour each way. He appeared to be occupying his time outside of work too, but Laura wasn't totally sure, because she never took the time to ask.

One subject Laura wanted to be perfectly clear about was sex. She knew she couldn't deal with it, so for the first time ever, she sat Kevin down and was extremely direct and straightforward about her needs.

"Kevin," she said, "there's something I've been thinking about, and I want to be very clear with you, so there won't be any chance of a misunderstanding. I have a lot going on right now—both in my head and in real life. I CANNOT handle sex right now. I want it to be perfectly clear that I cannot think about sex, cannot talk about sex...cannot handle having to refuse sex. I can't handle *ANYTHING* to do with sex right now. And I don't know what else to tell you. I will get back to you when things change for me, but for right now, this is where I'm at. Hannah's in bed with me, and you're on the couch, anyway, so we're all set there. But I'll also be changing clothes behind closed doors, and I'll be fully dressed at all times, so there will be absolutely no confusion about where I stand."

"Well, what do you think I am, some animal who can't control myself?"

Yes. "No, I just want to be very clear."

"Fine. Whatever. Was that all?"

"Yeah, that was all. As long as we understand each other."

"Yep. So I'm gonna go catch the Giants game at your Aunt Nancy's, if that's okay."

"Fine with me; see you later."

Since leaving the hospital, Laura was feeling more and more desperate to talk to someone who could relate to her—what she was going through, what she was feeling (or not feeling, as the case often was), and what she was actually doing day in and day out. While Kevin had some strong points as a husband, being an emotionally available partner was certainly not one of them. Once again, he confirmed that observation in early November. Hannah had yet another cardiology appointment at DHMC. After an unusually difficult couple of nights, Laura was concerned on the day of the appointment about trying to stay awake for the ninety-minute drive with Hannah in the car. She asked Kevin to take a bit of time off from work and drive them.

As she got into the car, Laura realized she would be stuck with Kevin for the entire hour-and-a-half drive to the hospital. She was prepared to stare quietly out the window, figuring any other action would likely lead to tension or arguments. Desperate to reach out to someone, Laura went against her better judgment and decided to try talking to Kevin.

"You know, it's really weird, but ever since I've been home, I've really missed Hannah being in the hospital. I mean, I like being home, I love that I don't have to leave Em with Rosie for so long, and, of course, I love the fact that Hannah is well enough to be home. But, I miss talking to the other moms and to the nurses. Plus, even though it isn't as hectic now that we're home, I'm actually more tired, now that I'm doing all of the feedings and meds on my own. I mean, I wouldn't ever wish sickness on Hannah, but I miss some of the stuff we had when we were still in the hospital."

"Huh. You're right; that is really weird."

Okkaaay, well, I feel like a fool now. I should have kept my mouth shut. Glad I didn't tell him about my temptations with the digoxin. Ah, he's probably right, anyway; it's pretty stupid to miss anything about having to stay in the hospital. Just keep your mouth shut, Laura. Nobody's going to understand the crazy thoughts you've been having lately—especially Kevin. Heck, half the time I don't even know where I'm coming from these days.

Laura wasn't looking forward to the long drive back home with Kevin. As it turned out, she didn't have to worry about it. Dr. O'Connor looked at Hannah and almost immediately informed Laura that he wouldn't allow her to leave the hospital that night. Hannah's weight was down, and she was experiencing more severe heart failure. *Ugh. Well, here we go again. Home for less than two weeks and we're back at the hospital. I wonder how long we'll be here this time. God, poor Emily. How long is this going to go on? Poor Hannah. Was there something I could have done to prevent this? I hope they aren't going to try to get an IV in. I don't think I could get through a round of pokes tonight. Crap, I didn't even put the wash into the dryer before I left. Oh, and I planned on making that roast for dinner. Who knows how long that'll sit in the fridge now. Ugh. I want to go home. I don't want to get so far behind with everything again. I don't want to let Em down again.*

Kevin had a smirk on his face. "Well, you're back in the hospital. I guess you got your wish!"

Laura was too crushed to speak. *How can he say something so cruel? But wait; he's right. I've wished my daughter into sickness and into the hospital. I am a sick, sick puppy. Isn't there a name for this? Munchausen's syndrome or something? Well, I take it back! I take it back! I want to go home to Emily tonight! I don't want Hannah to be sick! I just want to go home! Oh God, what have I done!*

Chapter VII

Torn to Pieces

The short four-day stay at the hospital was relatively uneventful, with the exception of Laura learning about something that gave her great hope for their return home. In a conversation with one of the nurses, Laura admitted to her severe fatigue, blaming it mainly on Hannah's hectic home-feeding schedule. The nurse remarked that Hannah should have been discharged with a feeding pump and assured Laura that the hospital would provide one for their next trip home.

Once she arrived, Laura needed a couple of days to catch up with all that had fallen behind during her four-day absence from home. With some hard work, she felt comfortable with the status of everything...except Hannah's condition. She was still a very sick little girl. Sweat dripped from her body constantly, as she struggled to deal with the extra fluid her heart could no longer handle. Her little chest puffed up and down so fast that counting her respiratory rate had become nearly impossible. The breaths that Laura was trying to count were more like vibrations. Her heart murmur was so loud now that one could literally hear it across the room. Laura learned later that it was considered a level-six murmur—the most severe category.

Unfortunately, the feeding pump wasn't working out at all as she had hoped. When the technician at the hospital had demonstrated how to use it, it seemed so simple. But now that Laura had to prime the tubing and set the rate on her own, she was fumbling, up to a half hour at a time, trying to get the machine to work. Her efforts inevitably ended with half of Hannah's feeding all over the floor. Through tears of frustration she would clean the wet, sticky, stinky carpet while cursing the hospital for teasing her with the allure of easy feedings. Then she'd grudgingly prepare yet another feeding, further stressed over the delay of the feeding she still had to administer by hand.

As it turned out, the few days Laura needed to catch up were the only few days she had at home. Two days after being discharged, Hannah was admitted back into the hospital.

"Hannah's in increasing failure, and her aorta is the culprit," Dr. O'Connor explained.

"I thought we addressed the aorta in her surgery—just a few weeks ago."

"Well, the echoes show that it has reconstricted—considerably. She's just not getting the circulation she needs, and she won't until we fix the problem."

"What do you mean *re*constricted? You mean fixing it wasn't... permanent?"

"No, unfortunately the vessel will sometimes reconstrict, forcing us to readdress."

Huh. I don't remember them mentioning that before. God, all the work done in Boston for nothing. Oh crap, Boston! "You aren't sending us back to Boston, are you?"

"No. I can do angioplasty here via catheterization. I'll enter her femoral artery with a catheter and feed it up through to the problem area in the aorta. Once I'm at the narrowed section, I'll feed through a balloon and "blow up" the aorta, so she'll get some blood flow back."

Yeah, I don't have any idea what you just said, but that's fine. You can do whatever the heck you want—just as long as we're not going back to Boston. "Okay, so when are we looking to do this?"

"I've scheduled her for ten o'clock tomorrow morning. That'll make her my second case. The plan from here is to get her on some IV fluids sometime this evening, and then stop her feedings at midnight, in prep for the cath in the morning. The actual procedure shouldn't take too, too long—an hour or so, if all goes well. Tonight you'll be on the floor, but after the cath, we'll move you into the PICU (Pediatric Intensive Care Unit) for a short time, probably overnight, until she's extubated. After that, you should be headed back home within a couple of days. Now she still very much needs the open-heart, of course, but this will make the wait much easier on her. She really needs it."

Whoa...tomorrow! He's not messing around here. Okay, get yourself up to speed; don't let this rattle you. So she needs this...whatever he called it...the uh...the cath something. No big deal. And it sounds like we should be home in plenty of time for Thanksgiving. It'll all be fine. And it's Dr. O'Connor; you know he'll take good care of her. Wait. He said extubated. That means breathing tube. Oh crap, that's right. This is a surgery! She's gonna need a breathing tube again. Come on, Laura, get with the program. Think. Oh, crap! She's gonna need an IV*—OH, GOD! Okay, okay, too much thinking. Take a breath. Don't let him see you panic. Just play it cool and get to the room. You can figure it all out later.*

They settled in on the pediatric floor relatively quickly, since it was becoming routine. This time, they had a semi-private room. Most of the rooms were private, making this a new experience for Laura. John (the twin brother of Jason, the preemie who had been next to Hannah in the ICN) was their roommate. Laura had never met the mom of the twins, but with all the time she had spent near the boys, she almost felt as though they were family.

Laura and Hannah moved into the treatment room that evening for the IV placement. Laura dragged her feet the entire way, comforted only by the thought that others, too, were dreading the task ahead. A policy had been put into effect, forbidding anyone other than certain members of the IV team to attempt placement. Members of that "elite team" knew the likely frustrations that lay ahead of them, and they were especially nervous that night. Dr. O'Connor had given strict instruction to get a line in—no matter what. They knew that Dr. O'Connor's unwavering demands and Hannah's consistent record of unsuccessful attempts would have negative repercussions, one way or another.

As usual, the first attempt followed extremely long and frustrated searches under extremely bright lights. Flashbacks of Hannah's very first IV attempt, back in the Littleton Regional Hospital ER, plagued Laura, as she helped to hold Hannah down. She tried to convince herself that the experience wouldn't be as traumatic this time. After all, a "two-poke maximum" policy was now in place to protect Hannah from becoming a human pincushion.

The first poke was to Hannah's left hand. Laura tried to focus on keeping the pacifier in Hannah's mouth, but she found it difficult to ignore what was happening elsewhere. Watching the needle pierce the skin wasn't that bad. But Hannah didn't have plump little veins that easily accepted the needle, making it necessary to "fish around" for a vein. Laura's stomach turned as the shard of steel would slide in, out, and from side-to-side under Hannah's paper-thin skin. Although the poke lasted only an instant, the searching, chasing, and digging with the needle lasted an agonizing number of minutes, making the experience a living hell. Predictably, the first poke was unsuccessful and a search for another site began immediately. Next, they tried for a halfway-promising vein in Hannah's right ankle. This time, Hannah was understandably more upset, although she didn't have enough energy to show the level of despair she must have been feeling. Her lethargy was a slight blessing, allowing Laura to pretend that Hannah's lackluster protests meant she wasn't in pain.

That attempt also proved to be a failed one. *There. That's two attempts. We're finally done here. They'll have to try tomorrow. Wait. They aren't cleaning up. Oh, my God! They're just switching off! They're getting someone else to try! I should say something. But you don't want to be "the problem mother." Just let them try one more time. She* <u>really</u> *needs this line, Laura, and they'll just be back tomorrow if they don't get it done tonight. Maybe this next person will have better luck. Take a deep breath. They're doing what's best.*

They spent a lot of time searching on Hannah's scalp. Nothing was looking good, so they settled for another spot on her right foot. Laura found it more difficult to hold Hannah down this time. Hannah wasn't fighting more, but Laura was feeling increasingly guilty, as if she were betraying Hannah by allowing this to happen. She tried to tune everything out, concentrating heavily on a poster on the wall, but she didn't succeed. Instead, she found herself painfully aware of the medical team's actions. As one team member stabbed Hannah's right ankle, two other team members were already simultaneously searching limbs for the next possible site, in complete anticipation of an expected failure. Laura's guilt morphed into a seething anger.

Laura's hands shook as she held Hannah down through the next attempt. When that poke failed, a different nurse was paged to make another attempt. Laura managed to survive two more pokes from the new nurse, but after the second try (the sixth one in total) she had reached her absolute limit. While choking down screams and wails and trying to remain as calm as possible, she finally spoke up.

"I thought we were supposed to stop after two attempts."

"Usually we do, but Hannah *really* needs this line. Dr. O'Connor insists on it."

"Yeah, but she's pooping out here. We've been in here for *two hours*. In two more hours, she can't eat until after the surgery. Even if you do get a line in tonight–which we both know isn't very likely–she's gonna be food deprived for even longer than she's supposed to be."

"Yeah, I hear you, believe me. Why don't we take a break? You can feed Hannah, and we'll call Dr. O'Connor and let him know where we're at."

Laura hoped Dr. O'Connor would abandon further attempts for the night when he got his update. She wondered how he could possibly live with himself if he were to order more. She was startled when Dr. O'Connor stopped by in person to explain.

"Hannah's my second case tomorrow, and unfortunately, I

expect my first case to run long, so she'll be going even longer without fluids than technically planned. At her size she can dehydrate quickly, and if an emergency crops up, we really need that access. I know that it's hard, but it has to be done."

Well, that sounds all well and good, but what if they can't get one in? Christ, don't you remember that they had to do cut-downs in Boston? Ugh, why can't we be the first case? Maybe then you'd just let us do this in the morning. "So how long do you expect that first case to run?"

"I fully expect Hannah to start two hours late—hopefully no later than that—but the first case is going to be a tricky one."

Laura uttered a defeated sigh. "Okay, if we're gonna do this, we'd better get going."

Once again they trudged back into the treatment room, and Laura was sick with dread. Hannah was too tired and weak to cry. She just whimpered, and tears streamed down her face as rubber bands were placed around her head and all four limbs as tourniquets. Three people desperately searched for a vein that might have somehow eluded them earlier. She already had two fresh bald spots on her head from unsuccessful tries, and they were shaving another. The spotlight bore down, blinding Hannah. *I've gotta get out of here. I'm not gonna make it through this one. What are you talking about! You can't just leave Hannah now! What kind of mother are you? It doesn't matter. I can't do this. Get out. Get out!*

"Would you guys mind...I mean, uh, is it possible...um could I step...uh...step out for a few minutes?"

The nurses were more than understanding and told Laura to go ahead, and they would bring Hannah back to her when they were done. Laura was slumped in shame, as she walked out the door. She was beaten. She wanted to cry. She wanted to scream. She wanted to run away. But she had no energy for any of that, so she just slowly shuffled back to Hannah's room and stared blankly at the TV.

Sometime before midnight, Hannah was brought back to Laura covered in Band-Aids, red in the face from crying, nearly unconscious from fatigue...and IV-free.

"We tried two more times," said the nurse, "but there's just nothing there. If Dr. O'Connor wants a line in tonight, he's gonna have to come in and do it himself. We refuse to touch her again."

Dr. O'Connor didn't show, and Hannah slept soundly through the night. Her procedure was scheduled for 10:00 a.m. the next morning. Ten o'clock came and went, and Hannah was growing increasingly cranky. In an attempt to quiet her, Laura took Hannah off the monitors, so they could walk around the unit. At about noon Laura headed back to the room to sit down and rest for a few minutes. On the way, Dr. O'Connor's nurse practitioner caught up with them and reported that Dr. O'Connor was finishing his first case and expected to be ready for Hannah by 1:00 p.m.

Once back in the room, Laura sat down with Hannah on her lap, and turned on the TV. Hannah was fidgety but relatively quiet. Laura settled into the chair, looking forward to a short rest. Before long Hannah seemed to settle down, as well. Laura looked down, expecting to see a sleeping baby in her arms. Instead, she found what she was sure was a dead one.

Hannah was limp and blue. Her eyes were open, fixed, and glazed.

For a second, an hour worth of thoughts ricocheted in all directions through Laura's head as she desperately attempted to process what was happening. *Oh, no! No! I didn't say good-bye. This can't be. No, no, of course not. Don't be ridiculous; your daughter doesn't just die in your arms. You must be mistaken. Her chest. Check her chest. No vibrations. No breaths. No movement. There's got to be an explanation for this. I'm sure there's a reasonable explanation. But, what if–no. Get a nurse. This isn't what you're thinking, so just stay calm and get one of the nurses.* Laura quickly scooped up Hannah and ran to the doorway. *Okay, now get their attention, but don't go looking like you're crazy. This isn't what you're thinking, so keep your cool. Just take this in stride, and it'll all turn out fine. Deep breath, now. Okay.* Laura directed her attention toward the nearby nurses' station and focused on speaking as calmly and quietly as she possibly could so as not to alarm anyone to a situation that certainly wasn't what she feared it was.

"Excuse me. I think she may have stopped breathing." Laura spoke the words almost in the form of a question, as if asking for the answer to the riddle of what was really happening.

A respiratory therapist shot his head up from his paperwork. "What did you just say?"

"I think my baby may have just stopped breathing." Laura was shaking now, and it was quite evident as she spoke these words.

"We've got a code over here!" the man yelled as he flew by Laura, whisking Hannah out of her arms. A flash of white followed him, as half-a-dozen doctors and nurses suddenly appeared.

Great. Now you've done it. You've got the whole staff in a panic. Look at that. They don't even have her in the right crib. They've put her in John's crib. They're gonna think they're working on John. This isn't right. Tell them she's in the wrong crib! Would you snap out of it, you idiot! Your baby may be dead over there, and you're obsessing about what side of the room she's on! You should have called the nurses sooner. You should have started CPR. Oh, my God, why didn't you start CPR? You moron! You choked! You should have done CPR! What were you thinking! You may have just killed her! Do you realize that? Wait...is that Dr. O'Connor over there? Thank God. He'll fix this. How'd he even get over here? Wasn't he just in the cath lab on the fourth floor a minute ago? Wow...he's like...superhuman. Ugh, snap out of it, Laura! Don't you see that this can't be good if he's here?

Laura never left the doorway. From there she watched, not wanting to be in the way, not wanting to say or do the wrong thing—and most of all, not wanting to think about, feel, or even see reality. She just wanted this part of their lives to be over. Her only hope was that Dr. O'Connor would somehow prevent the catastrophe she feared. She stood stock-still, awaiting their fate.

Time mocked Laura as it passed ever so slowly. While she ached in anticipation of news, one way or the other, the minutes appeared to mosey around the clock at their leisure. Somewhere in the world a proud papa was witnessing his baby boy's first steps; a couple was holding hands and basking in young, passionate love; and a little girl was taking her first ride on a pony. Most likely, all of them were wishing that their special moments in time could last forever.

Laura felt as if fate were ruling in their favor, allowing the moment to never pass. Minutes later, however, a faint sound restored her hope. She thought she had heard the glorious addition of Hannah's whimper beyond the buzz of the white coats working on her and the muffling effects of an oxygen mask. A nurse approached Laura.

"As you know, a common symptom of Wolf-Hirschhorn syndrome is seizure disorders. We're thinking that Hannah just had a seizure that involved apnea. In other words, she stopped breathing. Because she didn't have IV access, we obtained emergency IO access through which we were able to give her medication to stop the seizure, along with IV fluids. Right now she's stable, but Dr. O'Connor is still very concerned about her. He's taking her directly down to the cath lab for her procedure. Would you like to say a quick good-bye?"

Oh...uh...wow, okay...let me gather my thoughts. He–oh, oh–they're taking her right *now.* "Bye, sweetie. Mommy will be waiting for you. Be good for Dr. O'Connor."

As they wheeled Hannah by, one of the nurses gave Laura a reassuring squeeze on the shoulder. And then Hannah was gone. *Wait! I want to hold her! I want to tell her I love her! "Be good for Dr. O'Connor"? God, how stupid! Couldn't you come up with something better to send her off with? They didn't give me enough time! I need to hold her again! What if I don't get another chance? My God, what if I really* don't *get another chance! This could actually be real. Don't think that way, Laura. Come on; think about something else. Uh...wow, a seizure. I guess I knew this might happen, but I didn't picture seizures to be like* this– *not this scary...not this serious. Man, could this happen* again?

No...don't want to think about that...oh, that...IO thing. Boy, that sure would have come in handy last night. Why weren't they doing that then? "So what's an IO?"

"It's short for 'intraosseous.' Until a child is eight years old, access can be obtained through bone marrow. We were able to gain access through Hannah's shin. Of course, in true Hannah fashion, it took two attempts. The first one went too far in, but we have access now."

"So they...what...just...drill into her shin? Doesn't that hurt? Did they give her something first, so she wouldn't feel it?"

"Well it is, in essence, drilling into the bone, so I'm sure it would hurt you or me. I'd like to hope that Hannah didn't feel it. She was seizing at the time, so we can't know for sure. Unfortunately, nothing can really be given for pain. A child only gets an IO in an emergency situation when no other access is possible."

So if she did feel it, she had twice the pain, because they had to do it twice. Ugh...quick... can't think about that...too intense... too...too...something else...think about something else–Emily. Did I remind Kevin to give Em her vitamin this morning? Oh, Kevin. I should update Kevin. That's what I'll do. I'll call Kevin.

Laura did her best to explain calmly what had happened. Kevin and Emily had planned on going to the hospital to see Hannah after her procedure. Laura didn't want Emily to be frightened, so she advised him that it might not be a good idea. After all, they didn't know the condition Hannah would be in after the surgery–or if she'd even make it through the surgery. Kevin readily agreed. He said he would go directly to Tom and Susan's house instead, where he had planned to go with Emily anyway, after the hospital visit.

"That'll be fine," Laura said. "I'll call you there if anything else happens or to let you know how everything turns out."

Laura's emotions were scattered in all directions. She felt relieved about not having to see and deal with Kevin, yet disappointed about missing out on time with Emily. She was confused about the events earlier in the day and mind-numbingly sick with worry over Hannah.

"Laura?" Dr. O'Connor's nurse practitioner interrupted Laura's thoughts. "Hannah will be in the cath lab for awhile. Why don't we both go down to the cafeteria?" Laura agreed, but she didn't know if she'd feel up to talking when they got there. Making conversation was becoming more difficult lately, and felt like an impossible task this day. She felt more like hiding away in a corner, closing her eyes, and ignoring life until Hannah was out of surgery.

"How are you holding up?" the nurse asked as they sat down at a table.

"Okay, I guess."

"Laura, we're a little...concerned that you don't seem to be reacting to all of this...quite like we would expect. You're rather... quiet. We're worried about you."

Oh, I see. This isn't a gesture to help me pass the time; it's an intervention. Man, not reacting right—one more thing I'm doing wrong. God, Laura, you're such a loser. Well, how am I supposed to react! I thought I was doing so well keeping myself under control—obviously the wrong choice. What do they want from me? I can't do this! The one thing I think I'm doing right, and I've screwed it up. Does this mean they don't think I'm fit to have the girls? You'd better watch your step now. They might take the girls away from you. "Oh, sorry. I guess I'm just kind of...overwhelmed, maybe...I don't know."

"I know this is a lot—what's going on—this is a lot for any parent to go through, and all parents handle these types of situations differently. You have a lot on your shoulders, though, and it's okay to let some of it out. Use us. We're here for you. Allow us to help you through this. It's too much to take on all by yourself."

Laura thanked the nurse, with as much of a smile as she could muster, and walked away in a fog. She was finding it near impossible to formulate and maintain thoughts. She was a young, sleep-deprived, food-deprived, postpartum mother. Furthermore, she was attempting to prepare herself for her baby's possible death, yet somehow remain hopeful for an extraordinary recovery. Additionally, she was attempting to imagine and accept the reality of having a severely disabled child, *if* Hannah were to survive, while simultaneously mourning the death of the normal child she had thought she had. On top of that, with so much emotion and attention focused on Hannah, Laura felt as if she were completely ignoring Emily, which tripled her guilt load. She hadn't been prepared for such an extreme choice, in regard to the needs of her children. Thoughts of either of them were becoming too painful to endure and were ripping her apart inside.

In the meantime, her marriage was all but dead. Kevin was seldom there, and the few times he was, she was anxious for him to leave. When she tried to talk to him, not only was the sense of support she craved missing, but also he actually seemed to say the most hurtful things and take the most unsupportive actions possible.

For example, after Hannah was settled into the PICU hours later, Laura made a phone call to update Kevin. Considering the condition Hannah had been in prior to the procedure, Laura assumed he would be anxious to receive word about Hannah's status. Susan answered the call and told Laura she was babysitting Emily, because Kevin had decided to go hunting with Tom. *Hunting.* Laura was stunned. Having no cell phone, Kevin needed to be near the house phone for an update. Laura couldn't understand his decision to remain unavailable for the news of their daughter's life-or-death status. She was hurt, angry, and insulted that the father of her child would rather go hunting than find out whether his daughter lived or died.

After talking with Susan, Laura was livid. Her anger slowly simmered into the deepest resentment she had ever held toward Kevin. By the end of the night, those overpowering emotions had usurped what had been left of her limited energy reserves. She slipped further down the dark path of depression and self-hatred. She hated herself for her poor performance during Hannah's earlier emergency, for not being more available to Emily, for hating her life when Hannah was clearly much worse off, and for marrying someone who was capable of not loving his own child.

Laura scanned the rest of the faces in the PICU. Everywhere she looked, she saw sick children with parents sitting bedside, often hand in hand—not only moms, but dads too. All of these other mothers seemed to have what Laura desperately coveted—a shoulder to cry on, someone nagging them to have a healthy lunch when they didn't feel like eating, an understanding pair of eyes to look into when things were too scary for words. Most of all, though, Laura longed for someone whom she could trust to love and adore Hannah as much as she did—someone who would continue to fight for Hannah when she had no more fight left in her. Laura remembered the nurse's comments in the cafeteria and began to see how the nurse was right. This *was* a big burden for her to bear on her own. She wanted help carrying the load. But Kevin had repeatedly demonstrated he wanted nothing to do with Hannah. If Hannah's own father didn't want to be intimately involved in her life, Laura couldn't imagine anybody else would, either.

At 8:00 a.m. the next morning Laura used the phone placed just outside the closed double doors to the PICU to let the nurse know she was back from David's House. The unit coordinator told Laura someone would come out to get her when morning rounds were competed. More than an hour passed before Laura was given the okay to enter. Massively irritated by her lengthy wait, Laura's attention was immediately diverted to a group of white coats—surrounding Hannah's bed. She inwardly groaned at the implication of such a scene.

Hannah's nurse greeted Laura. "Hi. Sorry for the long wait out there, but, as you can see, we were pretty busy. After you left last night, Hannah had three more seizures. The first two only lasted a few minutes each, but the last one—this morning—lasted twenty minutes before we were able to successfully stop it, and it again involved apnea. The good news is her timing. First, she was still intubated, so not breathing spontaneously wasn't a life-threatening situation. Second, Dr. Romano—the best pediatric neurologist I know—happened to be leading rounds this morning, so she had the best possible person at her bedside when it happened."

But I wasn't at her bedside. That's great that she had a good doctor there for her, but I should have been standing there next to him. Why didn't you people page me last night when she seized again? Why didn't you let me in this morning when I first got here? Oh, I know. They don't trust you after yesterday, Laura. You're being pushed out of the picture. They don't want you involved. Stop it! Focus on Hannah! "Yeah, Hannah certainly has a thing for timing, doesn't she? So will we still be taking the breathing tube out today?"

"No, we'll be leaving that in for awhile longer. We've started her on a seizure medication called phenobarbital, but after this morning's events, we'll be leaving her breathing tube in until we're sure the drug is successful in getting her seizures under better control. Oh, here comes Dr. Romano. He can fill you in on the details and answer any questions you have."

Dr. Romano reiterated the details about using phenobarbital. He explained about the different causes of epilepsy and types of seizures, along with the role medication played. "Just to be safe, she'll need to remain intubated for at least a few more days, so we can get the phenobarb up to therapeutic levels and make sure that it's working well for her. In the meantime, we'll be getting an EEG, or an electrical study of Hannah's brain, which may help us in understanding why she's having these seizures, and also, how best to treat them."

Laura thanked the doctor for his time and settled in next to Hannah. *It looks like there's no way we'll make it home for Thanksgiving. Oh, come on. We might still make it. Today's Saturday, so we have four days to do what we need to do and get discharged. Once they get the tube out, I can kinda push to get out to the floor, or maybe even get discharged straight home from the PICU. You're fooling yourself, Laura. It's the weekend, and nothing happens on the weekend. Then we have three days. That's three days for Hannah to cook up some new complication. Let's face it. Thanksgiving is ruined. Ugh, being split up for the holiday is the worst! Do you even hear yourself? Little Christina over there will be lucky to even <u>live</u> through Thanksgiving. How dare you complain? And don't even think that you're going to get any sympathy from your family. I can hear it now: "That's what* *you get for going through with the heart surgery." Now what do I do? Do I go home to spend Thanksgiving with Em, or do I stay here with Hannah? Ugh, I'm so sick of this choice.*

Hannah's breathing tube remained in place even longer than expected, due to more seizure activity. When it was removed, her vocal cords became swollen and irritated, due to the extended intubation. Now, instead of being home for her first Thanksgiving, Hannah would be stuck in the PICU—with vocal cords that weren't working. Laura called Janet to discuss her holiday options. Laura, unfortunately, wasn't surprised when Janet informed her that Emily was an emotional wreck and *really* needed Laura home for Thanksgiving.

Laura stopped by the PICU to say goodbye to Hannah on Thanksgiving morning. On the way into the hospital she clung to hope that the doctors had made an overnight decision to discharge Hannah. She knew deep down just how delusional that hope was; Hannah was still an extremely sick little girl. Normally Laura wouldn't have minded being away from Hannah for a day, but the PICU was full to capacity and the nurses were exceptionally busy. She knew they wouldn't have time to rock Hannah or even answer all of her cries. No volunteers were available, either, since it was a holiday weekend. Worst of all was the fact that Hannah's strained vocal cords still weren't working; she was unable to utter a sound. When she cried, Hannah's face twisted in pain, tears streamed down her face—but the room remained eerily silent. Laura had never witnessed anything more heartbreaking.

Hannah was awake when Laura arrived at her bedside. *I could just scoop her up right now and run. She'd be okay at home. They'd try to convince me to bring her back here, but that wouldn't happen until tomorrow morning. What are you talking about? Laura, she's in the <u>intensive</u> <u>care</u> <u>unit</u>. She wouldn't be here if she didn't have to be. Look at her, though. Look at her tears. I have to pick her up. NO! If you sit down with her, you know damn well that you won't get back up. <u>Emily needs you</u>. I know, I know, but look at her. Yeah, I know, and if you could see Em right now, you'd feel just as strongly that she needs you this much, too. You've been here for days, Laura. It's time to be there for Emily. And I want to be, but it's too hard. I can't leave* *her like this. Stop it! You have to go! Just turn around and walk out. Hold your breath, close your eyes, and just do it. Emily's waiting. Go. Go. GO!*

Laura sped through Hanover on her way to the highway, while frantically searching with shaking fingers for a radio station with loud music that would help her escape. Laura had made the mistake of turning around to see Hannah one more time before she left the PICU. The nurses were unaware that Hannah had started crying, since they couldn't hear her muted sobs.

Laura had decided to leave anyway, knowing her willpower would fail her if she returned to Hannah's bedside. She struggled to rid herself of the excruciating memory of seeing tears streaming down Hannah's face as she had turned to walk away. Efforts to shake that image from her mind only offered a replacement vision of Emily wailing when Laura had last left home. The two images began to whirl around in her head—Hannah crying and Emily crying. The picture of the perfect family she had imagined the night Hannah was born had completely faded away. Instead, she was left with these gut-wrenching reminders of reality. The crying faces of her daughters were flashing by faster and faster, stabbing and ripping at her heart with each pass, until nothing else existed—no car, no road, no music, no Laura, just pain.

Wait. What are you doing turning the car off? Start the car back up. What are you talking about? This is Dad's house. Oh... huh...strange...I don't remember getting to the highway. No time for that now. Snap to it, Laura. You have a whole family to face and Em to...to...what do I need to do for Emily again? What exactly is it that I'm supposed to be doing here? Nurture her, I guess. Nurture might be a bit much right now. Be honest, Laura. You don't have it in you to be there for her today. But I have to be! I have to be there for her. Otherwise I've left Hannah behind for no reason. You idiot, I guess that's exactly what you've done then, because there isn't anything left in you for Em. Both girls are going without a mother right now, because you can't pull yourself together to be there for them. Stop it; this isn't helping anything! Maybe not, but it's the truth, and you know it. You should have just wrapped the car around that tree you were eyeing on the way here. No. No. Shake it off. I can do this.

As Laura walked into the house, she was crying hysterically—on the inside. To the outer world she was an empty shell of a person, and she could only imagine what she looked like when her father met her at the door. She had no energy left—no outward emotion. She felt certain that her soul had given up on her and left, too.

"What's wrong?" Stephen asked.

What's wrong! Where do I start? No! Hush. There's no winning here. If you talk to him, you won't feel any better. You'll just get the "I told you so" that they're all holding in. Take a minute alone to pull yourself together. Laura mumbled a few inaudible words and brushed past him on the way to her former bedroom. "Pulling herself together" was a much more difficult task than she had anticipated. She soon left the sanctuary of the bedroom, as painful images were, once again, a raging tornado in her head. She hoped the distraction of family would snap her out of this.

Laura met Kevin and Emily in the living room. Emily had come in briefly to make sure her mother was there before going outside to play. Laura felt relieved that Emily had not asked more of her at that time. Aware that she was now facing the rest of the family, Laura sat down in the rocker-recliner, trying to draw as little attention to herself as possible. *Who are all of these people? I know them, but I don't know them anymore. You're not one of them anymore. You're an outsider now. They're chatting it up about shopping, taxes, work, and hunting season. Go ahead. Just try throwing in a comment about something relevant in your life right now. You could tell them about Christina. Are you kidding? What a depressing story for a holiday. I can still talk to them, though. I can bring up...I can mention...ah, screw it. You're right. I don't belong here. Then you should leave, because your silence is making people uncomfortable.*

Laura retreated back to her bedroom again. Shortly thereafter, Kevin ascended the stairs, looking for her.

He spoke in his most particularly insensitive manner. "What's wrong with you?"

Laura was sitting on the edge of the bed. For a few moments, she pondered what he had said and how she might possibly respond. *Don't you know? Don't you know what's wrong? You're a parent of these two kids, too.*

"Can't you at least come down and make some small talk with the rest of the family? It's starting to get embarrassing."

Wow. He doesn't know. He really has no idea. Even if I could explain all that's in my heart right now, he still wouldn't have a clue. You're alone, Laura, all alone.

Kevin scolded her. "Laura—Jesus, snap out of it!"

I think he wants you to talk. If you can just think of something to say, maybe you can make it downstairs. Hmmm...say...what to say...saayyy...

"Screw it. Stay up here if you want." With a roll of his eyes and a disgusted sigh, Kevin went back downstairs to face the family.

He's right, you know. If you stay up here long enough, they'll come looking for you, and they might want you to talk—and open up about what's going on. Then what will you do? If you go back downstairs and just sit, maybe nobody will notice. No. I'm tired...too tired. I give up. Besides, if I rest, maybe I'll have energy for Em later on. Just rest. I wonder if I should call to check in on Hannah. NO!! Jesus, no. Don't start thinking about her! Quick... go downstairs. That'll distract those thoughts. Besides, maybe Emily's back inside.

Emily was still outside. In the meantime, Daniel had arrived. He and Kevin were sitting on the sofa in the living room. Laura sat back down in the rocker-recliner across from them, hoping that nobody would try to strike up a conversation with her. *Just get through the day, Laura. After this afternoon, you can have some quiet time with Em—maybe read a story together. But what if Hannah seized again? No, stop it! You've got to keep her out of your head! Focus on Emily. God, why can't I shut this off!*

"Laura, maybe you could go to the movies tonight—get your mind off things for awhile," said Daniel.

Laura looked up to find Daniel gazing at her with concern, as if he were reading her thoughts, as he so often seemed to do.

"*You* might as well take her. You always cheer her up. God knows *I* can't," said Kevin. The ever-familiar roll of his eyes followed his words.

Movies? I can't go to the movies when my girls need me. What kind of question is that? What kind of mother would I be? I came here to spend time with Emily. I left Hannah behind, so I could be with Emily. I...I can't...the movies. I haven't thought of going to the movies in months. I don't even know what's playing. With Daniel? Man, that'd be fun...but no...out of the question. But it's Daniel asking the question. He's so good at knowing what you need. Don't just dismiss him...but, no...I can't cheat Em out of more time.

"We could go to the late show—you know, after Emily's bedtime," offered Daniel, as if in answer to Laura's inner debate.

After bedtime...could that work? Of course not. What if the hospital calls? What if Em wakes up? What if...what if...oh, but time out with Daniel feels like the right answer. Come on, Laura, take a chance. It's selfish, though, to go out on a night when you should be there for the girls. But they won't even know. You can't be there for Hannah, anyway, and Em will be asleep. And Daniel wouldn't have suggested it, if it weren't okay to do. Go ahead. It's okay.

Laura spoke barely loud enough to hear. "All right." Daniel and Laura were going to the movies.

Chapter VIII

Healing Love

Laura and Emily spent some quality time together by snuggling up and reading a bedtime story. Laura realized how much she missed the special closeness of bedtime with Emily. If she hadn't planned to see a movie, she probably would have spent the entire night cuddled up with her daughter. Instead, Laura hesitantly kept to her plan, gave Emily one final hug, kissed her goodnight, and quietly left the room.

As they sat down in the theater, Laura was eager to open up to Daniel, yet she hesitated. Meaningful conversation for her had become awkward and uncomfortable lately. She questioned whether to bring up a subject that usually turned people away.

"Daniel, I have a question. When everything started to happen with Hannah, I called people to update them, and that was all fine. But if I tried to really *talk* to them about things and about how I was feeling, the mood would turn uncomfortable–really fast. Soon, even the updates, themselves, felt awkward. I would crave talking about everything, but dared not to, because it would leave me feeling lonely. Genuine communication with Kevin has been nonexistent. What else is new, right? So when I called you...I don't know...I guess I was hoping for something different somehow, but even with you, I still felt that...that disconnect, you know? What were you feeling when I first called you to tell you about Hannah?"

"Well, you left a few messages with one of my roommates, John, and while the messages that I got probably weren't exactly the messages you were leaving, I kinda knew what was up, before we actually talked. I felt horrible, too, because I really wanted to see you guys and to help, but school was starting up, and I was moving into the apartment with the guys and starting my classes— not to mention I don't have a car. But when you finally caught me on the phone and *really* filled me in on what was happening, God, I fought to hold back tears. And when we hung up, I cried and cried. I just thought that when I talked with you, I should...I don't know...be strong for you. Then there were a bunch of times when I thought of you and the girls and wanted to call, but I didn't know how to get in touch with you. I don't know if that was the right thing to do or not, but I was *definitely* feeling it with you."

Laura felt the lump in her throat that had been occurring frequently, but this time, a welling of tears accompanied it, which hadn't happened in weeks, if not months.

"You didn't do anything wrong. Thank you...thank you so much. But from now on, don't feel like you can't open up to me, because I feel like I have to be strong all the time—for Hannah and Em. And that's gone on for so long that I can't ever let my guard down, even when I want to. But just now I...I actually felt like I might cry...and... um...it's just good to know that you're still with me. We've always been so close, and...and...I was afraid that maybe we had lost that."

"Oh no, we haven't lost anything. I'm still here. I wish I had found a way to call you all those times I wanted to. Sorry about that. But whenever you need me, I'm here for you...that is, unless you need me somewhere I'd have to drive to. Or if you need me after Sunday, that's no good, because that's when I go back to school. And if you need me, but I'm out of the apartment, well, that's no good. But that's pretty much all the time. So, yeah, I'll be there for you but, you know, not so much *there* for you," he said. Daniel ended his words with the familiar grin that made everything feel all right again.

The following day, Littleton held a day-after-Thanksgiving Christmas parade downtown, followed by an after-party for the kids at the town hall. Since Kevin had made other plans for himself, Laura invited Daniel to join Emily and her for the festivities. The atmosphere that day was in sharp contrast to Laura's dark days leading up to it. A distinct nip in the November air greeted the occasional snowflake dancing its way to the ground. But the festive surroundings created a special warmth that kept them from noticing the cold temperature.

Emily was all smiles and giggles and Daniel was largely responsible for the sparkle in her eyes that day. He made her laugh and helped her relax, so she could enjoy the activities that she otherwise would have been too shy to participate in. With Daniel there, not only was Emily able to enjoy herself, but Laura was afforded the opportunity to finally relax.

For a few hours, life felt nearly normal again, and Laura didn't want it to end. She knew Emily needed to return home for a nap, and she planned to go back to DHMC for the night, but she wasn't ready to let this moment go. She wasn't ready to let Daniel go. A change was taking place. Laura was finally starting to feel her heart beating again. She was able to smell the air, to see in color, and to hear her own laughter. She couldn't bear the thought of going back to the way she had felt the day before.

While Emily was napping that afternoon, Daniel approached Laura as she was washing dishes. "Laura...uh...I got you a little something. I know it's not much..."

He handed her a bag, which contained a cassette tape of the soundtrack to the movie *Don Juan De Marco*. In a recent conversation, Laura had told Daniel how music helped sooth Hannah and mentioned a few tapes she intended to buy. Laura stood staring at the tape, stunned. Not only had he remembered a rather insignificant conversation, but he had also taken the initiative to find and buy the tape.

Laura reached under his arms and around his back for a hug. With her cheek to his chest she said, "No, no, Daniel, this is great. You're..." *Hold on now. Choose your words carefully. He's you're stepbrother, Laura. This is a mighty comfortable hug, and you're feeling a little too much excitement for the situation. He's gonna freak out, and you'll lose what you have with him. This is a guy who thinks of you as his sister. You are his sister! Oh, but these shoulders. I could rest on this shoulder for the rest of the day. I should have rested my head against this shoulder in the theater. And these arms...so secure. Maybe I could have felt the warmth of his arm around me or held his hand. This is the nicest, most considerate, and most loving man I've ever met. AND he's your stepbrother, Laura! He's a great stepbrother! It's a darn good thing you didn't do anything as foolish as trying to hold his hand last night. That would have been a catastrophe. Now hurry up and finish your sentence appropriately.* "...the greatest brother ever!"

She gave Daniel a quick rub on the back and respectably stepped away. *Let's review: "greatest brother ever." Yeah, that sounds legitimate enough. He'll never know what you were really thinking. But watch yourself. You're feeling some funky things for this guy. Don't go getting yourself into trouble. Trouble? No. I've had feelings like this for him before, and I controlled them. I can keep them at bay. But I'm just not ready to say good-bye yet. I want to spend a little more time with him. But how can I do that? I'm leaving later today for the hospital.*

Before Laura realized what she was doing, she blurted out an idea, as quickly as it had popped into her head. "You know, I'm going to the hospital tonight to check in on Hannah, and then I'll be coming back here tomorrow. Would you like to join me before you head back to school?"

He responded without hesitation. "Sure."

Thank God. What would I have done if he had said no? Do you hear yourself? This isn't going in a good direction. I mean, it's good that he's going with me, because then I'll be forced to come home to Emily, since I'm his only ride back. That way I won't get stuck at the hospital indefinitely, the way I always seem to. Don't kid yourself. You want to spend the night with Daniel. Don't be ridiculous. The room there has two twin beds. We've slept in adjacent beds loads of times at camp. Yeah, and you had inappropriate thoughts of him then, too, that nearly got the best of you. Yeah, but I was pregnant with Hannah, so my hormones were all out of whack. Besides, there was no danger of anything happening anyway. Let's face it. I was an absolute hippo when I was pregnant with Hannah. AND he thinks of me as a sister. It'll be fine. I'll just ignore any desire for anything more than strictly platonic contact, like I did back then. I've known him for two years, and I've really only had physical contact with him twice— the hug at camp last summer after Kevin's call and this hug now. That's respectable, right? Oh, there were the four-wheeler rides we went on together during our first summer, too. How I loved the excuse to wrap my arms around his waist and rest my cheek against his back. But I'm sure he doesn't even remember that, and I can't imagine that any jury would consider that shameful behavior, right? But after this last hug, maybe he thinks you want more. I mean, you just hugged a man and then promptly invited him over for the night. You've gotta say something to make it sound more PG rated. "And it'll work out well, too, because there's an extra bed in my room at David's House. They had run out of single rooms, so they put me in the Cow Room, which has two twin beds."

Daniel smiled. "Sounds great."

Yeah, he doesn't suspect a thing. He's just being the loving person that he always is. Now all I have to do is behave myself, and it'll all be fine.

After tucking Emily into bed for the night, Laura and Daniel headed out. Laura's drive to the hospital was transformed from the mundane chore it always had been to a joyous opportunity for more conversation with Daniel. "It's hard to believe that we've only known each other for just over two years," Laura said. "It seems like we've known each other forever."

"Yeah, but I remember the day we met like it was yesterday," said Daniel. "I was sitting in the living room, minding my own business, when a girl walked in, and I thought, 'Oh, great, now what am I going to do?' I never do well with girls."

Laura continued the memory. "You were watching *Empire Strikes Back* and I thought, 'Oh cool, *Empire Strikes Back*,' so I sat down to join you, and you changed it to *Beverly Hills 90210*. I couldn't believe it!"

Daniel continued. "And you said, 'Hey, what's the idea? Turn it back!' I couldn't believe it. A girl was actually okay with watching a *Star Wars* movie. That's when I knew we'd get along just fine–which was weird because I never had anything in common with any girl before."

"Yeah, but then you became quite the stud at school."

"Only because of the pick-up line that you taught me: have you seen a picture of my adorable little niece?"

"I guess you have quite a bit to thank Em for."

"Yeah, but being an uncle has been less than glamorous on a few occasions. Like, remember when I ended up eating that Desitin?"

"Oh, that was priceless. You came running out of the bathroom with your mouth all white saying, 'What's wrong with this toothpaste?'"

"I had never seen Desitin before. Man, that stuff was nasty."

"I guess that was a pretty tough summer for you. You moved from Manchester to your mom's new house, you suddenly have two more sisters plus an eight-month-old baby to contend with, and you don't even get a bed out of the deal–much less a room to yourself. You ended up having to sleep on the couch."

"Well, I don't know if I'd actually call it sleep. Emily was...uh..."

Laura finished for him. "Loud. Often. I felt so bad waking you up for work." *If only you knew how much I loved waking you. You looked so peaceful, so sweet. Sometimes I would imagine kissing you on the forehead or holding your hand. Oh, how I'd love to hold your hand right now. I could reach over and...Laura! Snap out of it. What has come over you? You are a married woman, and this is your stepbrother! Sweet as he is, you are not to touch his hand or any other part of his body.*

"Oh, I didn't mind. It had to have been much worse for you."

"Not really. I usually got to go back to bed until Em got up, but you had to go to work."

"It was all worth it. I love that kid. I wouldn't have wanted to spend that summer any other way."

When they arrived in the hospital parking lot, Laura was amazed at how fast the hour and a half had flown by.

• •

Hannah was right where Laura had left her in the PICU. Her voice had improved a bit and overall, she didn't look too bad. Laura and Daniel continued chatting as he rocked Hannah. Just as Laura had hoped, the conversation flowed naturally, as if they were sitting on a park bench on a sunny day. With no uncomfortable silences needing to be filled, she didn't feel as if she had to entertain him and, therefore, wasn't emotionally drained. In fact, Laura was able to rejoice in the precious sight of Hannah sleeping so peacefully in Daniel's arms while lovingly cradled on his lap, as they spoke. After spending a few hours with Hannah, Laura and Daniel headed to David's House. As they walked, Laura could feel her heart beating a little faster and her face becoming flushed with excitement. The moon seemed brighter, and the air felt crisper. The sound of the wind whispering through the trees touched her ears in a new way, and the scent of early winter on the late-night breeze somehow felt warmer and more inviting. Laura believed no one could have lifted her spirits the way Daniel had. *It's so nice to have this time with him. He completely turned around my mood and dug me out of the emotional pit I've been in. I'm so lucky to have him here with me. I wouldn't want to share this experience with anyone else.*

Laura gave Daniel a brief tour of David's House on their way to the Cow Room. As she pointed out various attributes of the breathtaking surroundings, she felt as if she were seeing everything for the first time. After entering their room, Laura desperately tried to occupy herself to avoid additional scandalous thoughts about Daniel.

Once the lights were out and they were tucked into their beds, she breathed a sigh of relief that she hadn't succumbed to yearnings that could have proven disastrous to their relationship. Lights out didn't mean the night was over. They continued to chat in the dark, as they had so many times at camp. However, this time, Laura had difficulty carrying on an active dialogue with Daniel. The conversation was wonderful, but Laura couldn't concentrate because of the simultaneous full-blown battle raging inside her head. *I simply must feel his arms around me again. Are you insane? Stop those ridiculous thoughts of hugs and handholding. Well, then I'll just sit on the side of his bed while we talk. We've done that before at camp. I simply have to be closer to him. Think, Laura. Think how much you would regret that later. But something tells me it would be okay. No, you are not to move an inch. Stay right where you are. No, I'm not sure why, but I have to take this chance. I'm going to ask him if he would mind if I lie down next to him. I just need to gather the courage and find the right moment.* "Ah, to heck with it." Before she could stop herself, Laura was walking over to Daniel's bed.

She was surprised when the situation didn't feel awkward at all. Laura slipped in between the covers, laid her head on Daniel's chest, and wrapped her arm around his waist. She felt as if she had jumped off a jagged cliff into a sea of warmth and comfort—a place where she most definitely belonged. Daniel held her close and stroked her hair as she breathed in a tranquility she had been missing all her life. After the long string of stressful days during the past few months, this new experience felt like a collective hot bubble bath washing away all of the previous tension. Laura never would have guessed that a simple embrace could be so needed or feel so wonderful—not just physically, but spiritually as well. His arms were like angel wings, lifting her spirits straight up to the heavens.

After a few minutes, Laura said, "I hope you don't mind me being here."

"No, definitely no. I always dreamed of this, but I never dreamed it would ever actually happen."

"You were feeling the same thing I was? I never would have guessed!"

"Are you kidding? I felt that it was radiating off me like a big neon sign. I thought for sure you'd hate me for being completely inappropriate. I mean, come on, I'm your stepbrother. I was doing all I could to contain myself. I have to say, though, that I was shocked when you came over here–incredibly thankful, but shocked."

"Oh, sorry about that. I was pretty nervous. I meant to ask first, but I guess I kinda skipped that part. Wait, if you've been feeling the same way I have, why didn't you say something?"

"Oh, I wanted to, believe me, but it had to be your call, you know?"

"Yeah, and I'm still a married woman. I don't want you to think I'm someone who would cheat on my husband. I know that sounds odd given the situation at hand..."

"No, no. I think we both know this isn't a sex thing. It's something else. I can't explain it, but it's perfect just the way it is. You feel perfect right where you are."

Soon they were saying goodnight, and as Laura looked up, searching for Daniel's eyes in the dimly lit room, she found him smiling down at her. He ran his fingertips down the side of her cheek. His expression was one that Laura had seen many times before when he was drawing. He studied her face, taking in every detail–every nuance. He was an incredible artist, and Laura always loved watching him at work. "I don't ever want to forget this moment," said Daniel.

"Me neither," said Laura. "I don't even want it to end."

Laura was certain she would never forget what happened next. Lost in the moment, they found themselves swept into a kiss. But, in Laura's mind, this particular kiss was, by far, the absolute worst kiss ever known to mankind. As the moments ticked by, her thoughts compared the two of them to two neurotic fish who had come face to face, after accidentally bumping into one another.

Then they sat frozen in place, having no earthly idea what they might possibly do next. They quickly pulled away laughing and decided they had been correct; this definitely was not a sex thing. The two of them snuggled into a warm embrace and drifted off to sleep. For Laura, it was a slumber more restful than she had experienced in months—if not years.

Chapter IX

Heart and Duty

Laura had a lot to think about on the way back to Littleton. *I need to get my head screwed on straight. What just happened back there? What an incredible night! Imagine waking up in Daniel's arms like that every morning—ahhhh! No. Stop it. Don't even try to imagine it. Any thoughts of further exploring a romantic relationship with Daniel would be totally selfish and would hurt the people you love most. You have to hold your marriage together for the girls. But I never knew there could be such magic between two people. Well, magic can't be counted on, and with kids to think about, you need to keep your feet on the ground. Plus, think of it from Daniel's standpoint. You aren't what he needs! Christ, Laura, he's young, talented, smart, and loving. He has so much to offer the world. He doesn't need a walking quagmire like you dragging him down. You have to stop this now. Anything less than a quick and resolute break is leading him on, and he doesn't deserve that. And you need to work on your marriage. Focus on the progress that you made last spring before Kevin left.*

As motivated as Laura *wanted* to be at working on her relationship with Kevin, she instead found herself immersed in a state of emptiness, and her dismal situation was consuming every thought. Up until that night in the Cow Room, she had recognized a longing for something more or something different in her life. However, she had never been able to identify exactly

118

what needed to change. The night in the Cow Room signified in abject crystal clarity what she needed, in order to live her life in perfect harmony. She now knew what she wanted, what she was missing, and what would remain out of reach, if she stayed with Kevin. *Maybe I would have been better off never knowing what could have been. Will I be able to live with the memories when it's highly unlikely that I'll ever experience anything like that again? What if I end up resenting Kevin even more because of the comparison I now have? Ugh, at least I can now tell Emily what love actually feels like.*

Meanwhile, depression continued to lock Laura in an unbearable stronghold. Memories of her Thanksgiving weekend were dreamlike, serving as an escape from her dark world. At night, she tried desperately to get to sleep, so the dream might continue. Laura hugged her pillow tightly, imagining and longing for Daniel's tender touch and caress. Her car trips to and from the hospital drifted by with far-away memories of their conversations. While rocking Hannah, her thoughts wandered back to the morning when they had returned to the PICU from David's House. Daniel had briefly stepped out to get them some breakfast. Laura hadn't asked for breakfast. In fact, she hadn't even thought about eating. But Daniel had said, "You need something to eat. I'll be right back." When he returned, he had presented to Hannah a small stuffed cow with angel's wings. "I got it to watch over her and keep her safe until I can come back...and to kind of...I don't know...'honor' our time in the Cow Room," he had said. Laura smirked while imagining how odd she must have looked to the nurses—rocking Hannah to the tunes of the Don Juan soundtrack as she longingly gazed toward the stuffed cow angel.

Struggles with Hannah, frustrations with Emily, and fights with Kevin dragged Laura out of her heavenly solace. With her baseline day-to-day stressors and the added stresses of the holiday season, sleep was becoming a rare commodity, and her eating habits were atrocious. She was frequently feeling weak and lightheaded. Her growing depression had seized every last ounce of energy. Life was spinning increasingly out of control, and thoughts of suicide were haunting Laura more often and more intensely.

Hannah was finally discharged two weeks after she had been admitted. Laura contemplated seeing Daniel again. *I'll call him and invite him for the weekend, just to see Hannah, now that she's out of the hospital. He could come and decorate the Christmas tree with us. Laura, you need to let this go. Let Daniel go. But when I'm with him, my haze and numbness are suspended for a little while. I've gotta see him again. No, that will just make this harder. And you're the last thing Daniel needs. It's not right to keep seeing him. But he wants to, and I need him! Emily needs him too. She lights up when Daniel's around. I'll just have to behave and try to remain as sisterly as possible.* Laura quickly made the phone call before second thoughts could take hold, and just as quickly, Daniel accepted the invitation.

Daniel's arrival drastically improved Laura's mood and energy level. By Saturday morning, she was feeling playful enough to partake in a spirited discussion with Daniel about which cereal was better, Cap'n Crunch or Kix. While sparring back and forth, each raised fine points for debate, but ultimately, they couldn't come to a mutual agreement on the better breakfast food.

Laura attempted to include Kevin in the light-hearted debate. "Well, what do you think, Kevin?"

"Think about *what*?" he asked. He was clearly annoyed by the request.

"Which is the better cereal, Cap'n Crunch—which Daniel argues tastes better, so it must clearly be considered the top choice—or Kix, which I contend is better for you and tastes good, too, so it must certainly be ranked higher?"

He scoffed at them. "Who *cares*?" Then he walked away with a disgusted look.

Later that morning, they all ventured out to a Christmas-tree farm. After struggling all week to communicate with Kevin, Laura felt relieved talking to Daniel—no worries, no battles, and no frustrations. The conversation simply flowed naturally. Laura reminded herself that she shared a special relationship with Daniel—even if only as a sibling. She desperately tried to convince herself that she should appreciate that privilege, and it should be enough.

Once the girls were asleep that night, Laura drove Daniel back to Steve and Janet's house. Laura stayed for a while, since she was only a five-minute drive away, in case Kevin needed her back home. They decided to watch the *Don Juan* movie. Daniel hadn't seen it, and since Laura was such a fan, he wanted to check it out.

Janet joined them for the movie, sitting on the smaller sofa, so the larger sofa was left for Daniel and Laura to share. Laura's favorite aspect of the romantic comedy was the colorful and passionate dialogue that had a particularly smooth and poetic cadence—a fitting backdrop for the drama unfolding on the sofa. Daniel had grabbed a blanket to ward off the winter chill. When Laura joined him on the sofa, he had thrown half of the blanket over her lap. As the movie continued and their seating positions shifted, Daniel and Laura soon felt their thighs touching under the blanket. *Mmmm...I can feel the warmth of his leg on mine. God, you're acting like a lovesick teenager. Just calm down. I can't! Should I be elated or petrified that this close contact is bringing back all of the wondrous sensations from last weekend? Try not to read too much into it; I doubt he's even noticing any of this. Oh, maybe I'm wrong.* Daniel had silently slipped his hand over Laura's. She glanced over at him and instantly knew he was feeling everything she was—the electricity, the excitement, the desire—along with the guilt and fear.

Laura found herself woefully unprepared for the movie to end. After all, she had to drive back home—to her husband. Daniel would be heading back to Plymouth the next day. She feared she couldn't face those realities. Then Janet inadvertently softened the transition for Laura. "Oh, it's snowing, guys. You two should go out to the hot tub."

Laura glanced at Daniel who had a smirk on his face. "Yeah, Mom. That sounds good."

The beauty of the night was a perfect setting for the hot tub. The snow fell magnificently from the sky, as the steam from the hot water rose to meet it just above their heads. Ice formed in their hair, creating a unique shimmer under the dim glow of the porch light.

"What are we going to do?" asked Laura.

"I don't know. I've thought about us all week, and I have no idea," said Daniel.

"Me neither. I had myself convinced that I should walk away from all of this and work on my marriage for the sake of the girls but, then I see you and fall head over heels all over again."

"Well, you have to do what's best for you and your family. I'm supportive either way. Obviously, I have a preference on how things should go, but you do what you feel is best."

"Thanks for saying that, but I don't even know what's best anymore. I've seen marriages break up and it's no good, but I've seen marriages stay together for the sake of the kids, and that can be just as bad. I feel bad telling you about this inner struggle I'm having. I know it must be hard for you to hear, but you're my best friend and the only person I can talk to. Even if I did have someone else to open up to, I can't imagine saying 'I think I'm in love with my stepbrother.'"

"Actually I've been having that conversation for a few years now. I was in love the first time I saw your picture—you know, the one on the piano where you've got that killer smile going on, and your eyes are all...wow...and your hair...well anyway, I saw it and thought, *Wow...who is that*! When I saw you in person, I was smitten. Then you'd visit me in the dorm at school, when you were living with Tom and Susan, and I couldn't help myself. I ended up talking to my roommate. I said, 'I know it sounds bad, but I think I'm in love with my stepsister.'"

"Oh, my God. What'd he say?"

"He said, 'Dude, that's messed up! She's married; you don't have a chance. And, *HELLO*, she's married to a *marine*!' I said, 'I know, I know. I just can't help it.'"

"That's funny. When we got back to California after that first summer we met, I told my friends stories about stuff that you and I had talked about or done. It was totally innocent, but at one point, my best friend, Janine, looked at me and said, 'Oh, my God, look at you! You're all flushed, and your eyes totally have that sparkle. Is there something you should be telling us?' I brushed her off and said, 'No, no. It was just a really fun summer.'"

Laura's last comments made Daniel think about his best friend, Will. "Will knows, too."

"He does? You told him, too?"

"Not really. He kinda figured it out on his own. Remember when he and I stayed over at camp this summer, and you ended up coming over to my bed to talk? Well, the next morning he said, 'Man, what's up with you and Laura?' When I asked what he meant, he said, 'You could cut the sexual tension with a knife!' I tried to deny it at first, but then I broke down and told him everything. Kelly knows, too, I think."

"She does? How would your girlfriend know!"

"I guess I'm not too good at hiding it. I went back to school last week and kinda had the perma-smile thing going on, and she matter-of-factly asked, 'You saw Laura this weekend, didn't you?'"

"I've thought about you and Kelly this week," said Laura. "I have to admit that I'm jealous when she's with you."

"Well, you might not have to worry about Kelly being around much longer. Things really aren't going well there."

"Oh, really?"

"Yeah. Things have been kinda rocky for awhile."

"Gee, I so wish I could say 'I'm sorry,' but I just can't seem to spit it out."

"That's okay. I'm not sorry either. I'm the happiest I've ever been right here, right now."

Laura agreed, as she rested her head on his shoulder. "Mmmm, me too."

They headed back inside. After dressing, they secretly shared a long kiss and embrace—no fish-kiss this time, but rather a tender, passionate, sincere, and breathtaking expression of love-filled emotion. Laura needed every ounce of willpower within her to pull away and walk out the door. Feeling anxious to check on Hannah certainly helped to propel her along. She walked to the car wondering if she could get through a whole week without Daniel.

• •

Utter exhaustion and depression continued to plague Laura. Physically, she was weaker than ever before and was having numerous fainting spells daily. She kept feeling as if she were drowning in a sea of duty and responsibility and couldn't rise up for air before the next crisis would drag her back down. In addition, irrational fears and paranoia were taking hold.

You should have been at home with Hannah Saturday night. What if something had gone wrong? That's abandonment... neglect. She could have died, and where were you? In a hot tub—with another man, no less. God, Laura, you kissed another man. Kevin could find out, file for divorce, and get custody of the girls on the grounds of adultery! What are you doing putting your children at risk like that? Do you really think Daniel would stand by you in the long run? Don't be ridiculous. If Kevin can't handle Hannah—and he's her biological father—what makes you think Daniel would stick around? You're screwing up, Laura. It's gonna get nothing but worse from here. But you could end it all now. The answer is right over there. It's as simple as a few swigs from those little bottles in the cupboard. You could rest. No, the girls need me. But they won't have you for long if you keep this up, and they get taken away from you. Look at your track record. You've given Hannah wrong doses of potentially lethal medications—and the nurses know about that. You left Hannah with Kevin, who didn't even take the time to learn infant CPR like you were both supposed to. This morning, you nearly killed Emily when you were carrying her to the car, because you had a fainting spell and fell on top of her. Heck, Em's over three years old now and not any closer to being potty trained than she was a year ago. What kind of mother are you? It's just a matter of time before people start catching on to your incompetence. No, I have to be here for the girls. I'm doing okay with parenting. I just need to talk to Daniel. He'll be able to lift this fog.

Laura's only salvation was a few stolen phone calls during the weekdays and the promise of Daniel's presence on weekends. He was fast becoming a drug that she was hopelessly addicted to. On a particularly bad day, she finally admitted to Daniel that she had a nearly constant preoccupation with rest, and she described the steady stream of fantasies about how she might reach that goal.

"Laura, whatever you do, promise me you won't touch Hannah's medicine or anything else that could hurt you. I don't know what I'd do without you. Promise that you'll keep yourself safe until I can get over there."

Laura answered listlessly with doubts still haunting her. "Yeah, I'll try." *Oh, you'd get by just fine without me—probably even better. You just don't want my death on your conscience. I shouldn't have brought this up. You idiot, Laura. Here's the one man who truly cares about you, and you're saddling him with all this crap. Just get over it, and keep your goddamned mouth shut.*

"No, that's not good enough. I want you to promise me that if you think you might do something—or even if you're just thinking about it again—that you'll call me. Can you promise me that?" The sincere nervousness in Daniel's voice made Laura nervous.

"I don't know. I'm sorry I even brought it up. I don't mean to trouble you with this stuff. I'll be fine."

"No. No, you won't be, and maybe I'm to blame for this. Would it be better if I left you alone? I'm so sorry if I've had anything to do with you feeling so bad."

"No, no...God, no. It's not you. You being around on the weekend is the only light at the end of a very long, dark tunnel that's my week. I can understand if you don't want to be around me right now, but I was having these thoughts well before Thanksgiving, so they're certainly not anything that you've caused. I guess I'm just tired. I need a good cry or something."

"God, I wish I could be there right now. I hate that I can't always be there for you. I still need a promise from you, though— that you'll call if you think about hurting yourself again."

"Okay. I promise I'll call."

"We'll get through this. Today's Wednesday. If you can just hold on until Friday night, I'll be there with you. Do you feel you can make it until then?"

"Yeah, I guess so. I should be fine until Friday."

"Will you call me tomorrow, anyway?"

"Yeah, I'll call when you get back from your two o'clock class, before Kevin gets home."

The conversation with Daniel gave Laura a lift, as always. Unfortunately, the events of that night and the next morning did nothing but throw her life further out of control.

At sunrise, Laura stumbled out to the living room and woke Kevin. "I was just up all night with Hannah. I'm beyond exhausted. We have to be at Dr. O'Connor's at ten this morning, and I'm really worried about driving, at this point. She's finally asleep. Would you mind trading places with me, so I can try to catch an hour or two of sleep? She might stay asleep, but I just want to make sure I get some straight sleep before I get behind the wheel."

Kevin agreed and went to the bedroom while Laura took his place on the couch. She was instantly out cold, swimming in the bizarre dreams that resulted from stress and sleep deprivation.

Gotta draw up Hannah's meds. I can't pull the stopper out of the syringe. Pull...pull...quick or you'll be late. Take a right at the exit. What's that tingle? This drive isn't supposed to feel that way. Where are we going? Who's driving? My hands are full of syringes. Wait, who's there? What's this man doing here? Gotta go. Gotta wake up. No, sleep. Just want to sleep. Go away; go away. Laura struggled to open her eyes, not really understanding why. When the fogginess cleared, she found Kevin on top of her. She shrieked, scrambling to slide out from under him and into a sitting position.

"What...what the hell are you *doing!*"

"You...you were giving mixed signals. I thought you wanted this."

"MIXED SIGNALS! What could possibly be mixed about asking to please let me trade places with you, so I can GET SOME SLEEP! How could you possibly read ANYTHING sexual into that?"

"Sorry. I thought you wanted it."

At that exact moment, Laura knew her marriage was over. She had made it abundantly clear that sex was out of the question until further notice. She had taken every precaution against coming across as a tease. If she couldn't feel safe and at ease sleeping in the same house as the man she had married, something would have to change. But she knew she would need to find a colossal amount of strength to finally end her dead marriage.

Laura's mind darted around aimlessly, yet frantically, as she drove to the hospital that morning. *It's over. Are you crazy? You can't get a divorce. How the heck do you think you'll survive on your own? You can't work right now. You need Kevin to pay the bills. Oh crap, did I send out that electric bill that was on the counter? Where would I live? I couldn't move back in with Dad and Janet. Oh, did I pack an extra set of clothes for Em this morning? I think she used her last back-up pair after yesterday's accident at Rosie's. I need to wash clothes and pack a new outfit for Emily. What was I supposed to remember? Was it groceries? Let's see. There was milk, cereal, A-1 sauce, laundry detergent...*

what else was there...what else...what...where am I? Right... take a right at this corner. Oh no, Hannah's fussing. Did I give her Tylenol with her early meds? Did I remember my notebook? What do I need to report to the doctor this week? God, you'll never be able to keep Hannah if you can't get your head out of your ass long enough to focus on what needs to be mentioned. Think, Laura...think...

Friday afternoon, Laura was counting down the moments until Daniel's arrival. The hardest part was knowing that he was in town. He would stay at Steve and Janet's house for a while, so it would appear to be a casual visit back home. Family members were already asking him why he was back home from school three weekends in a row. After a few hours at home, he called Laura and asked if she wanted to join him for the late showing of the latest James Bond flick. She actually had no interest in seeing it, but she certainly wasn't going to turn down the offer.

Daniel's interest in the movie quickly faded, after Laura's suggestion to leave the theater for another soak in the hot tub. As it turned out, however, their time in the hot tub was nearly as brief as their time in the theater. The temperature was well below zero that night, and they were uncomfortably cold, even in the hot water.

As they headed upstairs to get dressed, Laura realized they faced a decision. Steve and Janet were sound asleep. Laura wasn't expected home for at least another hour. *Do we pass up this opportunity and try to stay platonic, or do we move forward? My marriage is practically over, but I don't want Daniel to think of me as someone who cheats. And what if we forge ahead, realize that it's a mistake, and then I end up losing him altogether? I just don't know. I do know I've never regretted anything concerning Daniel, and I don't feel like having sex tonight would change that. But why am I even considering sex? I truly thought that my not wanting sex with Kevin had to do with the stress of Hannah. The stress hasn't changed, yet here I am—honestly interested...strange. <u>Honestly</u> interested? Or are you attempting to maintain Daniel's attention and affection by offering sex? No, it's not like that. Daniel's not like that. From day one, Kevin was all about obtaining the final goal of sex. But*

Daniel genuinely wants to spend time with me, and I think he'd see sex as a bonus, not a necessity, and certainly not a goal—and I'm so turned on by that! If anything happens, I think I'm okay with it. Or, if nothing happens, I'm okay with that, too.

The couple climbed the stairs, attempting to miss as many squeaky steps as possible. As a teen, Laura had memorized the quietest route from her late nights out after curfew. They turned right at the top of the stairs and entered Daniel's bedroom—the room that had belonged to Laura's father while he was growing up, the room where Laura had been conceived, and the room Laura had called her own when she lived there.

Earlier they had each separately changed into their bathing suits there, and now they searched for their clothes. In the darkness, they were guided only by the faint glow of the nightlight from the far end of the hallway. They could have shut the door and turned on the light, but dressing in the dark had somehow given them permission to dress in the same room a week earlier when the situation had first presented itself. On that occasion, they had remained facing away from one another until fully dressed. Nonetheless, Laura had found it incredibly exhilarating, back then, to be standing inches away from the man of her dreams—who was in the nude.

Laura found her clothes in the neatly folded pile on the foot of the bed where she had left them. She watched with amusement as Daniel canvassed the entire bedroom, retrieving odd articles of clothing from nearly every corner of the room. As they stood, they turned away from each other, and began to disrobe.

Laura trusted Daniel to be a gentleman, just as he had been the week before. Otherwise the experience would have been slightly less exciting and a little more worrisome. Laura fretted over Daniel's reaction to seeing all of her. After all, the body she was toweling off certainly wasn't the pre-children adolescent body that had occupied the bedroom the last time she had snuck up the stairs.

"What would it have been like if we had met in high school?" Daniel asked.

"I don't know. It would have meant a much more enjoyable high school experience for me, if I had had you to spend it with," said Laura.

"I don't know about that. I was never the guy that girls went for. You would have been the beautiful one that I would have admired from afar but would have been too afraid to talk to. I would have been the geek that you wouldn't have been caught dead talking to."

"I doubt that. I was never the beautiful one, and my closest friends in school were all geeks. I was a geek, too." Laura turned toward him. "I don't know what would have drawn us together, but something would have, and we would have gotten along great. I just think we were meant to be together." *Oh... I wasn't supposed to turn around.*

Daniel turned around when he realized Laura was facing him. Laura hadn't made a conscious decision to turn toward him. Instead, she had simply moved with a complete sense of familiarity. They stood silently for a moment and then slowly moved into an embrace.

Holding her face gently in his hands, while looking deep into her eyes, Daniel whispered to Laura. "You've always been the beautiful one."

He brushed a slow kiss across her mouth. She threaded her fingers into his hair and drew him closer. The kiss deepened, and then Laura swam into a sea of heavenly sensation as Daniel proceeded to slowly, tenderly, and passionately explore, paint, and sculpt her body with his hands and mouth. She had never felt more appreciated, nor had she ever appreciated anyone more for making it possible for her to feel that way. As their bodies joined, all thoughts escaped her. She did something she had never done before; she simply lived in the beauty of the moment. Tears slowly streamed down her cheeks, as she reveled in the perfection of their loving union.

The physical pleasure had been incredible, but the overwhelming sense of finding her way home after a long and difficult journey felt incredible. After a lifelong search for security, relaxation, and contentment, Laura had found it all, while wrapped in Daniel's arms. She was finally home.

While lying on top of Daniel in a relaxed embrace, Laura closed her eyes for a moment to bask in her blissful state. "Laura? Laura?" Daniel sounded a bit anxious.

"Yeah? Oh, my God, did I drift off?"

"Yeah. Sorry, I didn't want to wake you up. You were sleeping so peacefully, but...I can't...feel anything from my neck down, so..."

Laura apologized, as she scrambled off of Daniel. "Oh, I'm soooo sorry."

"No, no. Don't worry about it. It was totally worth it to hear you sleeping and feel you on my chest."

"Are you okay?"

"Oh yeah. My legs are asleep, but they'll be fine."

God, I finally have the best sexual experience of my life, and I literally fall asleep on the man I love—and nearly suffocate the poor guy. Way to go, Laura.

Laura felt she'd simply perish if she didn't see Daniel again before he left for school. She invited him for dinner the following night, but let him know he could arrive earlier. Daniel appeared the following afternoon, and Kevin soon left to watch football with Nancy. Daniel played with Emily while Laura took care of Hannah and did some laundry. Kevin returned when she was preparing dinner. A roast was in the oven, and Laura had started peeling potatoes. Daniel was comfortably seated in the living room with Emily, watching a video.

Kevin immediately joined Laura in the kitchen. "So, Laura... why has Daniel been hanging around here so much lately?" he asked.

Laura was struck by Kevin's exceedingly smug tone of voice. She brushed off the significance of the question. "Oh. I don't know. Because we're close, and he wants to help, I guess." *I'm not really lying, because it's partially true.*

"Well, your Aunt Nancy and Uncle Carl think he's spending too much time here."

"Aunt Nancy and Uncle Carl? Why would they have anything to say about it? What would they know about it?" *Oh crap...he's running his mouth off to the family. This isn't gonna be good. Brace yourself.*

"I was starting to feel like more was going on than you were telling me, so I talked to them about it."

Laura interrupted him. "Why would you go to them instead of coming to me? If you think something's wrong, just ask me; why would you go ask people who aren't involved?" *That's it—go on the offensive. But you're getting worked up. Just play it cool. Don't let him get a rise out of you.*

"I don't know; that's just what I did. Anyway, they didn't like what I had to say. They didn't think it sounded good at all."

"I'm sure it didn't. I can only imagine the spin you put on it." *Calm...easy...just concentrate on peeling the potatoes.*

"So I went to your father."

"What! Christ, Kevin, what did you do, hold a family meeting about me behind my back? Look, if you have a problem with me, you come to *me*. You don't go whining to my entire family looking for sympathy." *Don't worry. Dad knows not to overreact to stuff. Just relax. But he's got that smirk that I hate. I don't even want to know what that look is for.*

"If you'd let me finish...I went to your father, and he said I should send Daniel away, and he should be *forbidden* from the house from now on."

"WHAT!" Laura had never heard the word *forbidden* come out of her father's mouth. *Why would he say something like that?*

132

Kevin must have interpreted it wrong. Could Dad really be trying to take Daniel away from me? I can't do all of this without him! I won't be able to fight the urge to end it all. Without Daniel to look forward to on the weekends, what's left to live for? "You know for the past few weeks I have been trying my damnedest to work on things between you and me, but the more I try, the more frustrated and depressed I am." Laura was starting to yell. "And there's plenty to be depressed about these days. But *Daniel* is the one who's there for me! *He's* the one who listens! *He's* the one who cares about how I'm doing and how he can help, so e*xcuse me* for wanting to have *Daniel* around on the weekends!"

"Well, according to your dad, he needs to go away, and he needs to do it now."

Laura grabbed the phone off of the wall. With trembling fingers, she made a call to her father, as Kevin leaned against the counter looking quite pleased.

Laura demanded to hear an explanation. "What is this about you telling Kevin that he should forbid Daniel from being here anymore?"

"Well, Daniel's been spending a lot of time over there lately, and that can be a dangerous situation, so before anything gets out of hand, I think it's a good idea that things cool off a bit."

"Where do you come off deciding something like that–especially when you haven't even talked to me about it?"

"Well, maybe you're right there; maybe I should have talked to you about it, but it doesn't change how things need to be. Daniel needs to stay away from you for awhile and give you and Kevin a chance to work on things."

"Kevin and I have had *years* to work on things, Dad, and nothing changes. It just gets worse. You don't know what you're doing to me here. Daniel is the only one who has been there for me lately. You haven't been, Aunt Nancy hasn't been, and Kevin CERTAINLY hasn't been. And now you're trying to take him away from me! If you aren't going to help me, then just stay the HELL out of my life! GOD, DAD, are you TRYING to kill me!"

She slammed down the phone, feeling shaky and finding it hard to breathe.

Kevin was smiling. "So...I was right, wasn't I? Your dad wants him out, doesn't he?"

Quiet. Don't say anything; you'll just encourage him. Keep slicing your potatoes.

"Right?" asked Kevin. "That's what he said, isn't it? 'Cause this just isn't right having him around like he's been lately, and it has gotta fuckin' stop. This is my house, and I'm not going to have it."

Don't you dare say a word. Just finish making dinner.

"Right, Laura? You know I'm right. What'd your dad say to you? Huh? Talk to me. What did he say?"

Every word from Kevin's mouth burned like acid. *This is it. This is the end of you and Daniel. No! I haven't had time to prepare! Maybe with some preparation, I could face this, but not when it's just sprung on me like this. I thought God sent Daniel to me to help. I don't understand. I can't do it alone. Of course you can't. Everyone knows that. Stop wasting everyone's time. You just need to go away for good. You know what needs to be done.*

"A little too close to home, isn't it? You don't want to say anything, because you know it's true. Yeah, well, I'm not gonna be made a fool of in my own fuckin' house. I'm gonna go tell him right now that he's out of here."

After screeching some sort of response, Laura threw whatever was in her hands and ran out of the house—unable to face what could be happening next. Instead, she ran. She ran past the driveway and up the hill leading away from town.

• •

The snow is really starting to come down. I didn't hear anything about snow earlier. Earlier...did I give Hannah her early meds? Oh my God, what if I forgot? Wait...where is she?

Who's taking care of Hannah? What am I doing out here? Where am I, anyway? Oh, the girls are as good as gone now, Laura. You've really done it this time. You're never going to get them back now. Look at you...out in the middle of nowhere in the middle of winter. You don't even have shoes on, much less a coat. You left Hannah with two people who know nothing about her care. How do you think that's going to look? You're going to look like a whacked-out psycho woman, and it's your own damned fault. I wouldn't be surprised if something has happened to Hannah, and now she's back in the hospital. But I couldn't have been gone too long. I'll just wander back like I went out for a bit of fresh air. Yeah, that will work. I'm just out for an evening stroll. Or...you could not go back at all. Just keep wandering. If you go back, it's gonna hurt, and you don't want that. It's dark. Maybe you'll be lucky, and a car will drive by. I bet the driver wouldn't even see you, if you were to lay down flat in the road. But I should go back. I should at least say good-bye to Emily. And I need to make sure Hannah got her last meds.

Laura headed down the hill, back toward the house, but made many stops along the way to continue her inner debate concerning whether or not to return. She passed a house where two boys were playing in the snow with their father. The boys were giggling, running around, and throwing poorly made snowballs. Their lives seemed foreign to her. *Did we ever enjoy that level of innocence? Why do some people have it so easy?*

As she neared the house, Laura thought of different explanations she could offer for her absence and analyzed them in her head. Just before reaching the driveway, she spotted a car turning onto her street and starting up the hill. The vehicle was slowing down, and the driver was rolling down the window.

"Hey, Dad," said Laura. She wondered what her father and his friend, Paul, were doing there.

"Hey Laura. Whatcha up to?"

"Nothing much. I just took a walk to get a little air."

"Oh. Why don't you come back to my house with me for a little while?"

This is it. They don't want you to go back inside, because they're packing up the girls as we speak. It's really over this time. But don't make it worse for yourself, you fool. At least get some shoes on so, you won't look entirely insane.

"Okay, I just need to run in and grab a coat."

As Laura headed toward the driveway, she ran into Daniel on his way to meet her. "God, you had me so worried," said Daniel. "Are you okay?"

"Oh, sorry about that. Yeah. I'm fine. Just a little stroll to… um…get my head together." *Who am I kidding? Daniel's gonna see right through me. He always does.*

"After you threw that knife at Kevin, I wanted to run out after you but…it was so awkward…it was like he should have been the one to go…I don't know. If I'd had my way, I would have gone but…"

"I what? I threw a knife?"

"Yeah…you screamed something and then threw the knife you had been using…threw it right across the room at him. I was just coming into the kitchen, because I could tell that things were getting really heated, and I just wanted to leave, rather than make a big scene. I was just rounding the corner when it happened. Then you were gone so long, I didn't know what to do. So I called your Uncle Carl since he's a cop. I figured if anyone would know what to do, it would be him, but all he said was, 'Oh, she'll come back.' Then Kevin even got concerned, I think, because he finally said, 'Well you might as well go after her, because she certainly won't listen to anything I have to say.' I was just on my way out to look for you…oh, I'm just so relieved to see that you're okay. God, you must be freezing. Here, take my coat."

"I threw a knife?"

"Yeah. It didn't hit him, though. Where did you go, anyway?"

"I don't know."

"You were gone quite awhile—about an hour or so. You don't know where you went?"

"Not really."

Feeling dazed, Laura walked back to her father's car and got inside. *You just threw a knife at someone and then disappeared for an hour. You've gone too far this time, Laura. You've really lost it. This is the end. No more kids. No more Daniel. Everything's over. And to top it all off, you were just in the driveway, and you didn't even go into the house to check on Hannah. You don't remember giving her the earlier meds, and now that you've been gone so long, she's missed a feeding. Call it quits, Laura. It's too late. Game over. You lose.*

• •

Laura heard her father's voice echoing somewhere in the distance. "...and you're worrying us. It's gonna be okay. We're here to help with whatever you need. But you need to help me here. I don't know what to do to help. Laura? Can you just answer me?"

What am I doing in Dad's living room? I need to feed Hannah. It's way past her feeding time. Dr. O'Connor would kill me, if he knew I was screwing up her schedule like this. And Emily... did she have dinner? Is the roast still in the oven? That was an expensive roast, too. Oh, but Dad's here. Maybe he can help. "Dad, I need to go feed Hannah."

"Does Kevin know how and what to feed her?"

"Well...I think...well, I didn't...maybe..."

"I'll give him a call. What does she need?"

"Um...50cc of the formula on the top shelf of the fridge and the meds that are in the door in the jar labeled 8:00 p.m."

After Steve called Kevin, he continued questioning his daughter. "So you're having a rough time of it lately, huh?"

Laura nodded, while looking down at the floor.

"You had us pretty worried tonight."

"Sorry."

"What's going on? What's got you down?"

"Everything. Life." *I wish I could tell you. No...I wish I didn't have to tell you. I wish you could just understand. My head's spinning. I don't even remember, but I know there's stuff that's bringing me down—if I could only remember the stuff.*

"Is it Hannah?"

"Yeah, it's Hannah...Hannah, Emily, Kevin...everything. It's just all coming too fast, and I can't seem to slow things down enough to grab hold of anything anymore."

"What's going on with you and Kevin?"

"It's over. I'll be asking him for a divorce."

"Is it because of Daniel?"

"No. It's been over since it started. I just can't handle it anymore. He's driving me out of my mind and I...I just can't take it."

"Well, what's going on with you and Daniel, then?"

"I don't know. I don't know anymore."

"Have you had sex?"

"Yes. Once."

"That's it. You can't go on seeing him anymore. I'm telling you, Laura, I've seen this all hundreds of times before. Every marriage has its problems, and unless Kevin's beating you...is he beating you?"

"No."

"Then you need to suck it up and work it out. The grass is always gonna look greener somewhere else. I'm sure Daniel is great in bed, but it's not worth leaving your husband over."

"It's not like that, Dad. It's not about the sex—God! Things were over with Kevin long before Daniel and I even met."

"But why now? Sure Kevin's a little bit immature, and I'm sure he's definitely a dick at times, but give him ten or fifteen years, and he'll mellow out." Janet entered the room and sat down on the other sofa.

"But I'm sick of waiting, Dad. It's like...whatever stage I need him at, he's always three steps behind. He matures a little and he gets better, but he can never quite live up to what I need from him. I think, if anything, it's Hannah who's given me the backbone to face the fact that the marriage is over. With her, it's all about 'Live life for today, because you don't know what tomorrow is going to bring.' Well, why can't that motto apply to me? If something should happen to me now—or even five, six, or seven years from now—I don't want to die saying, 'Oh, I missed my chance at happiness. If only I could have held out for a few more years, I'm sure Kevin would have mellowed out, and things would have gotten better.' I've been waiting since we got together in high school for him to grow up, and I'm still waiting. I admit my mistake: I never should have married him, but I did. The damage has been done. It hasn't worked out, and now it's over."

"So what do you think you're going to do?" Janet asked. "You have two kids to think about now. You can't just go and leave your husband. What about them and what they need?"

Are you for real? Don't you have two kids? Didn't you just leave your second *husband—for another man, I might add*? "I realize that, Janet."

"So what will you do?" asked Steve. "Nobody's gonna want the baggage you have. You think Daniel's gonna stick around for that? He'd be nuts. How do you think you're gonna support yourself and the girls?"

"I haven't worked out all the details yet. I just know I can't go on living like this."

Janet continued. "You'll need a place to live, a way to pay the bills, help with the kids..."

"I know. I know."

"And you can't be trying to saddle Daniel with all of your responsibility, either." Janet's tone made it clear that this was her main point of the discussion. "He's just a college kid, Laura. He has his whole life ahead of him. He's just enjoying being your knight in shining armor right now. You can't expect him to take on all of this."

"I'm not expecting him to take any of this stuff on."

"Then how do you think you're going to pull it all off—especially with Hannah? You can't make it on your own."

"Well, I'll go on welfare, then. Okay? I need to sort it all out, but if I have to, I'll go on welfare until I can pull it together and do it on my own."

Laura's last comment left an all-too-familiar uncomfortable silence lurking in the room.

Steve began speaking in a frustrated, disappointed tone—one that Laura had never heard from him before. "I want you to understand, Laura, that if you leave Kevin, you can expect no support from me, okay?"

Janet desperately searched her mind for a suggestion. "What about counseling? Have you and Kevin tried counseling?" she asked.

"Not recently, but the last time it didn't do any good."

"How about holding off on any decisions until you can see a counselor?"

"Yeah...that seems fair. I can talk to a counselor first."

Janet summarized their conversation to make sure they were all in agreement. "So no decisions yet and no seeing Daniel until you've put in a solid effort to work things out with Kevin."

I've tried working on things with Kevin for nearly ten years. Just because counseling is now your idea—not mine—doesn't mean it'll work any better. Kevin and I were never meant to be. I've always known it. I'm now willing to face it and follow through. I know that Daniel and I share a real love—a rare love. But I know that I can't convince you of that now. So I'll humor you. I'll jump through your hoops—and you'll see. Someday, you'll see. Laura spoke up and confirmed the plan. "Yes—counseling, work with Kevin—and no Daniel."

Chapter X

Where Courage Lies

A counselor named Jim had an opening in his schedule and was able to see Laura right away. He wanted to see Kevin and Laura separately before starting joint sessions. Laura was happy with that plan—not necessarily because she'd be able to talk more freely without Kevin present. Anything she had to say about him she had already said to him, at one time or another. A private session, however, meant she wouldn't have to share the hour. That was to her liking, because she had a lot to say.

Sitting in the waiting room, Laura attempted to gather her thoughts and prepare a mental outline of areas she wanted to touch upon with the therapist. *There are lots of areas we're going to have to cover today, like Emily. I need to mention the disagreements we've had over stuff like potty training. But, besides the disagreements, something's going on with Em. She just doesn't seem to be picking up on things like she should be. There's the potty-training issue, her language skills, and the way she responds emotionally to people—or doesn't respond, as the case may be. I don't know; she's just different somehow.* The office door opened, and Jim invited Laura in. *Crap, I haven't figured out what I want to say yet. Do I mention I've been thinking about suicide—a lot—and that I was totally preoccupied with it this morning? Should I explain about Daniel? Where do I begin?*

"So...Laura...what brings you here today?"

With a deep breath, Laura attempted to explain why she was there, but she was having a difficult time. She had trouble recalling words, she struggled to remember what she was talking about, and she kept going off on a tangent. When she became aware of how she must have looked, she panicked and looked even worse, because she couldn't recall what she had been trying to say.

The session was nearing the end. "Do you have a local medical doctor?"

"Um...well the girls go see Dr. Michaels; he's a pediatrician..." *You idiot, what doctor do you see? I don't know...oh, when I was pregnant, he was a general practitioner. What was his name?* Oh ...Dr. Marks, I think."

"I want you to make an appointment to see him ASAP. I think you're dealing with some stuff here that you need help with. This is the first time I've met you, but judging from what I've seen here today, I'd say that you are suffering from post-traumatic stress disorder, generalized depression, and some generalized anxiety."

"Really—all of that? How...how can you tell all of that from just this one session?"

"Well, I'm noticing how you're having a difficult time staying focused and that your speech is pressed—that your words are just falling over themselves. In other words, your mind is racing so fast that your mouth just isn't able to keep up. There are other things too—little things, like your leg hasn't stopped shaking since you sat down."

"Oh...sorry." *What does all this mean? Am I really out of my mind? Will they really take the girls away from me now? Are we only having marital problems because I'm crazy?*

"No, no. Don't be sorry. I'm so glad you came in today. And it's nothing to be ashamed of, either. You've been through some pretty tough stuff lately, and I think you're going to need some help, including pharmaceutical help. But I think anyone in your shoes would need help. I'm not a doctor, so I can't prescribe medications, but I'm sure that Dr. Marks would be happy to prescribe something that might help you through this. In the meantime, I'll meet with Kevin, and then I'll see you individually again next week."

• •

Dr. Marks walked through the doorway of the examination room. In an instant, he, too, was able to make a quick diagnosis. "Hello, Laura. How are—wow, you have thyroid issues!"

"Excuse me?"

He walked over and felt her neck. "Has anyone mentioned your thyroid before?"

"After I had Emily, someone mentioned that my thyroid was enlarged, and I got it tested, but it was fine, if I remember correctly."

"Well, we're going to check it again. We usually have to feel a patient's neck as they swallow, in order to judge the size of the thyroid gland. But I could see yours from across the room."

"So what does it mean for me?"

"Likely hypothyroidism. It's not at all uncommon among women. You should be noticing a slowing down of your metabolism as the thyroid pumps out less and less hormone. You might feel cold more often, and tired, like you just can't get enough sleep. You might have problems with drier skin and hair, or even hair loss. You might be more irritable or suffer from depression, maybe have memory problems, and maybe a decreased sex drive. You might be gaining weight or having trouble losing weight. Like I said, the whole body just slows down. Luckily, though, it's easily treated with artificial hormones."

"Well, a lot of that is sounding accurate." *So this could explain why Jim thought that I have depression, anxiety, and post-traumatic stress disorder.*

"We'll check those thyroid levels; I should have results for you in a day or two."

At home, Kevin appeared giddy after his initial session with Jim. "I wasn't too keen on going," he said, "but after talking with him for a little while, I discovered a few things about myself—a few things that are really good to know."

Laura tried to be supportive without invading his privacy. "Oh yeah? That's good."

"Yeah. For instance, I now realize I never loved you. When I was talking to him, it just hit me that all I wanted when we got married was sex. I never wanted to get married. I just wanted sex more often."

No shit, Sherlock. You're telling me you just figured that out? You're just saying out loud what we've both known forever. You just want to be hurtful. Sorry, pal. I'm not up for that game right now. I'm too tired to let this affect me. "Wow. It must feel good to have some clarity about your true feelings."

"Hell, yeah! It feels good to say out loud what I guess I've been feeling all along."

Laura agreed. "I'm glad that Jim was able to help you out."

At Laura's next appointment with Jim, the focus was more on the marriage, rather than Laura's emotional health issues. "So I met with Kevin the other day."

"Yeah, he told me that he had a good session with you. He said that he now realizes he never loved me and that he was never interested in anything other than sex."

"Well, in our last session you had told me about some of your marital issues. You talked about various problems that you and Kevin were having, and about the many attempts you've made to solve some of these issues—failed attempts, I should say."

"Uh-huh."

"Well, after talking with you and talking with Kevin...I have to say that...there's no way you can stay with him. You <u>have</u> to leave him. Otherwise he's going to drive you to your death. With all of the very difficult things you are facing right now with the girls, you need support. Not only is Kevin unable to provide you with that support at this time in his life, he's more like an 'anti-support' for you. Being with him is driving you deeper into your depression."

Laura was surprised at how quickly he had come to the same conclusion she had come to some time ago, and she was glad to feel validated. She fully intended to take her counselor's advice. She began searching for the courage to follow through.

The following day, Kevin's mother dropped by the house, which was actually hers. Just before Hannah was born, Laura and Emily had moved out of camp, which wasn't suitable for winter living. Kevin's mother, Linda, in turn, moved in with her mother, whose health was failing and had begun needing round-the-clock care. The plan appeared to benefit everyone. Overall, the arrangement had been working out fine—for everyone except Linda. While she was happy to help out her mother, Linda was tired and stressed from the extra workload. She began complaining that Kevin and Laura hadn't shoveled the walkway the way they were supposed to.

"I know," Laura said. "Before it started snowing, I told Kevin that the driveway and walkway were his responsibility. I've asked him a few times to get the job done, but he keeps putting it off. I finally called the plow guy to do the driveway the other day, but I

146

haven't been able to get to the walkway. I was hoping that Kevin would take care of it over the weekend, but..."

Linda persisted. "Well it can't be put off. It builds up and ices over, and then it's a dangerous situation."

Why are you yelling at me? Tell your son that. Let him be responsible for something for once. "I know. You should talk to Kevin. Maybe he'll listen to you."

"Well, if you two are going to use my house, you're going to have to deal with maintaining the house the way it needs to be maintained."

Look, lay off. I can't take any more pressure. Take this fight to your son. "I know...but that's Kevin, not me."

Linda continued. "You know, I didn't ask much from you two when you moved in here. I just asked for a few simple things to be done."

With frustration, Laura recognized that Linda was on a rant and was hearing nothing that Laura was saying. She hated that Linda was lumping her in with her son's irresponsibility. She was already doing everything she could to keep Linda's house in top condition. The realization that Kevin's failures and shortcomings reflected on her in a negative way, as long as they were together, hit her hard. The thought became too much to bear, and Laura snapped.

Laura started yelling at Linda. "I KNOW, Linda, but that's KEVIN's responsibility–NOT MINE! I have enough going on! Stop hassling me about stuff that is UP TO KEVIN! If he can't get the GODDAMNED driveway and walkway dealt with, that's between YOU AND HIM!" Laura stomped her feet. With her head shaking back and forth wildly between her hands she continued to wail. "I CAN'T DO THIS ANYMORE! I CAN'T DO IT! JUST STOP IT! STOP IT! STOP IT!"

Laura heard Emily's voice echoing from across the room. She had joined the two women and was petrified.

Emily was shaking and starting to cry. "Mommy...please don't..."

Laura ran over to her, fell to her knees and hugged her daughter tightly. "I'm so sorry, sweetie. Mommy didn't mean to yell...and it won't ever happen again. I'm going to change things, so that this will never, ever happen again."

The courage Laura had been searching for was suddenly staring her in the face—through Emily's tear-filled eyes. Laura could now see that she and Kevin brought out the worst in each other. The girls deserved better; they deserved the best their parents could give. Hannah had given Laura strength. Now Emily had helped her find her bravery.

After an extra long cuddle with Emily at bedtime that night, Laura sat down in the living room with Kevin. "You and I have sat down many times to discuss divorce, but we've never followed through. Either it would be too expensive, or we'd get busy with something else, or it'd be time for you to leave on a ship for six months. Well...this time...I'm saying to you that I...I want a divorce. We're done here and we both know it. We can't afford to go on trying to make it work. Splitting up will be for the best—for both of us. So, I'll stay through Christmas for Emily's sake. Then I'll get an apartment and be out of here by the first of the year."

"Wow. So this is it, huh?"

"Yeah. This time it's real. But I want to do it right for the girls' sake. No matter what's going on with you and me, I want to make sure you'll be a part of the girls' lives. My door will always be open, and you'll be welcome for meals, to read bedtime stories, and things like that. You and I need to split, but that's just us—not you and the girls."

"Hmm...you're really serious this time. Do you have a place to go yet?"

"I think so. There's a place on Union Street that was listed in the paper that sounds like it would work. I need to call the real estate agent in the morning."

"Huh...so...is this about Daniel?"

"No. This has been coming for a long time. We both know that. It's just time. You're miserable. I'm miserable. We'll both be a lot happier if we're not together."

"But you and Daniel are together, right? I mean, now that we have nothing to lose, we can be honest about it."

"Yeah, Daniel and I are very close. But that's not why we're having this conversation."

"Have you two had sex?"

Hmmm...how should I answer that? There's no reason to be dishonest, but the whole Daniel and me thing has nothing to do with sex. If I say yes, it'll be all about sex, in Kevin's eyes, because that's what he's about. That would just distract him from the real reason we're here.

Laura decided to lie. "No." Attempting to steer the conversation away from her sex life, Laura turned the focus back to him. "Now that we have nothing to lose, how many times have you cheated on me, other than the one I already know about when you were in Thailand?"

"None...until now. I've been banging this chick up in Berlin for awhile now."

Wow, I wasn't expecting that answer. I wasn't even really sure about Thailand. Oh well, I shouldn't be surprised. I wonder if he happened to mention this to Aunt Nancy and Uncle Carl when he was whining about the time Daniel and I were spending together. "Oh, really? So this woman really makes you happy, then?"

"We have a lot of fun together. I mean it's not a serious relationship or anything, but she's a mighty fine fuck. She lets me do things you'd never dream of letting me do."

"Well, good for you. Sounds like you've found a soul mate. See? I knew there was one out there for you somewhere. Maybe you and this woman will make a relationship of it, or maybe you won't. Either way, I know you're going to be much happier, once I'm gone."

"Yeah, I think you're right. But I want to go on the record as saying that I'm willing to stick it out and try to make it work. I wouldn't leave you, you know."

What I know is that in order for him to be the good guy here—in order to be the victim—he has to say that he's willing to work on things. But he's not. He's not willing to change anything. If he were, he wouldn't have been "banging some chick up in Berlin for awhile now." "I understand that, and I appreciate that, but we're still done here."

"Well, there's always a chance that we could work things out, right? This is just a separation, right? Nothing is final, is it?"

Wow, maybe the idea of change actually scares him a little bit, but I know for a fact that he'll never look back, once he gets a taste of freedom. I think he just needs a sense of security to feel comfortable about letting go. "Oh, yeah, anything could happen. We just need some time apart. But I'm willing to keep an open mind. There's nothing final yet."

Her words seemed enough to appease him. Laura was amazed at how little she felt. She did feel somewhat betrayed by his cheating, but not hurt. In fact, she was happy he had some sort of distraction that made her leaving easier. She felt a bit guilty about lying to him, but she knew she'd soon get over that. All in all, she could not have expected the conversation to go any more smoothly than it did—a testament, perhaps, to how overdue it was.

Life had already been running at a fast pace. Now, having committed to leaving her husband in less than two weeks, Laura was whirling within a new flurry of activity. She had a lawyer to meet with and a real estate agent to sign papers with. She had the oil company, the telephone company, and the electric and cable companies to call. She had credit cards to adjust, the post office to notify, and the bank to call. She had boxes to pack, belongings to separate, and furniture to move. In the meantime, she still had Christmas shopping to do, groceries to buy, dinner to make, clothes to wash, dishes to do, bills to pay, medications to give, doctors' appointments to get to, tube feedings to hang, Early Intervention personnel to meet with, and maybe most importantly, Christmas cookies to make with Emily as she had promised.

Days had become nothing more than a blur. However, one late afternoon when Laura was rushing around town, the entire world appeared to slow down to a standstill. Just days before Christmas, when Laura was making as many stops as she could before picking up Emily at Rosie's house, it had begun to snow. As she drove toward the grocery store, she was mentally reviewing her shopping list when something caught her attention out of the corner of her eye. Daniel was walking down Main Street between the Jax Jr. Theater and the Coffee Pot Diner. Laura's mind raced. *Do I stop? Do I drive on? I could pull over and be in his arms in less than a minute. No. I promised not to have any contact with Daniel for now. If we want respect from others, we're gonna have to follow the rules. Pass up this opportunity, and you can be back in his arms before long—and then it'll be legal.*

That afternoon could have continued on as any other afternoon, but instead, something made Daniel turn and look back over his shoulder, just as Laura was approaching. He smiled and tentatively lifted his hand for a nervous half-wave.

Although Laura had faith in what she and Daniel shared, their time apart left room for doubt. She knew that their family was not encouraging their relationship and that they were trying to persuade Daniel against it. She wanted to believe that his feelings for her hadn't changed, but if their family had succeeded in changing his mind, she didn't want to interfere. Despite what her heart was saying, her logic told her she was not right for Daniel. Yet she could not imagine walking away. However, she had promised herself that she wouldn't make it difficult for him, if he were to end it. But the look in his eyes that afternoon set her heart at ease. Nothing had changed between them. Laura wanted to let Daniel know that her feelings hadn't changed either. *What should I do? Should I stop? Should I keep going?* Not knowing what else to do, Laura blew him a kiss. *Since he's been just as careful to play by the rules as I have, I don't want to get him into trouble.* Daniel brought his hand back down and placed it over his heart, as he stood still on the sidewalk and watched her slowly pass by. Laura would cherish that vision of Daniel in the falling snow with his blue coat and brown hat forever. She longed for his touch, his voice, his laugh, his scent.

While a busy schedule usually protected Laura from wallowing in loneliness, there still seemed to be plenty of time for self-doubt. *You're never going to be able to pull this off. You're in way over your head. What if the whole plan flops? Mom's in Kentucky, so you won't be able to turn to her. And Dad said to expect no help from him. You can deny it to everyone else, but you know you're counting on help from Daniel, and that's just asking for trouble. Daniel is wonderful, but it's just a matter of time before he realizes what he's gotten himself into and walks—or runs—away. If and when he does leave, you can't stop him. So you might as well get it through your head that you CAN'T count on him. And that will be it. If it doesn't work out with Daniel, you're not going to be opening your door to a bunch of other guys and expose Emily to that. Without exception, there will be no other men. The idea of leaving may be right in theory, but whether or not you can make it on your own in the real world, remains to be seen. Well, there's no turning back now. This is either the best decision I've ever made—or a fatal mistake. I guess I'll soon find out.*

• •

On Christmas day, Laura went through the motions for the girls. She was thankful that Hannah was home for the holiday, but her mind was certainly not on the festivities of the season. The family gathering at Steve and Janet's house was awkward. Kevin didn't attend, but Daniel did. At the table, he was conveniently positioned across the room from Laura and the girls. They barely felt comfortable making eye contact with one another, much less speaking. Then, as soon as everyone opened their gifts, Daniel was whisked off to visit his aunt and uncle, and Laura headed out to drop in on Kevin's grandmother (or Gram, as everyone called her).

Laura's visit at Gram's house was difficult, too, because Laura had many fond memories that had taken place in that home, and she knew this could be one of her last times there. Adding to the emotional impact of that day was Linda's presence. Linda and Laura had developed a special relationship. Linda had always treated Laura like a daughter, and Laura knew the dissolution of their relationship was going to be extremely hard.

Christmas was an emotionally exhausting day, but Laura got no reprieve afterwards. Next, she had to face an absolutely grueling week of hard work as she made her final preparations for the move. The two-bedroom apartment she was moving into was part of an old house that had been built in the early 1900s and later split into two separate dwellings.

Laura began by washing down all of the walls, as she was sure the previous tenants were smokers. Hannah's quietest time was usually between 12:00 a.m. and 2:00 a.m., so she drove to the apartment at about midnight, after getting Hannah settled, and began moving items inside.

Kevin unknowingly rewarded Laura with a pleasant surprise after an incredibly hectic and demanding week. He suggested she invite Daniel over for New Year's Eve, as he wanted to "go party with his chick" in Berlin for the night.

"Okay, that sounds like a plan. I don't know if Daniel will be able to come over, but feel free to go out for the night. I certainly won't be going anywhere."

Daniel did stay overnight on New Year's Eve. Laura was sure her night with Daniel in no way resembled Kevin's night in Berlin, but she was equally certain that her night was far superior to his. In fact, it was the most romantic New Year's Eve she had ever experienced—despite routine interruptions from Hannah. After the couple's extended separation, the bliss that Laura associated with Daniel's warm embraces, tender touches, and passionate loving shined to more brilliant and brighter hues than Laura could have ever imagined. The perfect world he had swept her off to had no room for any kind of negativity.

The next morning Kevin was kind enough to share some of his experiences from the night before. "Last night was fuckin' awesome!"

"Oh yeah? That's good."

"Man, I had forgotten that sex could be so good. She had moves that were so fuckin' hot! She's quite the screamer, too."

Oh, come on. That's way too much information, thank you. He's either totally clueless, or he's trying to get a rise out of you. Keep your cool, Laura. Just brush it off.

"I didn't know how I'd feel about that, but I think I like it. And, holy shit, the things she could do with her legs—wow. And then she let me —"

"You know what? I don't need to know the details. I'm glad you had fun. We'll just leave it at that." *God, I'm glad I'm leaving today. I'm definitely doing the right thing. I might be worried about what lies ahead of me, but I'm sure glad about what I'm leaving behind.*

Chapter XI

Letting Go of the Past

Laura looked at her new home with pride and thought, *I did this. This is all mine.* Something else that was now all hers was the responsibility of the girls, which was actually nothing new, but more issues were cropping up with both girls. Emily was showing signs of stress—having nightmares, bizarre bursts of anger, less bowel and bladder control, increased separation anxiety, and more frequent asthma attacks. Hannah was having an increasingly difficult time digesting food again; her breathing was worse; she was having five- to thirty-second seizures hundreds of times per day, despite getting her daily phenobarbital; and her bottom was bleeding again from chronic diarrhea.

Laura made every effort to help Emily cope with the move. Relocating was something Emily had experienced before. In fact, this particular move was number six in Emily's three-year lifespan. Laura also hoped Emily wouldn't be too bothered by the separation from Kevin. After all, he had already been gone for nearly half of her life.

Part of Laura felt like shielding the girls from Kevin and his hurtful ways, but the rational side of her knew that maintaining some sort of relationship would be best for them. Emily would need to make up her own mind about her father. Laura realized that talking negatively about him or preventing her from seeing him would only make Emily resent Laura later on. She hoped that an open-door policy with Kevin would mean Emily could have him share times that were important to her—meals, story time, playtime, etc.—and that Kevin might develop an interest in Hannah at the same time.

Laura strongly believed that Kevin should form a bond with Hannah. By this time, Hannah looked and acted like any other infant. She appeared younger than she actually was, but people couldn't immediately determine she was different in any way, just by looking at her. She cried, wore diapers, and couldn't walk or talk yet—like any other baby. But those similarities were not going to last long. Forming a relationship with her at this point would be much easier than trying to create one in later years when barriers associated with her disability would be obvious. For instance, trying to bond with a twelve-year-old who is still in diapers and unable to walk or talk would present a more significant challenge.

Laura was thankful that Hannah was home, so she could maintain a daily routine to help Emily feel as calm and secure as possible. She worried how long Hannah would last at home, though, because of the multitude of problems that had recently surfaced. She continued her hectic pace of staying up late to get things done and sleeping little. She knew she wouldn't be able to manage this way forever, but she felt she had no choice at the time. Now that she was head of the household, she was even more paranoid about some authority figure taking the girls away from her, if everything didn't appear perfect. Therefore, Laura needed to wash, dry, and put away every dish, pick up every piece of clothing, put every toy in place, line up every throw pillow, finish all of the sweeping, have all of the boots in a row by the front door, and make sure the girls were neatly tucked in bed before she could feel comfortable acknowledging the day's work had been done. At that point, sleep wouldn't last long. Laura would climb into bed right about the time Hannah would need another feeding or her diaper changed. Then Emily would often wake up crying, and Laura would need to comfort her.

Her weekly sessions with Jim continued, and she shared with him what she could not share with her family. She certainly could not tell her family about her worries and frustrations concerning single parenting; most of them thought she was absolutely insane for leaving Kevin in the first place. She figured they were disappointed in her and most likely saw her relationship with Daniel as an insignificant fling.

In fact, Janet was especially infuriated. She didn't want Laura to simply straighten out her relationship with Kevin before getting involved with Daniel. Janet didn't want Daniel and Laura together—at all. She even went as far as telling Laura and Daniel she was embarrassed to have a son involved with his stepsister. But even if Laura had been a stranger to her, she felt Janet wouldn't have been impressed with her, and Laura certainly couldn't blame her. *Let's face it; I'm nearly five years older than Daniel, divorced, and not only the mother of two children by another man, but also the mother of a severely handicapped child. As Dad pointed out, I'm not exactly considered a fine catch.*

Daniel's interest in Laura totally stumped everyone. He was a college student who routinely missed his 9:30 a.m. class, because that was an "ungodly hour of the day." He was a person who worked just enough hours, in order to buy the latest video game. He was someone whose biggest responsibility had been to find what he described as a "cleanish" pair of underwear every morning. Many people would probably assume that this type of guy would never last with a woman suffering from depression with a non-potty-trained three-year-old who had chronic ear infections and asthma attacks, along with a newborn who had multiple daily seizures, was dying of heart failure and would be 100 percent dependent on others for the rest of her life—if she were to survive at all.

But Daniel was there for them. He continued to have an uncanny sense of exactly what Laura needed from him. When he walked into Laura's apartment, he could instantly gauge what state of mind she was in. If he had to step over toys or move aside half-empty bottles of formula, he was prepared for a different type of visit than he would have had if he had found a tidy, quiet house, instead.

Daniel somehow concluded that Laura's fatigued and overwhelmed state of mind was largely responsible for her obsessive housecleaning behaviors. Housework was something she actually did have control over, and she was going to control it to the hilt. Whenever the house looked cluttered, Laura's mind felt more cluttered, which was unbearable. Even her uncluttered mind felt constantly inundated. Half-empty bottles and unfolded laundry translated to a fraught and fragile Laura who would need a different kind of attention than the relaxed and content Laura sitting on an orderly couch in a perfectly tidied living room.

In contrast, Daniel lived in student housing with three roommates who had trash that flowed from the trashcan, across the kitchen, and into the living room. They had socks that had likely been on the floor since September, which were dirty enough to get up and walk away on their own. They had food in the fridge that cockroaches wouldn't touch. Laura wondered how Daniel could possibly relate to how important a clean home was to her when it obviously meant nothing to him.

Daniel was still able to set Laura's mind at ease, even when issues he couldn't identify with were involved. For example, she was quite stressed about finances. Kevin was paying $550 per month in child support, but Laura had no other source of income. Her rent alone was $550 per month. Kevin and Laura had split roughly $12,000 in savings. Beyond her $6,000, Laura had nothing else.

Daniel spoke with raised eyebrows. "Six grand? Well, that's great, then. You're all set!"

Wow, he's clueless. "Well, I might be all set this week and this month and maybe for a few months after that if I'm careful, but with no other income I'm screwed after that."

"No. You'll be fine."

"How could I possibly be fine? I'll still have a household to run and no money left to run it with."

"I know it doesn't seem like I'd know anything about this, but trust me; I do. You're a good person. You use money wisely. When you need money, it'll be there for you. It's like...good karma. And even if I'm wrong–which I'm not–there's still no sense in worrying about it, because there's nothing you can do about it right now, anyway. Right?"

"I guess so." *Boy, my head tells me that you are way out in left field here. But you're certainly right that I can't do anything about it now, so there's no point in stressing. Man, even when I think you're full of it, you still know just what to say.*

Daniel was indispensable, in regard to overseeing the girls, as well. He was able to instantly grasp the details involved in Hannah's routine care. For instance, Hannah's feedings were time-consuming and often had Laura feeling frustrated. The process required much thought and attention. First, Laura would offer her formula by mouth, and then she poured the remainder into a syringe and attached it to Hannah's G-tube, so gravity would cause it to flow into her stomach slowly. However, for some unknown reason, severe gas had become a problem for Hannah. Therefore, the height that Laura held the syringe at, during the feeding, had to be closely monitored.

Laura had to allow enough time for gas bubbles to escape, without permitting too much time, since the next feeding would be due in one to two hours. A poorly monitored syringe could result in vomiting or an overflowing syringe. Pregestimil mixed with stomach acid smells rancid on clothing; plus vomiting or spillage meant guessing how much was lost and having to make more replacement formula. Finally, even if the feeding was completely successful, Hannah still had to be held perfectly still for up to forty-five minutes afterwards to further prevent vomiting.

Not only did Daniel quickly develop the knack for tasks like feedings, medications, diaper changes, recognition of seizure activity, and pain assessments, but he also performed them with a bright and cheerful attitude. If Laura began to stress about whether or not she should call the doctor, he'd offer a comment, such as "Well, I think she needs 10 cc of ...amperheferneferine ... uh...stat."

They would have competitions to see who could get Hannah to eat more by mouth. Daniel would proclaim himself the feeding master when he'd catch a particularly long series of gas bubbles. In the kitchen, he'd commentate with a French chef's accent as he mixed up formula. Accents were actually one of his specialties, and he had a number of characters that visited quite often—the ever-romantic Pierre Jon Luke, the bold and spicy Muy Macho, and Laura's favorite of all, the rugged and manly McHaggis. She requested his presence so often that Daniel actually started to get a little envious.

Daniel had a similar calming effect on Emily who often became stressed for seemingly bizarre reasons. When watching television, sometimes she would suddenly begin screaming. Daniel and Laura eventually realized the problem had to do with transition. Emily didn't seem to recognize the conclusion of a storyline, so the end of a show took her by surprise. The rolling credits served as her only means of understanding the show was over. If they went unnoticed, and a new show started unexpectedly, she would be devastated. Daniel quickly learned (as Laura had known for some time) that arguing, punishing, or attempting to reason with Emily during those times was useless. Distraction worked best every time, and Emily was soon a huge fan of Daniel's slapstick-style comedy. All he had to do was trip or hit his head on the way into the living room, and the problem would be instantly solved.

During the month of January, Hannah remained healthy enough to stay home for the longest length of time since her birth, while Emily was settling into their new routine. Daniel was out of school for the winter break during most of the month, so he was able to spend that time with them. Kevin had moved into a small place of his own in the neighboring town of Whitefield and visited Emily a few times throughout the month. Mainly, he saw her during Emily's weekly evening visit with Linda and Gram. He still hadn't seen or expressed any interest in Hannah. The few times Laura had seen Kevin since moving out, his constant tales of late nights out while partying annoyed her. Laura was having many late nights of her own—but they were not any fun, and they were starting to wear on her.

February brought a challenge Laura had feared most: Hannah was admitted back into the hospital with pneumonia. Since she was on the pediatric floor, not the PICU, Laura had to stay with her. With some creative planning—and the help of Daniel, Janet, and her sister—Laura successfully arranged the weekend, so that both girls had someone with them at all times. She was even able to include a previously promised trip to Plymouth State College with Emily, so they could watch Daniel perform in the play, *Peter Pan.*

Kevin didn't offer any assistance during the weekend. However, he did mention his availability on Monday. "I have to drop off some paperwork at the hospital on Monday, anyway, so I can pick Em up and take her to Rosie's," he said.

Laura had hoped he would spend time with Emily on Sunday, instead of her being stuck in Hannah's hospital room with Laura, but that didn't happen. Daniel was able to stay at David's House with Emily on Sunday night. When Kevin showed up at the hospital on Monday morning, he bragged about partying the entire weekend. Laura was not impressed.

Soon after Kevin, Emily, and Daniel left the hospital, Dr. O'Connor arrived. He spoke apologetically. "I hate to say it, but we're seeing another reconstriction of her aorta."

Laura was bewildered. "*Another* one?"

"I know. It's unusual to see this happen so frequently, but I should be able to correct the flow again with angioplasty."

"But this is the third time this has happened–in less than six months! Like...how many times can this happen? I mean...how many times do we put her through these surgeries?"

The doctor sighed. "Well, this becomes the real question. Unfortunately, I don't have the answer for you."

"Well...I think...I mean...we'll definitely go ahead with this one...but...I don't know...I guess...I guess this should be it. I mean...if she does this more than three times...I just don't think it's fair to keep sending her into the operating room. What do you think?"

"I think that's a very reasonable plan. I've scheduled her for this Friday. And I'd like to keep her here until then, so we can get her pneumonia well treated before putting her back under anesthesia."

Laura called Kevin that night to update him on the plans. Upon hearing the news, he informed Laura that he would tell his commander he wouldn't be able to work the day of the surgery. Then Laura scrambled to find someone to take care of Emily, since Kevin certainly wasn't volunteering to take her for the week. Luckily, Janet agreed to pick her up from Rosie's house that evening and keep her for as long as necessary.

Laura called Kevin on Thursday to let him know that Hannah's procedure was scheduled for 8:00 a.m. "Yeah, I won't be able to make it," he said. "I have to work, and I'll be on the road, so I don't know where the hell I'll be, if you try to get in touch with me."

What the hell do you mean, "I can't make it"! You're home on humanitarian leave specifically so you can make it for these things! Ugh...why am I even complaining? I didn't want your sorry ass here, anyway. Kevin said he would call the next afternoon.

The next day was a tough one. Laura didn't receive the page to meet Hannah at the PICU until 2:30 in the afternoon. By that time, she was in a total panic, imagining everything that could have gone wrong, while trying desperately to believe there could be a reasonable explanation for the delay. Her worrying was justified. The nurse practitioner explained that Hannah had coded on the table, and they needed extra time to stabilize her before they could complete the procedure.

Laura's worries continued as she looked around the unit to find an overwhelmed nursing staff. A helicopter had just flown in two kids, and two others were in severe respiratory distress. One was little baby Christina. Tears were streaming down her mother's face. Laura realized this could be the end of Christina's valiant struggle for life. *Oh no, I told Em I'd pick her up today and stay at David's House with her. What do I do now? Do I really want to leave Hannah alone in the PICU when the nurses are so busy? The last time I was here, Hannah seized and they didn't call or page me. What if she codes, and I don't find out until later? What if she codes, and they can't bring her back? I'm not leaving. What about Emily? Should I go get her? If I do, then*

I'll have to find someone to stay with her at David's House; that doesn't make any sense. But how many times last night did I say "Mommy will see you tomorrow"? What an idiot I am! I should know better than to promise her anything, at this point. Let's see...Linda should be available to pick her up after work. Emily spent last night with her, so that would make sense to have her go there again. Crap...I don't have Linda's work number. Well... maybe Dad's home. Maybe he can look up the number for me.

Janet answered the phone and said she could pick up Emily. She had recently bought a new Disney movie that she thought Emily would like. Laura breathed a heavy sigh of relief, knowing Emily's night was all planned, and immediately called Rosie to inform her. Then, Laura settled in next to Hannah.

Kevin called that evening with no explanation or apology for not calling earlier. His casual tone was irking when he asked about Hannah. Laura explained that the procedure had gone poorly, but Hannah seemed relatively stable at the moment, and they were even thinking about taking out her breathing tube.

Kevin's tone became more forceful. "So what's the deal with Emily?"

Laura explained that Emily was still in Littleton.

Kevin grew more demanding. "Where do you come off making decisions like that when I'm in charge?"

What do you mean by "in charge"? You said you wouldn't be available, even by phone. So how the hell could you have been in charge of anything? "Well, I didn't think it was a good idea for Emily to come here as planned, so I made alternate arrangements. If you're unhappy with them, then feel free to pick her up at Dad's."

Kevin was clearly on a rant. "You don't go making decisions like that when I'm in charge. You should have called my mother."

The conversation was wearing on Laura. "Yes. You're absolutely right. It would have been easiest for Emily to stay with Linda. But I didn't have her work number with me. I hadn't heard from you

163

this afternoon and it was getting late, so I did the best I could at the time and made other plans for Emily."

"This is bullshit."

This isn't about trying to solve a problem. This is some kind of power play. Well, I'm not going to tell you I was in the wrong, because I did the right thing. "I'm sorry this bothers you so much, but it can easily be fixed. Just go pick her up."

"No. When Janet gets an idea in her head, there's no changing it."

There isn't even any logic in his argument. He just wants to fight. Laura stood her ground. "Bull. Emily is our daughter. If you want to spend time with her, that's your right."

"Well, when I'm in charge, I won't have you going around making—"

Laura interrupted. "Since when are you in charge, Kevin? You were out of town; you were unavail—" Laura heard a loud click. *Wow...he's never hung up on me before. I wonder if he'll pick up Emily. He won't. He doesn't want Emily. That's not what it's about, at all.*

The next day brought a stroke of good luck for Hannah. Overnight they extubated her as planned, and in the morning, they actually discharged her. Laura figured the decision had more to do with too many patients and too few beds, and less to do with how stable Hannah was. But she certainly wasn't going to question it, so she headed home instead.

Unfortunately, the problems with Kevin didn't end as quickly and easily as the hospital admission. On Monday evening, Laura and Emily ran into him at the grocery store. He mentioned having spent much of Friday evening with Carl and Nancy. He then rambled on about partying since then. Laura felt her suspicions were validated. Kevin had not only passed up the chance to pick up Emily Friday night, but he had also failed to even visit her when she was literally right next door.

Emily asked, "Daddy, can I go with you in your car?"

"No, pumpkin," he said, "I have a lot to do tonight. I'll see you another time."

Wednesday was Valentine's Day, and Emily went to Gram's for her weekly evening visit. When she returned home, she seemed upset and kept asking and then crying for Daddy, which, incidentally, she only did after spending time with Kevin's mother.

"Would you like to call him, sweetie?" Laura asked.

Emily screamed in response. "NO! I need to see him!"

"You might be able to see him. I can call and let him know you want to see him tonight." Emily screamed hysterically for nearly an hour before she finally agreed.

Emily took the phone. "Daddy, I want you to come read me my story."

Despite Emily's weekly requests to see him (after every visit with Linda), Kevin had only come one time to Laura's place unannounced—at about 11:30 p.m. Laura was in bed, talking to Daniel on the phone. She heard the front door slam and footsteps quickly coming toward her room. A moment later, Kevin was standing in her bedroom doorway. Laura had already hung up the phone.

"I heard Daniel slept over here this weekend. Did he?"

"Uh...yeah, why?" Laura asked.

Kevin yelled at her. "I refuse to have other men sleeping in the house with the girls!"

Where the hell is this coming from? Didn't you suggest that Daniel spend the night with me on New Year's Eve? "Excuse me? This is my place. You have no say over who sleeps here."

"They're my kids, too, damn it, so I do have a say about what happens where they're concerned. Plus, I thought you said we might see if we could work things out between us."

What? He can't seriously think there's any hope for us anymore. And with all of the "banging" going on in Berlin—and who knows where else—he can't possibly be jealous of Daniel and me. For all I know, he's probably drunk now. "Frankly, Kevin, it's too late to have this discussion right now. Yes, I said I would keep an open mind about us, but neither of us ever said anything about staying monogamous. You know all too well that I'm with Daniel, and I know you're with other women. Now, I said I would leave the door open for you to see the girls anytime—not so you can come and harass me late at night."

"Well this is bullshit, and you haven't heard the last from me on this."

Then he turned and left, slamming the door behind him. A week had passed since that incident, and, after it occurred, Laura began locking the door each night. She told Kevin he'd have to call—or, at least, knock first. Now Laura was hoping he would come through this time for Emily.

Seconds later, Laura realized Kevin was declining to see Emily once again, and Emily was back to crying hysterically. Laura scooped her up and rocked her back and forth.

"It's okay, sweetie; it's okay."

Emily continued crying with the phone still up to her ear. Laura could hear Kevin on the other end asking, "What's wrong, pumpkin? Emily, *what's wrong*! Daddy loves you. Do you love Daddy?"

Emily cried harder with every question. *What do you think is wrong, you asshole! Your daughter wants ten minutes of your precious fucking time. What the hell is your problem?*
"Sweetie, would you like Mommy to ask?"

Emily shook her head yes and handed Laura the phone. "Kevin, why do you keep asking her what's wrong? You're not *here*. That's what's wrong!"

"Well it's too late," he said. "I'm not coming over."

Laura wasn't about to argue with him in front of Emily. That week, Emily didn't see Kevin until Sunday. When he dropped her off, he mentioned his upcoming plans to Laura. "Oh, by the way, I'll be taking a week of leave from February 24 to March 2 to go down to Massachusetts and party with Mary Jo (his cousin), so I won't be around that week. Right now, I'm headed over to Carl and Nancy's to hang with them for awhile."

"Boy, you hang out with them quite a bit, huh?"

"Yeah. They're totally disgusted with you right now...you know...for ripping my family away from me and everything."

"You know...excuse me for saying this if I'm wrong, but you said yourself that you never loved me or wanted to be married to me. And it's obvious that you don't want the responsibility of a family right now. That being said, it seems like you would be desperate to be out of the marriage and out of the family. But you didn't want to have to be the one to leave me, because you didn't want to look like an ass who would leave his wife and kids in a bad situation. So, instead, you made my life such a living hell that it would force me to leave you, so then you could go to both sides of the family and cry and complain that I've 'ripped your family away from you.'" *Oh, you shouldn't have said that. He's gonna be pissed.* As it turned out, Kevin wasn't angry after all. Instead, Laura was shocked and a little frightened by his reaction.

He replied with the most evil, sadistic, and smug face she'd ever seen. "Yep...and it worked great, didn't it?"

Kevin left, and Laura then had to face the rest of her Sunday evening. Sunday nights were particularly hard on her. Daniel had been by her side for nearly the entire month of January, but since he had returned to school, he was only home on weekends and some occasional isolated nights during the week. Without his visits on a regular basis, Laura was quickly deteriorating. She was having a harder time holding herself together emotionally, and the hardest times, by far, were Sunday nights after Daniel had left for school. He was her lifeline, and his absence made her feel as if she were suffocating—almost as if she were gasping for air, and the emptiness of the quiet house was smothering her.

When Daniel was with Laura and the girls, she tried not to waste any of their precious time together by worrying about her mental instabilities, but the situation was getting harder to hide because of her declining state. She was so happy and relieved to see him on Friday nights that she usually felt good. But she was like a ticking time bomb, and Daniel knew it. Anything stressful had the potential to put her over the edge—a frustrating confrontation with Kevin or another family member, a trying situation with Emily, an unsuccessful feeding with Hannah, or a disturbing number of bills in the mail—and no one could foresee what would do it.

When she would plummet into a depression, she didn't have the energy to crawl out of it. She would sit, usually in the rocker, glassy-eyed and staring off into the corner for extended periods of time, sometimes hours. Daniel would take her far-off stare as his cue to pick up where she left off with the girls, and would then attempt to make her feel better. Laura hated herself during those times, mainly for putting him through that.

She could usually hear him talking to her. He would say, "Laura, I'm worried about you. It's going to be okay. We're together now, and it's all going to be alright." Then he'd stroke her hand.

She would hear him speaking, but the emotional sensations in her head muffled his words. Pent-up feelings of panic and despair about Hannah coding, Emily crying, Janet fuming, or Kevin yelling would bubble up to the surface and infiltrate Laura's thought process when she felt safe enough. Daniel's presence was what made it safe, and she hated feeling as though she was somehow saving up her worst times for him.

Daniel would sometimes verbalize his frustration. "If you could just say something...anything...to me right now, I'd feel so much better." But she couldn't. She was an empty shell with no voice and no words. During those times of darkness, her soul could think of nothing but flying away—going home to be finally free from the daily pains and trials. She longed to escape from the anguish that was pouring over her in an ocean of waves, as her endless stream of responsibilities continuously intensified.

Suicide remained awfully tempting. The only thought that kept Laura from following through was envisioning the girls with Kevin once she was gone. Thoughts of overdose shifted to new, vivid images of physical pain. Recurring daydreams featured her catapulting through the kitchen window, headfirst, into the oak tree that stood some thirty feet away. She felt the glass slicing and gouging into her skin. She heard the wood splintering and cracking, as she made contact. Then she felt the warm flow of blood washing over her, and for those few moments, she felt no other pain.

Daniel soon convinced Laura to call Dr. Marks. Without hesitation, the doctor prescribed Prozac. Laura had previously refrained from trying an antidepressant, hoping that treating the diagnosed thyroid issue would resolve the problem. She anxiously awaited feeling the benefits of the drug during the two weeks it took before it would begin working. Secretly, she had her doubts as to how much it might actually help. In Laura's mind, the only cure for the depression would be a drastic reduction in her stress load, which was just not in the foreseeable future.

Laura's depression didn't dictate all of her time with Daniel. They went for drives and played with Emily in the snow. They hung out and played video games with Daniel's friends. Laura and Daniel shared quiet candlelit desserts after the girls were in bed, cuddled on the couch and shared pints of Ben and Jerry's while enjoying movies, or they'd just lie in bed, dreaming about their future together. As rocky as those times were, the couple was able to find total sanctuary in each other's arms.

The better Daniel made Laura feel, the more she worried he would end up feeling she had taken advantage of him. *He shares so many of my thoughts, feelings, wishes, and dreams. I feel like he's an angel sent straight from heaven, exclusively for me. With all he does for me, how can I possibly return the favor? Do I even deserve him? What could I possibly do for him? What could he possibly see in me? What if he tires of the workload and leaves? Will he suddenly wake up and think, "What the hell am I doing? No woman is worth all of this!" This feels too perfect to be real. I keep waiting for the inevitable to happen.*

Daniel always seemed to read Laura's mind and would set out to calm her fears. He would often bring her gifts—flowers, poems, and desserts for them to share, but the gifts she loved most were his drawings. One Friday he walked in with a large drawing in hand. Rather sheepishly, he tried to explain. "This is for you. I uh...I sat down and tried to...tried to put to paper just how it is that you make me feel. Laura, I love you so much that...that it doesn't even feel real sometimes. I can't really explain it, but...I don't even know what I did before you. I don't know what I'd do without you. I just know that I don't ever want to be anywhere where you aren't. So...anyway...here it is...and...I hope you enjoy it."

Not only was it an absolutely beautiful drawing, but also the artwork communicated perfectly what Laura needed to know at the time. No words could have spoken stronger or clearer. Ironically, in the drawing, Daniel actually was an angel. Any worries Laura had, about Daniel feeling differently than her, had melted away and had been replaced with an absolute faith she had never before experienced. She realized then that Daniel hadn't exactly been sent to her, but rather, they had been *brought together*. She knew deep inside, they were meant to be together— hopefully forever. Laura wondered if maybe they were meant to be together just for the short term. Although their length of time together was unknown, Laura did know something with absolute certainty: Should Daniel ever feel the need to move on, in the future, nobody else could take his place. This was a once in a lifetime deal. Perfection can't be duplicated. And Daniel was perfect for Laura.

Chapter XII

End of an Era

March began with a bang. Laura received a surprise call from Boston Children's Hospital informing her that Hannah's open-heart surgery was scheduled for Wednesday, March 13. She had mixed feelings—glad to finally be moving on, but (with Hannah's most recent coding episode still fresh in her mind) worried about the prospect of yet another surgery.

Laura feared the logistical nightmare she faced. They wanted Hannah in Boston for a Tuesday afternoon presurgical checkup, but they weren't going to admit her the night before surgery, like they did at Dartmouth. Laura and Hannah would have to leave the hospital after the appointment and return at 7:30 a.m. the next morning for surgery. Since the drive to Boston took nearly three hours, that translated to roughly nine hours of driving time in less than an eighteen-hour period.

Laura decided that driving back and forth to the hospital would be too hard, so she investigated other options. The Ronald McDonald House wasn't available, and local hotels were not in her budget. Furthermore, she had no idea what she was going to do with Emily. Meanwhile, Kevin had returned from his trip to his cousin's place. Emily called him a couple of days later, asking for a visit. He said no, but he'd see her the next day when she went to Gram's for her weekly visit. He also told Laura he had requested a new position in the southern New Hampshire town of Bedford, so he would be nearer to his cousin. Laura informed him about Hannah's scheduled surgery, and he said he'd be in touch soon with a new contact number.

On Wednesday evening, Emily went to visit Linda and Gram as usual, but Kevin never showed up. He never called with the new number, either, so Laura had no idea whether or not he planned on being at the hospital for Hannah's surgery. She had little time to be irritated, though, because she was too preoccupied with preparations for the trip.

Luckily, Laura's best friends from the Marine base in California, Ben and Janine, had recently moved back to their home state of Massachusetts with their three-year-old son, Cody, and luckily, they lived relatively close to the hospital. Unfortunately, they were temporarily staying with Janine's parents while they looked for a place of their own, and Janine's parents still had Janine's younger sister living with them, too.

Laura knew how stressed and cramped the household must be, but feeling absolutely desperate, she asked Janine if there was any possible way they could stay with her family Tuesday night. Janine and her mother told Laura they were welcome to stay, and Laura hoped it wouldn't be too much of a strain. Laura picked up Daniel as she headed south. He wanted to be there for Hannah's surgery and to help Laura, so he decided to skip his classes for the rest of the week. At Janine's parents' house, Laura set up camp in the basement rec room. She tried to stay out of their way, but attempting to be subtle was difficult with an IV pole, medications, and formula that needed to be drawn up in the kitchen. Worst of all, Emily's asthmatic cough and wheeze were escalating, despite the asthma medication she was taking.

When they got to Massachusetts, Laura called Linda. She had a contact number for Kevin, so Laura finally got it. She wanted to ask him to take Emily for the day, if he wasn't planning on going to the hospital. Kevin dashed that plan when he announced he wanted to be at the hospital for Hannah's surgery.

Laura explained the arrangements. "We have to be at admitting by 7:30 tomorrow morning. Then she'll actually go to surgery between 8:00 and 8:30, so that would give you up to an hour with her."

"Great," he said. "I'll just meet you at admitting at 7:30, then."

Despite Laura's disappointment with Kevin's decision not to take care of Emily, she didn't want to discourage him from being there for Hannah. Laura wasn't looking forward to seeing him in the morning, though. She and Daniel had been through so much with Hannah that it actually felt as if Kevin would be intruding.

Laura still had to find someone to watch Emily. The wait during surgery would be too long for her, and seeing Hannah after surgery would be too stressful. Swallowing her pride, Laura asked Janine to take her for the day. Janine said yes again, but this time, Laura sensed a little more tension behind her words. Laura promised Janine that this favor would be the last she'd ask, and thanked her repeatedly.

Laura and Daniel endured a long night with neither of the girls sleeping well. At 7:30 a.m., Laura and Daniel were sitting at the hospital admitting desk with Hannah. Kevin wasn't there. At 7:45, they met with the surgeon, Dr. Hillard. By eight o'clock, they were in a room waiting for the nurse to take Hannah into the operating room for anesthesia.

Laura was thankful to have Daniel with her. Without his support, the situation would have been beyond difficult. Unlike past surgeries, Laura was all too aware that Hannah might not make it this time.

She and Daniel had already had the "what if" discussions. What if Hannah didn't survive? What type of funeral would they have? Who would they want there or not want there? Should Emily go? What songs should they play? Burial or cremation? What if Hannah survived, but was on life support? Under what circumstances should they discontinue the mechanical support and let her go? What if the surgery goes well, instead? What will Hannah's future be like?

Vivid images of walking into the hospital with Hannah and then, walking out without her haunted Laura. Recollections of

Hannah's code, during her last procedure, left Laura fearing she would soon be facing that dreadful walk. Whatever the scenario, Laura felt she absolutely needed Daniel by her side, and he felt the same way. Laura had no idea what had happened to Kevin, and she didn't care. All of her focus was on Hannah. Too many times in the past, they had wheeled Hannah away, and Laura had regretted not saying enough. She wouldn't let that happen this time.

"Sweetie, today's going to be a long day," said Laura. "It's going to be hard to get through today, but it'll make all the days to come so much easier for you. You might feel like it's not worth it—like you want to let go. And if you do—if you just can't hold on any more—it's okay. Mommy understands. But if you can just make it through this hard time, we'll have so many fun days to look forward to! You just need to be Mommy's brave little girl—like you always are."

Then Daniel chimed in. "We love you, kiddo. You make us proud every day. You'll do great in there; I just know you will."

Then the nurse came to take Hannah to the anesthesia prep room. Reluctantly, they each gave her one last hug and kiss goodbye. Laura took an extra moment to hold Hannah close, so she could memorize every aspect of how she felt in her arms. Just in case she never got to hold Hannah again, she wanted to be sure she wouldn't forget a single detail—her warmth, her smell, or how smooth the hair on her head felt against her cheek. Then Laura passed Hannah to the nurse and clutched Daniel's hand. Hannah looked back at them, as the nurse carried her away. Hannah's eyes seemed to question where she was going and why the eyes looking back at her were so sad and so scared.

A good portion of Laura's anxiety stemmed from the fact that she wasn't too numb to feel the gravity of the situation. Up until now, many of the critical moments in Hannah's life had occurred as total surprises, with Laura feeling completely unprepared. Not only was this a planned event, but it was also happening after a long stretch of hospitalization-free time at home. Of course, Hannah was still very sick, but having her in the comfort of her home, Laura had been able to focus on Hannah as a person and daughter, rather than the one in need.

Hannah had turned into the one in need of a feeding, medications, a diaper change, a doctor's visit, an IV, or chest x-rays. She was Hannah, the patient, or at times, Hannah, the chore, instead of Hannah, Laura's precious little girl. Although Laura had become an expert at understanding the significance behind Hannah's vital signs, spotting subtle seizure activity, and judging the level of her gassiness, Hannah, the person, was practically a stranger. With some quality time at home, Laura was finally getting a chance to meet her daughter. And the reality of what she could lose scared Laura like never before.

Later that morning, Kevin surprised Laura and Daniel with his presence. "Sorry I'm late," he said. "I stayed at my cousin Mary Jo's last night, and the cat must have batted my keys behind the counter, because I got up and couldn't find them anywhere this morning."

Any other time, Laura might have been irritated by his tardiness and weak excuse. This time, however, she couldn't have cared less. Maybe he just didn't want to be there to see her off. Maybe there really was a mischievous cat, or maybe he had partied a little too hard the night before and he was too hung over—or too drunk—to drive earlier. None of that mattered. She and Daniel had gotten their private moments with Hannah, just as they had wished.

At about 11:30 a.m., a nurse who had been providing updates said Dr. Hillard was finishing up and would soon be out to talk to them. "This is a good time to get something to eat or stretch your legs," she said. "Just be back by noon, so you can speak with the doctor."

As they parted ways, Kevin said, "So I'll see you around 12:30."

Minutes later, Kevin's words struck Laura. "Wait...did Kevin say he'd be back at 12:30? He had to have heard the nurse say that noon was the time to be back, right?" she asked Daniel.

"Yeah, I thought she was pretty clear."

Daniel and Laura couldn't wait to hear from Dr. Hillard. The minutes dragged by. Finally, the doctor approached them, and he had a good report.

"Everything went according to plan," he said. "Hannah remained stable through the entire procedure. She didn't need any more blood than we expected. I was able to successfully patch up the ASD and VSD and repair the malfunctioning pulmonary and tricuspid valves. The tricuspid valve wasn't as bad as we had thought. Uh...everything went really well. Do you have any questions?"

"So does this mean that her heart should be good from here on out?" Laura asked. "If her aorta doesn't tighten up again, does this mean she's out of heart failure for good?"

"Yeah, I think that it would be reasonable to expect a full and speedy recovery from here. Everything is looking good. Now, at this point she's being settled into the cardiac ICU. She'll stay there until she's extubated, possibly even as early as tomorrow; then she'll be moved out to the cardiac floor where she'll stay until she's stable enough to head home. You have a little time before they'll be ready for you to visit her. I would expect they might be ready for you in about an hour and a half. And keep in mind that she'll look different than when you dropped her off this morning. She'll have chest tubes that are draining off the excess fluid, she'll have a Foley catheter in for urine, she'll be pale and cool, and a little puffy, too..."

Laura tried to save him the explanation. "I know. It was the same when you did the bypass surgery a few months ago."

"Well, take care, and if you have any other questions or concerns have me paged."

Man, what do you say to the man who has saved your daughter's life–again? "Thank you, Dr. Hillard. Thank you so very much."

True to his word, Kevin returned to the waiting area at around 12:30, just after the doctor had left. Laura filled him in.

"...and Dr. Hillard said we could see her in an hour and a half."

Kevin rolled his eyes dramatically.

Laura was annoyed. "Well, you don't have to stick around, if you don't want to."

He seemed relieved to have gotten permission to leave. "Okay, then; I'm gonna take off," he said. Laura was glad to see him go and wondered why he had come at all. He never even once saw Hannah.

After Laura and Daniel had paced their way through the long and difficult wait, they made their way to the CICU. The nurse pulled them aside, so she could remind them, once again, how Hannah would look. Laura was so anxious to see Hannah that she wasn't paying attention to what the nurse was saying. When they finally got to Hannah's bedside, Laura proved how grossly unprepared she had been. Technically, she had known what to expect, but emotionally, she was far from ready to handle the sight before her.

A flood of feelings caught her off guard. The first to sweep over her was a profound sense of relief. She rushed to Hannah's side and took hold of her baby's hand. Hannah was ice cold. Somehow Laura had forgotten about that from last time. And she was so pale that she was nearly as white as the sheet she was lying upon. Laura wasn't sure whether Hannah had looked and felt this way last time or whether Laura's defenses had kept her from absorbing it all, back then. Her vision narrowed, her knees buckled, and she could feel the blood draining from her head.

She whispered to Daniel. "Oh no. I'm passing out."

"Do you want to go sit down?" Daniel asked.

Laura shook her head no; she wasn't ready to leave Hannah's side. Daniel quickly sidestepped his position, so he was against her and wrapped his arm around her waist for support. "It's okay. Just take a few breaths. It's gonna be okay."

Later that day, Laura's sister, Jen, arrived at the hospital. Ben and Janine were kind enough to drive Emily into the city to meet up with Laura and the others. After they left, Daniel, Jen, and Emily took a cab to the Ronald McDonald House to spend the night. Kevin called, so Laura gave him a quick update, and then she sat with Hannah for a few more hours before heading to the CICU parents' room for the night.

The next morning, when everyone returned from the Ronald McDonald House, Laura was shocked to learn from Daniel how much the taxi ride and one night's stay had cost. She was thankful she had given the bulk of their cash to Daniel the night before. Otherwise, he wouldn't have had enough to pay for everything. But she panicked when she realized she would deplete the food fund from her tight budget, if they stayed another night. Laura had been told that Hannah could possibly be moved to the cardiac floor as early as the next day. If Laura could devise a plan for the night, they would soon have a room to themselves.

Children weren't allowed in the CICU parents' room. However, each pair of cots was sectioned off with curtains. Laura figured they could probably make it through the night unnoticed, if she could sneak Emily into the room and get her to sleep quietly through the night. Even if they got caught, they would, most likely, be transferring to a regular room the next day, anyway.

The seemingly brilliant plan did not go well. Emily wouldn't go to sleep. She didn't like sleeping on a cot, and she was dreadfully overtired—after not sleeping well at the Ronald McDonald House and also missing out on a nap in the afternoon. Laura tried to be patient and comfort her, but comforting soon turned into tense shushing.

Laura knew they faced getting kicked out and having no place to go, if they were to upset any of the other parents. After more than an hour of unsuccessful attempts, Emily finally fell asleep and Laura continued to hope no one would realize Emily was there.

Later in the night, the challenge to keep Emily quiet became an issue, once again. This time, Emily's asthma was in full force and shushing certainly wasn't going to work. Laura was afraid that some of the parents who had put up with the noise earlier would now be angry. Not only were Emily's coughing and wheezing episodes disruptive enough to keep others awake, but she also sounded sick—as if she could be contagious. No parent in the cardiac intensive care unit would want to be near a sick child. With every sigh she heard or the sound of weight shifting on a cot, Laura imagined an enraged parent. Somehow, they got through that night without anyone complaining to the nurses—or, at least, without the nurses blaming them for any problems. However, the stress of the situation took its toll on Laura.

Trying to manage Emily's needs while simultaneously attempting to cope with Hannah's surgery was wearing her down both physically and emotionally, but the most exhausting aspect of that hospital stay was her constant fear of upsetting people. She hated feeling like a burden, and that's how she had felt from the moment the trip had begun. Laura felt horrible asking for so many favors from Janine and her family. She hoped Janine understood the depth of her gratitude. But the person Laura most worried about stressing out was Daniel. *Will this be what sends him running? It's bad enough that he has to go through Hannah's ordeal, but now with Emily having issues, too... The poor guy was having the time of his life in college, and then I come along and suck him into this vortex of stress, fatigue, anxiety, and trauma. It's too much to ask of anybody. You should be ashamed of yourself for bringing him here. God, I hate feeling this way.*

The next day, Laura and Daniel alternated duties. One sat with Hannah in the ICU, while the other sat with Emily in the parents' lounge, and they would periodically change places. Throughout the day Emily's cough worsened. By afternoon, she sat listlessly in Laura's arms—coughing, wheezing, and struggling to breathe. After sitting across from them for a while, another mother suggested that Laura take Emily to the emergency room.

Laura was furious at herself for not thinking of the idea on her own. But she hadn't even realized that Boston Children's had an ER! In her mind, it was the "surgery hospital." She began to feel lost in a sea of questions that she couldn't answer yet. She worried about Emily's medical condition and how it might play out. Then she worried about what she would do if something happened to Hannah while she was stuck in the ER with Emily. Laura bashfully thanked the concerned woman for her suggestion and set off to find Daniel.

Daniel stayed with Hannah while Laura took Emily to the ER. Emily received some breathing treatments and was having her respiratory status checked about every hour. She wasn't improving much, so they were there for the rest of the day. Daniel periodically went downstairs to give Laura updates on Hannah. He found out she would be transferred to a room in a few more hours.

"What's your other daughter's diagnosis?" asked Emily's ER doctor.

"You've probably never heard of it. It's a rare genetic disorder called Wolf-Hirschhorn syndrome or four-p-minus."

Most doctors who asked about Hannah's diagnosis became embarrassed when they didn't recognize Wolf-Hirschhorn syndrome. This doctor responded in a way Laura never would have expected.

He smiled. "Oh, that's my dad."

Laura looked down at his name badge and read *Dr. Hirschhorn*. She couldn't believe her eyes. The son of the doctor who had discovered one of her children's disabilities was actually treating her other child! As surprising as that was, Laura was even more surprised at what the young Dr. Hirschhorn had to say next.

"Emily's respiratory status has improved some, but not so much that I would feel comfortable sending her home. I think she needs to stay with us—at least for the night."

Laura couldn't even process what he was saying. "What?" she asked. "She has to be...admitted!"

"Yes—probably just overnight for observation. She has a pretty bad wheeze, and she's not responding to breathing treatments well enough for us to feel comfortable discharging her."

Now Laura had more to fret about. She already had concerns about Hannah being moved and was wondering if they were pushing her out of the ICU too early. Adding to her state of anxiety was the decision to keep Emily hospitalized. Laura was quickly feeling totally overwhelmed. Not only was Emily sick, but she was also acting totally obnoxious. She was literally bouncing off the walls—running from one side of the examination room to the other and bouncing with her shoulders.

The medication used for the breathing treatments was albuterol, which had side effects that included increased heart rate and hyperactivity. Emily had so much of it in her system that Laura worried she'd actually hurt herself. She had been treated with albuterol in the past, but she had never received that much before. When Laura held Emily, she could feel Emily's heart racing away; yet the doctor said she still needed more treatments. That thought scared Laura.

Daniel brought up another concern that Laura hadn't even thought about. "I asked around upstairs about what would happen if they admitted Emily, and apparently, the area where kids with asthma get admitted is at the opposite end of the hospital from the cardiac department."

Laura stared at him blankly for a moment or two and then began to giggle—not an "Oh, there's nothing you can do in this situation but chuckle" kind of snicker, but an "Oh my God, I'm totally losing my mind, and I can't even respond to what you've just said" kind of laugh.

Daniel gave her a hug. "Don't worry about it. I'll take care of everything. You just stay with Emily. I'll be back soon."

Daniel was on a mission. He said he was determined to get the girls placed in the same room or, at least, in rooms close to one another. Laura was skeptical. After all, this place ran like a machine. She was sure the hospital's policy and procedures wouldn't allow for such a family-specific request.

Daniel returned about an hour later and reported that he had successfully procured a single room for both girls, after speaking with the nursing supervisor. Laura was amazed, grateful, and relieved. She hugged him and thanked him for saving her from the stressful situation she would have been in, trekking back and forth from one end of the hospital to the other.

They soon settled into their room, and Emily was calming down, since she was requiring fewer breathing treatments. Laura tried to track down Kevin and let him know that both girls were now admitted, but all she got was his answering machine, so she left a message.

That night finally offered them a little peace. Hannah was quiet for the night, and the energizing side effects of Emily's albuterol had completely worn off, so she was sleeping soundly. Laura and Daniel lay in each other's arms, totally exhausted from the long, trying day.

Emily was discharged from the hospital the following day. The nurse said that Hannah was ready to be discharged, too, but she was awaiting a signature from one of the doctors. He didn't end up signing off on Hannah's chart until late in the evening, so they didn't actually leave until the next day.

Laura couldn't believe it. What a difference a working heart had made! Hannah had always had such a difficult time recovering from past surgeries, but after her open-heart surgery, she was being released just four days later! She looked great, too. She was awake, alert, and not in any apparent pain. And Emily was breathing easily. The double ordeal appeared to be over, and they happily headed home.

As they rode north that afternoon, Laura tried to get used to the idea that Hannah was no longer in heart failure. That was a bizarre feeling. *I guess this is the end of an era. Where do we go from here? What will we face next?*

Chapter XIII

Life Is But a Dream

Laura wasn't able to get in touch with Kevin until a week after returning home from Boston. With both girls now out of the hospital, Laura was irritated by his lack of interest in the condition of each of his daughters. But irritation quickly turned to shock.

"Hey, just wanted to let you know that it looks like I'll be moving to California next month on the fifteenth."

"Oh...okayyyy. What brought this on—and what about the Marines?"

"I'll be out of the Marines by then, and I don't know...I like it out there; I thought it would be fun to go back and do some partying—you know, have a little fun while I'm still young."

"And you remember that we have a court date set for April 26, right?"

"Shit...I had forgotten about that. I'll have to see if I can get that changed."

"Why? Is there a reason you can't wait a few days? And what will you do for work?"

"No. I just want to get out there, and the fifteenth works well. And I have some leave time saved up that I'll cash in, so I'll have some paid time to look around for what I want to do next. Gotta go."

With mixed emotions, Laura hung up the phone. She was petrified that her main source of income (Kevin's child support) would soon decrease or disappear all together. However, based on his habitual refusals to see Emily—which resulted in her heartbreaking meltdowns—California was as good a place as any for Kevin.

Later, after a particularly insightful support group meeting, Laura excitedly called Daniel.

"Apparently we could get much better services in Plymouth. Hannah could get the block nursing hours that she qualifies for, which would mean that a nurse could stay with her, so I could work. And there's no reason for me to stay up here anymore, now that Kevin's moving away. So, if I look into the rent situation and find that it's feasible, what do you say to us moving down there?"

"I say, 'When can you do it, and why haven't we done it yet?'"

Laura discovered that rents were actually cheaper in the Plymouth area. She and Daniel discussed the exhilarating possibility of moving in together.

"My dad pays for my housing, along with my school cost. The rent for these apartments is about what he's now paying for my on-campus housing. I'll talk to him and see what he thinks."

• •

Kevin called in the morning on Easter Sunday. "When's Emily going to Gram's?"

"About five," Laura said, "after her nap and dinner."

"Oh, I thought it'd be earlier," he said casually. He continued speaking in a tone that clearly implied the true meaning of the call. "Would you ask your lawyer to change that court date from the twenty-sixth to another date? Maybe before the fifteenth, so it won't fuck up my California plans?"

"I'll mention it to her, but I doubt there's much we can do. Today is already the seventh."

"Well, just see what you can do."

Emily mentioned that night that Kevin hadn't been at Gram's on Easter. He called a few days later to see what Laura's lawyer had said.

"She said that she wouldn't be able to change the court date," said Laura. "Did you go to Gram's for Easter?" she asked.

Laura posed the question out of curiosity, and also, to change the subject from the court date. Her lawyer had actually laughed and said it was ridiculous if Kevin expected her to do him any favors.

Kevin simply said, "No, I didn't go over there." Later in the conversation, though, he elaborated that he had been too drunk to see Emily on Easter, so he had decided to quit drinking.

Kevin did see Emily a few nights later. He picked her up the night before leaving for California and spent a few hours with her, so he could say goodbye. Apparently the court date wasn't important enough for him to alter his travel plans. When he dropped off Emily, he stayed for a little while to discuss the separation papers that would soon be finalized in court.

"I notice that I'm 100% responsible for any medical costs that insurance doesn't cover. I would appreciate you changing that to 50/50, before the final papers go through."

"Kevin, I'm in the hospital with Hannah all the time. I can't work right now. How can you expect me to come up with 50% of any uncovered medical costs?"

"Well, that's not my problem, and I want it changed before it goes through."

She ignored him.

At the beginning of May, Kevin called Laura, informing her he was back in New Hampshire for the week. The fact that Kevin was back in town so soon seemed bizarre to Laura. *Why would he leave New Hampshire, right before our court date, and then return just days later? Maybe to complain about the outcome of the court hearing?*

Kevin was fuming that Laura hadn't changed the provision about health insurance for the girls. Laura couldn't believe he was complaining. She had submitted the separation agreement the way it originally had been written. But because of Kevin's absence in court, Laura could have asked for more—alimony, additional child support, health insurance for herself, etc. In her eyes, he should have been thankful that she didn't take advantage of the situation.

Kevin breezed out of town as fast and randomly as he had breezed in. Laura now had no contact information for him. All she had heard was that he now had a job escorting strippers. Meanwhile, Emily brought up the subject of her relationship with Kevin, as well as her relationship with Daniel.

"Mommy, is Daniel my daddy, too?" she asked.

From the time she first thought about divorce, Laura had planned on making it quite clear to Emily that she had only one daddy, and he was Kevin. But her original plan was based on envisioning an involved, caring, and supportive Kevin. Instead, she was dealing with someone who remained completely uninvolved with his daughters, and had even gone to the extreme of nonchalantly moving across the country. "Kevin is your father, and you'll always have only one father—just like Grandpa Steve is the only father I'll ever have. And because Kevin's your daddy, he has loved you very much from the time you were born and will always love you for the rest of your life. But then Daniel met you and he thought, *Wow, this little girl is so special*, and he began to love you *like* a daddy, too. So that makes you a very lucky girl. You have a daddy who loves you and Daniel who loves you like a daddy."

"So he's like a...Daddy Daniel?"

"Yeah, I guess you could say that."

When the conversation ended, Laura didn't get the sense that Emily had taken it any more seriously than when she had asked about why the sky is blue or what animal chicken comes from. However, this time, their chat must have had an impact on Emily, because she began referring to Daniel as Daddy Daniel when talking to other people. She had another name for Daniel, though, when she wanted his attention. Daniel and Laura called each other hon, so whenever Emily wanted Daniel, she typically yelled, "Hon! Come here, please, hon!" Laura was agreeable to whatever Emily called Daniel, as long as she was happy. However, Linda and Janet were much less pleased with the Daddy Daniel title. For Linda, it was a reminder that her family was slipping away, and for Janet, it was a sign that Laura and Daniel weren't going their separate ways.

After a rocky start, the spring of 1996 was brightening. With Hannah's heart surgery out of the way, Laura was able to slip into a more stable routine. Even Emily was calming down. Best of all, she saw some semblance of a connection between the two girls for the first time.

One afternoon in May, Daniel joined Laura and Hannah to pick up Emily up at Rosie's house. The scent of new growth and rich soil filled the air. Since the weather was so nice, Daniel stayed in the front yard with the two girls, along with another little girl whom Rosie cared for. Laura went inside to chat with Rosie. Meanwhile, Daniel pretended to be a monster, and the girls were darting to and fro, winding through his legs as he roared and stomped his feet.

After a few minutes, Daniel called Laura outside. With Hannah cradled in one arm, he howled and took a few more giant steps. Once again, the girls began to run wildly around him, laughing and squealing. At first, Laura wasn't quite sure why Daniel had called her. A second later, though, he motioned toward Hannah with a nod of his head. Then she saw it. When the girls screeched and laughed as they swung through Daniel's legs, Hannah was laughing, too.

Tears filled Laura's eyes and she caught her breath. The article she had read about Wolf-Hirschhorn syndrome said she could expect Hannah to learn to smile. But to hear her laugh...she didn't dare dream she'd ever have the pleasure of such a delight. Hannah's laughter was the most wonderful sound—a deep, hearty laugh that was completely infectious and a direct response to the girls. When they stopped laughing, she stopped. When they started up again, so did Hannah. What a joyous event! Emily was extremely proud that she was the first person to make Hannah laugh. Laura and Daniel were happy that Emily was able to claim that position, too. Most of all, Hannah's laughter filled them with hope. Not only had she demonstrated the physical ability to laugh, but she was also apparently aware of her surroundings—and was responding appropriately.

Laura had a lot to be thankful for that spring and was looking forward to a great summer, as well. Emily was happier, Hannah was healthier—and, oh, to be in love in the springtime! Daniel and Laura talked, they laughed, they played, they worked together, they cried together, they held each other, they made love.

Laura felt like a better person with Daniel by her side. He added new color and excitement to even the most mundane daily chores and activities. Daniel introduced Laura to a level of joy in life that she had never known—like when she was a child and the eye doctor put glasses on her face for the first time. She had been so accustomed to seeing a blurry world that she couldn't believe everything around her was actually crisp and vibrant. She felt complete with Daniel, and she never wanted to be without him again.

Of course, enjoying a new love is easy when you happen to be with a hopeless romantic. Daniel would buy her flowers for no reason. He'd say wonderful things, such as, "Emily, how does it feel to have the most amazing woman in the world as a mom?" He literally lit candles and sprinkled rose petals on the bed. Laura wondered how she ever got so lucky. But, insecurities still got to her from time to time.

Frustrated with what she saw in the mirror, Laura thought about her pre-motherhood body. "I just wish you could have seen me before all of...this...happened," she said to Daniel.

"I'm sure you were beautiful then, but I can't imagine you looking any more beautiful than you do now," he said. "You're absolutely perfect."

Laura assumed those were mere comfort words, but Daniel proved that beauty was truly what he saw when he looked at her. One night he picked up his sketchbook while she slept, and he drew what he saw. When he showed Laura the drawing, she scarcely believed it was a picture of her.

"No, hon. There's no way I look like that!"

"What are you talking about?" he asked. "That's exactly what you look like. See? Beautiful, right?"

For the first time in her life, Laura honestly felt attractive.

Spring was blooming along marvelously until they hit a sour note on Mother's Day. Laura's day had started off with some sweet cards and gorgeous flowers from Daniel and the girls. Then Daniel called Janet to wish her a happy Mother's Day. He let it slip out that he and Laura were planning to get a place together. Janet had already been displeased with the idea that Laura and Daniel were a couple. Now she officially declared war. And they braced for the impact.

Chapter XIV

Waking to a Nightmare

Janet was determined to do whatever it took to keep Laura and Daniel from living together. She pounced upon every opportunity to argue her point.

"Laura, you need to stand up on your own two feet and make an independent life for yourself and the girls."

"I know. I have no intention of relying on Daniel for support. That would be crazy; he's a full-time college student. He couldn't support us even if he wanted to. Moving to Plymouth is best for the girls and me right now, and I plan to fully support us independently."

"Well, how do you think you're going to support yourself in your situation? You need to find yourself a man who can help you through this—to get the bills paid and food on the table. You don't need to be fooling around with a college kid at this point in your life!"

You just said I need to be independent; now I need a man. Man, Janet, just be honest. You don't want Daniel with me; I get that. Sorry, but it's going to happen anyway.

As frustrating as it was to be at this incredible impasse with Janet, Laura actually gave her a lot of credit. Despite her obvious objections to Laura's relationship with her son, Janet had routinely stepped in to help Laura. Many times she had readily taken Emily when Laura was stuck in the hospital or at an appointment with Hannah. Laura realized how hard that must have been for Janet when she had such conflict in her heart. Laura felt bad that she was inadvertently putting Janet in an uncomfortable position, but she certainly wasn't going to appease her by walking away from Daniel.

By the end of May, Laura and Daniel found a two-bedroom, one-bath apartment in Plymouth, which was off-campus student housing in a three-story apartment house. The apartment had its pros and cons. First and foremost, the rent was reasonable at $475 per month and included heat and hot water, which was cheaper than what Laura was currently paying. Also, it was a great location in town and less than a block from Plymouth's hospital and pediatrician's office.

On the down side, it was on the third floor. Laura envisioned dreadful hikes with Hannah's carrier seat plus groceries or other store-bought items to carry inside. She'd also be lugging laundry to and from a laundry room in a nearby building. When bringing clean laundry back home, she'd have to first hike up a hill, and then climb the stairs. Laura feared the thought of winter days when she'd also be battling snow, ice, and cold.

Before signing the lease, Daniel spoke to his father and then called Laura. "So I have the skinny on what Dad intends to do about school next year," said Daniel.

"Oh yeah? What'd he say?"

"That I wasn't the first one to call him about it. Mom called him last week insisting he cut all school funding, as long as you and I insist on living together. She's worried that you want to control me, that you're using me as some sort of sex toy, and that I'm just getting off on being your knight in shining armor."

"Sex toy?"

"I know...I know...she has no idea. Don't worry about it; she just doesn't know what's going on and she's worried, so she's making assumptions."

"So what did he say? I don't want to be responsible for you losing your school funding."

"No, no. He said he won't be able to give me any more money for room and board, but he won't take any money away from me, either. He said he trusts my judgment about where I live and who I live with, and as long as I'm continuing to go to class, he'll continue to fund it."

"Wow. Thank God for that. But this sheds new light on how serious your mom is."

"Yeah, but I'm sure she'll calm down once the shock wears off a little."

"I hope so. But Janet still has the summer to work on him. What if August arrives and your dad says, 'Gee, maybe she has a point,' and takes your school money away?"

"No. Dad wouldn't do that. He said he'll give me the money for school, and he will. Mom will probably keep calling him, but he won't change his mind. However, we'll have to get through the summer, before his money will come in."

"Right. I just don't know if I'm going to be able to pull off the whole summer. There's about a thousand dollars left in savings. That'll cover the first month's rent and the security deposit. I'll be getting my $550 security deposit back. Kevin's child support will only cover the rent plus a little extra—but with daycare for Emily, and groceries, and new tires for the car, and...ugh. But that's not your issue to deal with; these are my expenses. But there's that 4p- national conference coming up, and I really wanted to make it."

The second national conference ever held for families of children with Wolf-Hirschhorn syndrome was scheduled for mid-July in San Francisco. The plan involved organizing a conference every other year in a different area of the country, so as many families as possible would have the opportunity to attend. Laura desperately wanted to see other 4p- kids, especially the older children. She had so many questions for the other parents. What would she be facing? What did she have to worry about? Unlike parents of typical children, who have a general idea of what lies ahead—the terrible twos, the eager-to-please four-year-old, the shy and awkward twelve-year-old, and the hormone-driven fifteen-year-old—Laura felt unprepared regarding Hannah's future development. Laura also longed for companionship and a sense of belonging—even if it were temporary. The trip would be expensive, though.

Daniel reassured Laura. "We'll make the trip, hon," he said, "and we'll survive the summer. I'm not going to leave you high and dry. I'll get a job and help with the expenses. I know you don't want to feel like you're taking advantage of me, but I'm not going to live rent-free at your place, either. We'll manage...somehow. Don't worry."

When they signed the lease for the apartment on the following day, the landlord told them they were lucky, because he had made a mistake. He generally rented to students, so he was used to drawing up leases per person. However, this lease had both Laura's and Daniel's signatures on it, so they had essentially gotten the place for half price.

Later that evening, Laura packed some of the nonessentials from the kitchen, but she wasn't able to get much work done. Hannah was fussier than usual and seemed to be coming down with a cold. Laura was having difficulty consoling her, but Tylenol at bedtime seemed to help. Laura and Daniel finally settled into bed at around eleven o'clock. All too soon, an exhausted Laura was aroused from sleeping.

"Laura," said Daniel, "I think Hannah might be seizing."

Daniel had placed Hannah on the bed next to Laura. Her arms and legs were jerking rhythmically, she had drool trickling down her cheek, her eyes were staring to the right, and her eyelids and lips were twitching.

"Yep. It's a seizure. Crap."

"She seemed pretty hot, too, so I gave her some more Tylenol," said Daniel.

"What time is it?" Laura asked.

"One."

"Okay. Um...I'll call Linda and ask her to stay with Emily, so we can take Hannah in."

Laura wondered if being more diligent with fever prevention could have averted the seizure. She scolded herself for not setting her alarm to give Hannah a second dose of Tylenol at midnight.

Linda was only a three-minute drive away, but it seemed like hours until she arrived. Hannah's arms and legs were jerking harder by then, and she was growing increasingly pale. She wasn't crying or making any noise—just twitching, jerking, and burning with fever. Her limbs were stiff and her hands remained clenched, yet she was completely limp when Laura picked her up. Although she still required head support when being held, Hannah had always had some degree of head control, until now. She didn't make eye contact with Laura. In fact, her eyes didn't search the room at all. They continued to stare to the side with a haunting emptiness, as her eyelids and mouth twitched unremittingly. Laura had never witnessed such violent seizure activity for such a long period of time.

Linda had to leave by 5:00 a.m., in order to get to work on time. Laura thanked her for coming and assured her that someone would relieve her on time. Daniel sped along during the mile and a half ride to the hospital. The ER waiting room was empty, so they were ushered right in. Soon Laura was offering a nurse a brief history. Eventually the ER doctor came in to examine Hannah and ask a few questions. It was approaching 2:00 a.m. As the doctor walked back to his desk and Hannah continued to seize, Laura and Daniel grew confused and frustrated over the lack of treatment. Finally, the nurse returned with a suppository, explaining that it was a rectal medication to stop the seizure.

About fifteen minutes later, Hannah's seizure began to subside. Laura and Daniel were greatly relieved. But Hannah soon vomited, and then nearly stopped breathing. Her respiratory rate dropped down to 8...6...4... A normal respiration rate for a child her age and size was 30 to 60. Her oxygen saturations were dropping, as well, from the high 90s to 100, down to the high 70s and low 80s. The nurse began administering oxygen and went to alert the doctor. In a few moments, the doctor came by to report that he had called Dr. Michaels, who would soon be in.

Laura looked down at Hannah's tiny eight-pound form, lying flat on the gurney, totally motionless after more than an hour of exhausting grand mal seizure activity. Wearing only her diaper and still quite warm with fever, Hannah's G-tube was vented to the side of her body, in case she vomited again. She had monitor leads stuck to her chest, an oxygen probe on her hand, and an oxygen mask on her face. *So much has happened during the past nine months, but here we are again, right where we began, waiting for Dr. Michaels. Can I do this again? I was just getting used to things calming down; I need more time to rest. Oh, relax, Laura. The seizure stopped. Dr. Michaels will send you home soon. Just take a deep breath; it'll be over soon.* But the ordeal didn't end there. Within minutes, Hannah was seizing just as violently as before receiving medication. Laura's heart sank. Daniel put his arm around her and gave a reassuring squeeze.

Dr. Michaels was soon standing next to Laura, asking a few brief questions. He then laid out his plan. "It would be best, of course, if we had IV access to give her medications that would likely succeed in stopping this seizure activity. However, we know that IV access is all but impossible with Hannah, so for now, I won't even waste time trying that. Instead, I'll give her an intramuscular shot of a seizure-stopping medication called Ativan. It'll be fast acting, so if it doesn't work, we'll know right away. I'm hoping it'll be successful, so we won't have to worry about another plan."

As the doctor walked away, Daniel turned to Laura. "Hon, you're exhausted. After the nurse gives this medication, I want you to go home, so you can get some sleep."

"No, no. I'll be fine. I'm just —"

"You're stressed. You're worried. You were just starting to feel like you could take a breath again, and now you're back here. The difference is that now you have me, and tonight I'm not going to take no for an answer. Dr. Michaels is here, I'm here, and we'll take good care of Hannah. You need sleep, so you can be the mother you want to be for the girls. Besides, Emily will be less stressed when she gets up, if you're there to get her ready for Rosie."

"No...I can do it. I can handle this. I just needed a minute to kinda switch into gear."

"I know that you can do it; I'm saying you don't have to. I want you to save your energy. You know that more stuff will surely pop up for you to handle. Tonight I'll handle this one."

Laura's mind reeled with "what if" questions. She was imagining different scenarios and possible consequences to her leaving. She knew being home for Emily in the morning would be best. She even saw some benefit to possibly getting caught up on housework. But she couldn't get herself to leave, despite the demanding tone coming from Daniel.

"Laura, you'll literally be two miles away. If anything happens, I'll call you. If we need anything, I'll let you know."

"Promise?"

"If you'll promise to actually sleep when you get home—no housework."

Aww, man! You know me too well. It's almost annoying the way you can read my mind like that. "Okay. Deal. I'll go, after Hannah gets her medicine...and I'll sleep."

Within a few minutes after the injection, the seizure stopped again. Laura hoped that the drama had ended and that Hannah would be released later on. She kissed both Daniel and Hannah goodbye, and then headed back to the apartment.

After thanking Linda for her help and peeking in on Emily, Laura headed to bed as promised and fell right to sleep. At eight o'clock, she heard Emily turning on the TV. Laura quickly got Emily ready for daycare, threw on some clothes, and left the apartment. When she returned to the hospital around 9:00 a.m., Hannah had been moved to a room. Laura didn't take that as a good sign. She had hoped to find Daniel and Hannah in the ER, waiting for a ride home. As Laura approached the room number she was looking for, she heard voices from within. She turned from the hall into the room and stepped around the drawn curtain. Fear completely swept over her. A group of doctors and nurses were surrounding Hannah's bed. Daniel stood a few feet from the foot of the bed with his face tense and pale, and his eyes welled up with tears. Voices hushed as Laura approached, but she realized all too quickly that the quiet had nothing to do with her arrival. Beyond the squeak of her shoes on the recently mopped floor was the unmistakable sound of crunching bone. Laura immediately came to a stop. She couldn't see Hannah through the crowd, but did see Dr. Michaels and observed his arm making a screwing motion. He was placing an intraosseous line (IO line) in Hannah's shinbone, just as they had done at DHMC.

Laura felt sick. She was weak and shaky. She wished she could do a retake of the scene. She wanted to walk down the hall again, but go slower, so she would have found the room about five minutes later. She desperately wanted to erase what she had just seen and heard. Unfortunately, after every attempt that she made, to clear those last few seconds from her memory, the horrendous cracking of fragile bone seemed to echo louder in her ears. Considerable time passed before her body reacted to the scene unfolding before her—a bizarre, yet uncomfortable feeling of adrenaline spiking and spirits plummeting.

Laura stumbled over to Daniel's side. He looked horrible. The night had obviously been hard on him, which caused Laura to regret not staying with him overnight. She reached out and hugged him. "So, what's going on?" she asked.

Daniel answered with an exhausted sigh and a shaky voice, while rubbing his hands over his eyes and face. "Ugh…it's been a long night. Let's see. You left after she got her first dose of Ativan. That worked for a few minutes, but then she started seizing for a third time, so they gave her another dose. That stopped it again— for a few minutes—so another dose. It stopped again for a bit, but then she started up for the—what—fifth time, I guess. Then they tried to put in an IV. That took awhile but, of course, no luck, so they wanted to do this IO thing, so they can give her other meds that will hopefully get the seizing to stop and stay stopped."

"It's after nine now. Hannah started seizing sometime before one this morning—and she still hasn't stopped?"

"Nope. They're still trying. They're going to transfer her to Dartmouth, but they want to try to get her stable first. Were you able to get some sleep?"

"Yeah. I got to sleep faster and slept better than I thought I would. Thank you for staying. If we're headed back to Dartmouth, at least I had this morning with Emily. I just...I just can't believe that Hannah has been seizing all this time."

"I know. I know." Daniel rubbed Laura's shoulder as she held Hannah's tiny, jerking hand. "Just try to stay as relaxed as possible. They're doing everything they can. Dr. Michaels has been working with her, and he's had Dr. Romano on the phone to help. Now they can give her the other meds, so maybe we'll finally have some success."

Laura stroked Hannah's head, hoping desperately that Hannah hadn't been able to feel what they had just done to her leg, but that she might, instead, sense her mother's love through her touch. Hannah's head was positively burning up.

"Geez, what's her temperature?" Laura asked a nurse.

"It was 104.6 the last time I checked. We've placed her on cold, dry blankets and I just gave her Tylenol and Motrin to bring down the fever." Within a few minutes, Dr. Michaels was back in the room. He informed Laura that they were going to give Hannah another 100 mg of Dilantin through the IO line. If that didn't work, they would have to intubate her for transport to Dartmouth.

The nurse administered the Dilantin, and they all watched anxiously for any response. Ten minutes later, Dr. Michaels left the room to begin making arrangements for intubation, but finally, at about 10:00 a.m., Hannah stopped seizing.

But her condition was still a concern. With the sedating medications in her system and such prolonged seizure activity,

Hannah was now totally unconscious. Laura touched her, picked her up, and held her, but she was completely unresponsive.

· ·

After Hannah made it to DHMC seizure-free and had an uneventful two-day stay, Dr. Romano decided to discharge her from the hospital.

"The blood and cerebral-spinal fluid cultures that were collected in Littleton are back," said Dr. Romano. "Everything has come back negative. With the slight nasal drainage that you reported Hannah having just prior to the seizure, it is likely that she had a viral illness. That may have triggered the seizure; however, it is entirely possible that there was no reason for the seizure, other than her underlying epilepsy. Sometimes these kids can fall into a seizing pattern if the seizure disorder is not sufficiently controlled."

"How often do they have these big seizures when they do that?" Laura asked.

"It depends on the child. For some, there's a year or more between events, and for others, it can happen again in months or even days later. It is important for us to continue working on controlling the epilepsy medically, so as to avoid these large events. I have written prescriptions for you to continue Hannah's phenobarb at 20 mg twice a day, and I have added a script for a new medication, Tegretol. She is to get 15 mg of the Tegretol three times a day."

· ·

Once they arrived back home, Laura had to return to moving mode. She needed to pack, notify the utility companies, and change her mailing address. A flurry of last-minute activity meant hastily packed boxes, but Laura made it out of the old place before the lease was up. The move to Plymouth began well for everyone. Emily liked her new room that looked out onto their quiet street, Laura liked her new kitchen that was more than twice the size of her last one, and they both loved having Daniel living with them.

Of course, not everything was rosy and bright. Just before leaving Littleton, Emily came down with another ear infection. Visiting Dr. Michaels, one final time on her way out of town, seemed rather fitting to Laura. He prescribed an antibiotic for Emily, and they proceeded with the move. On their first morning in their new home, Emily woke with swollen joints and was covered in hives. Unfortunately, it was a Sunday and the pediatrician's office was closed. Within twenty-four hours of arriving in town, they began trekking their way to the Plymouth ER for the first of—what Laura anticipated to be—many ER visits.

Chapter XV

Making Contact

Emily soon recovered from her ear infection and allergic reaction to the antibiotic. Life became calm enough during the next few weeks for Laura to unpack and settle into her new home. She even received some good news, following the move. Her father had some friends who traveled extensively. When they heard Laura and Daniel were trying to attend a conference, they offered them two free frequent-flyer tickets. Daniel was right again; fate had found a way for them to get there.

Laura thought she had worked out their travel schedule perfectly, but the night before the trip, she discovered she had written down the wrong departure time. They wouldn't be leaving Logan International Airport at 3:00 p.m. That was the time of their connection flight. Instead, they were leaving at 6:00 a.m. Since she realized this at around midnight, she faced a tremendous last-minute scramble that included very little sleep.

Laura worried about Hannah tolerating the flight. She had grown much more irritable with each recent change in seizure medication. By the time they reached San Francisco, Laura and Daniel were exhausted from lack of sleep and the long day of travel, but thankful that Hannah had actually handled the flight quite well. During the shuttle ride from the airport to the hotel, they happily chatted with a couple from North Carolina who had a 4p- infant daughter. Although the baby was blonde and blue eyed, in many ways, she looked like she could have been Hannah's twin.

Their heads were shaped the same, and their noses, eyes, and mouths were the same. Beyond that, though, they even had the same movements and mannerisms. Laura was mesmerized. She wanted to know more about what this family had experienced, so far. But she felt so tired, she could barely speak without slurring her words, so she decided against delving into the questions she had.

After getting their room key and discussing what to do about dinner, Laura and Daniel entered the elevator with Hannah and soon found their room. With a groan of relief, Laura dropped the suitcase onto the floor, set up the IV pole, and was about to adjust the temperature of the air conditioner. Daniel let go of the porta crib and placed Hannah, who was still in her car seat, onto the bed. Before Laura even opened the control panel of the air conditioner, Daniel needed her attention.

"Uh, hon...is this a seizure that she's having?"

Laura walked over to Hannah and watched her seizing. "Maybe it's just a short one. Let's give her a minute and see if she comes out of it."

"I can't believe this," said Daniel. "We no more than walk through the door, and she starts. What are we going to do if she doesn't stop?"

"I don't know—call 911, I guess. I can't believe this, either. What if we miss the conference?"

"Let's not think about that right now. Maybe she'll pull herself out of it."

Laura recognized Daniel's attempt to console her, but she could plainly see he was just as skeptical as she was, as they watched Hannah's seizure worsen. Reluctantly, they called 911 and were instructed to meet the paramedics downstairs.

The elevator doors opened to a busy lobby. Laura discretely explained to a gentleman at the front desk that Hannah was seizing, and an ambulance would be arriving shortly. Another parent attending the conference overheard her.

"Seizure, huh? Can I get you anything? Can I do anything for you?"

Laura felt slightly embarrassed. "Thanks, but no," she replied. "The paramedics will be here shortly."

"Oh...you called the paramedics?" The mother's surprised expression had judgmental undertones. "Is this her first seizure?"

"No, she's had many," Laura said, "but her last one ran rather long and was difficult to stop, so we just wanted to get her to the hospital, in case it happens again."

Word of their situation spread fast, and soon parents were approaching left and right offering help and advice. Laura appreciated their concern, but she felt more uncomfortable with each offer of help. Each parent seemed to fall into one of three categories.

First, the eager type would offer comments such as, "My car's in the parking lot. I can drive you guys to the hospital if you'd like, or just give me a call, and I'll pick you up when you're done."

Then there was the curious type (the crowd that Laura guessed she would have belonged to, had she been an onlooker) who tossed out one question after another: "Does she seize often?" "How long are her seizures?" "What are her seizure meds?" "How old was she when she had her first seizure?" "Does she have apnea with her seizures?" "Is this a typical seizure for her?"

Finally, the condescending parents—with their heads cocked to the side and expressions like that of an experienced parent witnessing a new parent struggling with her first diaper change— would ask, "So she's having a little seizure, huh?"

Not exactly a little seizure. We're now going on twenty minutes to a half hour. "Yeah, her last big seizure went on for hours, so we want to get to the hospital and see if we can get this one stopped sooner." *See? I'm not just some inexperienced idiot. If this were a little thirty-second seizure, I wouldn't be waiting for an ambulance.* They didn't respond to reason.

"You're taking her to the hospital? Does she stop breathing when she seizes?"

"Well...no...not recently...it's just that she..." *Didn't you just hear me? Her last seizure lasted for hours. Why* <u>*wouldn't*</u> *we go to the hospital?*

"Have you tried an ice cube on the back of her neck?" asked one of the parents. "That often provides enough of a jolt to stop the seizures we've dealt with. I'll go get some ice."

Another mom spoke up while the first mother was searching for ice. "I find the ice trick only works if you do it just as the seizure is starting. Have you tried Ativan? Ativan works well at stopping seizures for our kids."

"Yeah, I...I think they tried that the last time. I think they tried everything. Nothing seemed to work." *And if all the drugs haven't worked to stop her seizures, I can't imagine ice will.*

"Well what about Valium...have you tried Valium?"

"I'm not sure...I think so, but I'm not positive." *God, where is that ambulance?*

The ice mother returned with a cold, wet washcloth. "Well, I couldn't find the ice machine, but here; we can try this." They ran the cold cloth over the back of Hannah's neck...and she continued to seize.

Finally the ambulance arrived. Laura and Daniel made as gracious an attempt as possible to bow out of their little powwow that was beginning to feel more like a heated press conference.

• •

They soon arrived at the University of California at San Francisco Medical Center, which offered a very different experience from any of the East-Coast hospitals Laura had frequented. While Hannah was being treated, Laura and Daniel were pulled aside to answer insurance-related questions. On the East Coast, that phase had always been handled only after the emergency situation had settled down. Adding to her stress, Laura was unsure about New Hampshire Medicaid covering an out-of-state hospital visit.

However, what stunned and upset Laura the most was being asked to go to the waiting area when they finally finished all of the paperwork. She spoke firmly. "But my baby is back there. I need to be with her. She can't speak up for herself. I'm her voice," she said.

"I'm sorry, ma'am. The nurse will be out for you when they are ready for you."

God only knows what they're doing to her. They don't even know Hannah. Wouldn't it make sense to have a parent there to give them her background information? The minutes ticked by without any word from the doctors behind the closed doors. Worries were consuming Laura. *I bet they're trying to get an IV in. They don't know what a tough poke she is. What if they're trying an IO? It's obvious that she's had them before. What else are they doing to her? What if this seizure lasts longer than the last one? What if they can't stop it? No. They'll stop it, but I'm sure they'll want to keep her at least overnight. What if they keep her all weekend or longer? All that money wasted on a conference, just to spend the whole time in a hospital room. Will we have to buy new tickets to get home? What will I do with Emily...Ugh...*

Daniel pulled her into a hug, interrupting her panicked train of thought. "It'll be okay, hon. I'm sure they'll be out any minute, and I'm sure it'll all work out just fine."

"Thanks, hon. I just can't stand not knowing what's going on. I can't believe we're even here. I can't believe this is happening again. Did you notice anything different about her today? Maybe this trip was too much for her—too stressful or something."

"Maybe. Maybe it was the pressure changes on the plane or temperature changes between air conditioning and outside. I don't know what's scarier—that we might need to anticipate what might throw her over the edge, like a cold or environmental stress, or that she might just do this from time to time with nothing provoking it."

"That's true. It might have nothing to do with anything that happened today. Remember Dr. Romano said kids sometimes get into a seizing pattern with these bigger seizures?"

"Yeah. Let's see; it's been about six weeks since her last one. We'd better circle the calendar at home, so we don't plan any cross-country travel six weeks from now," Daniel said with a smile.

About an hour after arriving, a nurse came out to the waiting area to get them. "We're having some trouble getting Hannah's seizure stopped," she said.

"Unfortunately, that doesn't surprise me," Laura said, while being escorted to Hannah's bed. "Her last one lasted more than nine hours; she seems to have stubborn seizures." *You would have already known this, if we'd been allowed back here earlier.*

While Laura was relieved to be back at Hannah's side, she felt she wasn't much help to the doctors. Their questions were specifically related to the medications used when attempting to stop the last big seizure. Laura felt more and more useless as she repeatedly replied with empty responses.

"I'm not sure...I didn't notice...I don't think they mentioned that...I don't know...I don't recall."

Laura may have actually known some of the answers, but her emotional and fatigued state was preventing her from thinking clearly. Between feeling grossly overtired, eating nothing more nutritious than pretzels during the past sixteen hours, having her confidence shaken by a few (well-meaning) parents at the hotel, becoming anxious due to the unfamiliarity of the hospital, and simply worrying about Hannah, she was coming up with nothing. She was barely able to comprehend the questions, so formulating useful answers was way beyond her capability.

The remainder of their time in the ER was no different than it had been back home a few weeks earlier. Miraculously, they were able to place an IV, but ultimately, it made no difference. Hannah seized for about five hours, and why the seizure stopped was unclear. The doctor wanted to keep Hannah overnight for observation, promising she would be discharged as early as possible, if she remained stable. Because Hannah was in the ICU, Laura and Daniel weren't allowed to sleep bedside, so they called a parent who had offered transportation back to the hotel.

After a full night of uninterrupted sleep, Laura awoke the next morning feeling energized and excited to meet the other 4p- families. Hannah had remained stable overnight, so she was released. One of the parents had offered Laura and Daniel a ride to the hospital, and they were soon on their way back to the hotel—where the conference had already begun. They arrived just in time for the lunch break, allowing time to socialize with the other parents and to meet some of the children.

Laura could have sat and watched the kids all day. In fact, she felt some pressure to absorb as much as she could while there. This would be her last chance, for at least two years, to see children like Hannah. This was her opportunity to observe, ask questions, compare, and share personal experiences. Once they returned home, there wouldn't be any reference books to turn to or advice lines to call.

After the lunch break, everyone began scattering to meeting rooms for the educational classes that were led by professionals. Laura attended one led by a neurologist, while Daniel went to one specifically for fathers. As Laura's class was ending, another mother approached her and ended up giving her the most helpful piece of information from the entire conference.

First, she introduced herself. "Hi. My name is Lindsey. I'm Mark's mom. I understand your little Hannah had a seizure yesterday, and it was a pretty long one. You know, my Mark has big seizures like that. Seizure disorders are typical for Wolf-Hirschhorn kids, but I haven't found too many others who have them quite as severe. We've found that the only drug that works for him is paraldehyde. Have you tried it?"

Man, I guess I'd better pay closer attention to what they're giving her at the hospital. "I'm not sure. I know we've tried Ativan and, I think, Valium, but I'm not sure."

"Oh, you'd remember this drug. It's really nasty, but it works. And it's the only drug that works. Mark can seize for hours on end, just like your Hannah, but paraldehyde stops the seizure activity within five to ten minutes."

Wow, it sounds like this woman really knows what we're going through. I wonder if the docs did try this drug, and I just didn't know about it. I mean, if it works that well, I don't know why they wouldn't have tried it. "That's amazing. What's it called again?"

"Here. I'll write it down for you. When you get home, you can ask your doctor about it." Laura politely thanked her.

At the end of the day, Laura and Daniel excitedly compared notes and commented on the day's events. Daniel marveled at the similarities among the kids. "It's hard to believe how alike they all are when the only thing they have in common is just one tiny, missing piece of one single chromosome."

"Yeah, and it's nice talking to families, too, instead of just getting information from doctors who really don't know any more about Wolf-Hirschhorn syndrome than we do."

"Some of these families are amazing—or just crazy. There's one from somewhere in the Upper Midwest, I think, and she has a 4p-kid, but then she has about eight other kids, too."

"I really want to get back home and be with Emily again, but part of me doesn't want to leave. I finally feel like I have people around me who understand what we've been through and can relate to our lives," said Laura.

"Yeah, I see what you're saying." Daniel continued, slowly and thoughtfully. "But there were a few things that made me a little uncomfortable around the other parents."

"Oh yeah? Like what?"

"Well, first of all, I think I'm the youngest one here, so that never helps, because I'm always afraid that people are looking at me like I couldn't possibly know what I'm talking about. But the other thing is that I feel like...I feel like parents are putting up fronts here."

"What do you mean?"

"I don't know. Like when they're telling you their kid had to have this surgery and that procedure, and then they say, 'But I'd never change a thing,' or 'She's absolutely perfect just the way she is.' I mean, I can understand loving your child, and these kids are definitely deserving of unconditional love, but to say they're perfect or that you wouldn't want to change anything...I love Hannah, but in no way do I think she's perfect the way she is. If I could somehow align the stars, so she wouldn't have any more seizures or turn back time and give her a healthy heart, I'd do it in a second—no question. She's had a rough start in life, and I think it would be almost disrespectful to her to glaze over the fact that she has seen way too much pain and suffering in her short, little life. These parents talk about their kids, and they have proud, beaming smiles on their faces, but you can see the pain in their eyes. Yet they don't speak of the pain—like it would hurt too much. Then that makes me uncomfortable because I don't necessarily feel the way they say they're feeling, and I honestly don't believe they're feeling the way they say they're feeling, either, so it leaves me not really knowing what to say."

"Yeah, I guess I saw that, too, but I was just so happy to be with these people that I didn't want to rock the boat."

They continued to chat in bed for a few more minutes. Hannah slept reasonably well that night, so they were blessed with another rare full night of sleep. The next morning brought a whirlwind of activity—group pictures; last-minute introductions; and many, many good-byes. They learned about planned regional get-togethers during the years between the national gatherings, so they looked forward to seeing all of the New England kids the following summer.

Chapter XVI

Doctor's Orders

Once back home, Laura shifted her attention to getting services for Hannah, getting Emily into preschool, and getting some sort of income for the household. However, by mid-August, her focus was back on seizure control. Hannah had been hit by another big seizure—just four weeks after her prolonged seizure in California. Laura had mentioned the paraldehyde to Dr. Romano, but since it was an old and rare drug, he was having trouble accessing it. When they arrived at the hospital, Laura spoke to the ER doctor.

"I'm pretty doubtful that we'll have much luck with getting this seizure under control. She's done this a couple of times now, and no matter what we try, the seizures don't appear to respond. Would it be possible for me to just take Hannah home and monitor her there?"

"No, you definitely needed to come in. Even if the rescue meds we're using aren't fully effective, it's best for her to be on oxygen. Oxygen won't necessarily limit or stop the seizure, but it can make her more comfortable and limit brain damage. The body uses tremendous amounts of energy to sustain a seizure. The danger involves the brain using up oxygen very rapidly—especially when the seizure activity is sustained for such a long time."

Before long, Hannah's new pediatrician, Dr. Wheeler, arrived to take over her care. They medicated, they struggled, they waited, they watched, and they medicated some more. Five hours later,

Hannah's seizure finally subsided. Dr. Wheeler decided not to keep Hannah overnight, and they got back home just after 1:00 a.m.

"I think I'm going to like working with Dr. Wheeler," Laura said to Daniel. "I think most docs would have had us stay overnight, just to be on the safe side, but he seems to have a pretty common-sense approach. She didn't have problems recovering from her last two big seizures, so he didn't expect this one would be any different. It's so much easier to recover at home...for both of us."

"That's good. Considering how often she's having these seizures, I'd hate for you to have to spend a night in the hospital every time."

"I know. There were six weeks between the first two and four weeks between the last one and this one. Does that mean the next one will be in two weeks?"

"God, I hope not. That'd be the worst."

In between these attacks (or status seizures, as Laura had learned to call them), Laura and Daniel were desperately attempting to adjust Hannah's medications, so they could stop the madness and get on with their lives. Not only had they been having no luck, but also, the medications, themselves, appeared to be creating problems. After increasing the phenobarbital dose in the spring, they had noticed Hannah was more cranky than usual. They wondered if that was a side effect or something else, typical and benign, such as teething. But when they had increased the dose again, after the June status seizure, the fussiness progressed to all-out irritability. Then, when they had added Tegretol, she went from irritable to downright inconsolable. They had stopped the Tegretol, soon after returning from California, and had replaced it with Neurontin. However, Hannah was still irritable during most of her wakeful hours, and unfortunately, that was nearly all of the time, because it was growing harder and harder for her to settle into sleep.

Determining what was bothering Hannah had become a frustrating challenge. As the summer wore on, Laura and Daniel grew increasingly confused and weary. Laura frequently updated Dr. Romano. She knew something was drastically wrong, but she was finding it more and more difficult to articulate exactly what they were seeing, exactly what was bothersome about Hannah's behaviors, and exactly what seemed to help or hinder them.

When Hannah had been in heart failure, Laura had to track and report her cardiac symptoms. She simply counted Hannah's heart rate and respirations, determined how lethargic she was, and observed whether or not she was sweaty or needed to work particularly hard, in order to breathe. But now they were dealing with behaviors, and interpreting them was more perplexing. The details of their observations were much more muddled and subjective: how much crying would be considered normal in a day–for a newborn? For a toddler? For a 4p- child? For a typical child? How much of Hannah's behavior was due to physical discomfort? What might that discomfort be?

Laura was rocking Hannah about two weeks later, on Emily's fourth birthday, when Hannah suddenly stiffened in her arms.

"Oh, come on, sweetie, not tonight. You don't want to do this tonight."

Hannah's head and eyes were turned to the left and her mouth was twitching. "Hon! Quick–go get some ice, and let's see if we can stop this before it really gets rolling."

Daniel placed some ice on the back of Hannah's neck, but her head and eyes remained deviated to the left, and her arms were starting to jolt rhythmically. Laura sighed. "Okay, I'll take her in. The chicken and rice is in the oven and should be ready in about twenty minutes. Emily's bedding from last night's accident is in the washer. The basket next to the door has enough quarters for the dryer. Hopefully, we'll be back tonight. If not, I'll give you a call so we can figure out tomorrow. Thank God we had a birthday party for both of them last weekend, huh? I'm so glad I don't have to miss cake and ice cream with Emily tonight."

Dr. Wheeler met them in the ER, and he was clearly annoyed. "Why did you bring her here?" he asked.

"Because she was seizing and it wasn't stopping at home." *Isn't it obvious?*

"Well, what do you expect us to do for her here?"

"Uh...the last time we were here, the ER doctor told me that we should continue to come in, because oxygen helps during the seizure and minimizes brain damage."

"Next time you should just stay home and let her seize it out. We haven't been able to stop the seizures, and it's not like the seizures are going to change her overall picture in the long run. You should just keep her home where you both can be more comfortable."

"Can you write a prescription for oxygen at home, then?"

"No. You have another child at home, and oxygen can be dangerous. You don't want to end up with too much hospital equipment at your house."

No wonder why he was so easygoing last time. He didn't even want her here to begin with, so of course he wasn't going to keep her overnight. He might be right about the seizures not changing her long-term picture, but she still deserves treatment. What will happen the next time I bring her in for a seizure? Will he turn us away? Will he yell at me? Despite multiple doses of medications, the seizure continued. Dr. Wheeler called Dr. Romano, who wanted Hannah transported by ambulance to DHMC. Dr. Wheeler obviously disagreed with the plan, but he sent them anyway. The seizure finally stopped (after a total of roughly three hours), just as they were arriving at DHMC. They ended up staying for four days and were discharged with yet another change in Hannah's medication regime.

As bad as that entire experience had been, things became much worse the following day—when Kevin unexpectedly appeared at their front door.

"Hi! I'm back! I've decided to go to college and get a degree."

"W...Wow. That's a switch—and a rather sudden decision, isn't it?"

"I figure I have the GI Bill, so I might as well use it."

"So...where are you taking classes?"

"Here at Plymouth."

Oh shit. "Oh good...good for you."

"Yeah, I'm just commuting from Littleton. I got all Tuesday and Thursday classes, so I'll still have my Mondays, Wednesdays, and Fridays."

"So you have a job up North, then?"

"No. I have a full load of classes, so that'll take up all of my time."

"But you just said you have your Mondays, Wednesdays, and Fridays."

"Yeah, well, I'll have homework and stuff to keep me busy."

"Soooo...how are you going to pay child support?"

"Well, the checks will be dropping down to $155 a month because I'm not working. So this check here will be the last bigger check."

Keep calm. Don't panic. "But, Kevin, I can't work—at least not enough to get the bills paid. I have to take Hannah to the hospital all the time lately. Even without the frequent trips to the ER, Hannah has clinic visits in Dartmouth at least once a week, plus the local pediatrician once or twice a week. And I have to be here for home visits from all of the therapists. Even though we just got approved for forty hours a week of home nursing care, there's no guarantee we'll even find nurses to fill forty hours each week. It took a while just to find one nurse who's available a few days a week. She'll be starting on Monday. And if Hannah starts seizing, the nurse can't go to the hospital with her; I still have to go. I hope to start earning some money soon, but I can't make enough right now to handle all of the expenses on my own. I depend on the child support to make sure the rent gets paid every month."

Kevin shot back indignantly. "But I'm doing this to better myself, so I can get a better job and make more money for the girls. I can't believe that you can't see this is for their benefit."

Nothing you do is for them. Everything you do is about you. "That's a fine plan, in theory, but we can't survive without an income. If we were still together, there's no way you'd be making this decision to just drop everything and go back to school. One of us has to work right now. I can't, because of Hannah's health. The fact that we're not together doesn't mean your responsibility to the girls is any less."

"Let Daniel go out and get a job. If he wants to play the dad, let him work."

"It's not Daniel's responsibility. It's ours. They're our kids."

"Well, I know that you got Emily calling him *Daddy*—which I'm not at all appreciative of, by the way. And believe me, I'm not gonna be putting up with that shit, now that I'm back. I'm her dad, her only dad, and she's gonna know that."

Ugh, I knew this argument was going to come up eventually; we might as well get it over with. Let's see...I need to politely say, "Unfortunately, she knows you're her father, you dickhead. Maybe if you had attended to her a little more when you were here, maybe if you hadn't ignored her sister, and maybe if you had never left to go party on the west coast, things would have been clearer to her. You don't really care what she calls Daniel. You don't even want the kids—or, at least, not the responsibility of the kids. You're proving that by quitting your job and going off to college, like some carefree kid who has the choice. Stop concentrating on making everything a power struggle, and start concentrating on the welfare of your daughters." "Kevin, I never coached Emily to call anyone by any name—except for Janet, I guess. It's more natural for me to say Grammy, but Janet wanted to be called Nana, so I try to remember that, when I'm referring to her. As far as Daniel's concerned, Emily has been happy with what she calls him, and Daniel has been happy with it, so I'm happy with it. She knows the difference between you and Daniel. Any time your name comes up in a conversation, she knows you are her father and that you are her only father."

"You're so full of shit. You coached her to call him that, and you know you did. You just want to edge me out of your nice, neat little family, but that ain't gonna happen. Emily will know the truth, no matter what lies you're filling her with."

Ugh, I don't want to play this game today. "Well, I guess there's nothing else for me to say, if you think I'm lying. We'll just have to leave it at that."

Kevin left in a huff, and Laura was left in a panic regarding finances. Daniel had gotten a job at a grocery store, soon after they returned from California. He worked a few nights a week and wasn't making much money. Plus, the available cash from his weekly check was further reduced by his savings plan for the Nintendo 64 video-gaming system he was extremely anxious to buy. Fifty dollars from every check went toward the $250 cost for the system. The remainder covered his share of groceries.

Later that night, Daniel approached Laura. "Are you okay? You've been quiet tonight, and you have that empty look in your eyes that you sometimes used to get, up in Littleton."

"No, I'm all right. I'm sure I'll feel better in the morning after some sleep."

Laura knew she wasn't being honest with Daniel. She was chronically exhausted, but physical fatigue was just the beginning. Once again, fears and worries were rolling in like a rapidly rising tide. She wasn't sure what she had expected after Hannah's heart surgery, but certainly nothing like this! The doctors had told her to possibly expect seizures, but that didn't prepare her for the struggles of the turbulent life they were now experiencing. At least the heart failure had ended with surgery, and that was a huge relief for Laura. There was no such end date of hope in this madness.

Laura felt overwhelmed by much more than just Hannah's medical issues, too. For instance, she was growing frustrated with Hannah's multiple services. At first, she had been pleased to learn that Hannah would receive such benefits as occupational therapy, physical therapy, early intervention, and guidance from a nutritionist. But Laura was now struggling to keep up with appointment planning and weekly goals, regarding each form of therapy. Furthermore, she worried about everything–from the appearance of the apartment, as numerous people trudged in and out on a daily basis–to feelings of ineptitude, as various therapists explained theories or techniques that she didn't fully understand. And Laura looked forward to the support of home nursing care, but she was stressed at the idea of these strangers coming into her home. They would be there for hours at a time to judge her parenting, her housekeeping and her lifestyle. She wondered if the assistance was worth the lost privacy. Her thoughts continued to spin out of control.

What if Hannah's always going to be a cranky, crying baby and there's just nothing we can do about it? What if the seizure meds are causing the fussiness? Then we'd have to decide whether we want her seizing uncontrollably, but happy during the few hours a day that she isn't seizing, or if we want her to have better-controlled seizures, but be chronically irritable. Either way, she's miserable, and I can't stand watching her suffer like this. And now, on top of everything else, there are worse financial problems and Emily to worry about. She needs to know her father. But he hurt her badly before he left for California, and he hasn't changed a bit. I can see her becoming an emotional mess again. I should be talking to Daniel about all of this, but I don't want to pile my woes onto him. He's carrying enough, as it is. My biggest worry, by far, is that this will eventually be too much for him to handle, and he'll take off. Who could blame him?

Daniel's voice pulled Laura out of her train of thought. "Did Kevin say why he came back? I thought he was having the time of his life out West. What was it he was doing for work, again? Wasn't he working with prostitutes or something?"

Throwing a pillow at him and smirking, Laura corrected him. "Driving and providing security for exotic dancers."

"Oh yeah. Can you imagine Emily inviting him to career day for that one?"

"I know, but at least it gave him good money to pay the child support. We were even getting some extra money every month from tips that the women got and shared with him. That's all gone now. I'm still trying to figure out what I'm going to do."

"I've said it before, and I'll say it again. The money will come from somewhere. Don't worry about that. You –"

Laura interrupted with more explosiveness than she had intended. "I don't know where you get all of your optimism about our financial picture. Don't you understand what's going on here! I'm out of savings, I have no idea how I'm going to get a job or how I'll be able to keep one, and my main source of income is now less than a third of what it was. Hannah's SSI money will help every month, but if I use that toward rent, I'll have no money to go toward Toddle Town (Emily's daycare). That's $110 per week that I have to pull out of thin air."

"Yeah, I know. I know what's going on. But things will work out. They always do."

That's what you think. I don't see how it can work out this time. Over the summer I was just incredibly lucky that Hannah's SSI money came through. I can't count on luck every time things get tight. Well, there's no point in arguing about it. "Sorry, hon. I'm just stressed out."

"Yeah, like I was saying earlier, I can definitely see that you've been down lately. You're doing a good job, hon, considering how hard it is with Hannah. And things are hard with Emily, too. I mean...she's a sweet kid and I love her, but she isn't your typical four-year-old—between the constant potty accidents and the weird outbursts over totally bizarre things—like when I sat in your chair at the table the other night, she had a total meltdown. And when I pick her up at Toddle Town, she starts freaking out, and I end up carrying her to the car, kicking and screaming. It's exhausting. I'm starting to feel terrified to pick her up. Even though I don't pick her up until three, I'm already totally tense by ten in the morning. After I get her, I'm completely worn out from stressing over it all day. Plus, everyone there probably thinks she doesn't want to come home, because we're beating her or something."

"Oh, I'm sorry, hon. I didn't realize it was affecting you that much. But I don't think it has anything to do with her not wanting to come home. It's the transition she can't handle, just like when we have to leave the house, or a TV show ends, or it's bedtime. I just try to offer lots of warnings. I also try to call Toddle Town ahead of time, so they can start preparing her for the pick-up. Or if I get there unannounced, I sit down and hang out for a few minutes, so she has a little more time to adjust to the transition. Sometimes she still melts down, but usually those things help."

"Okay, but you shouldn't have to do that; know what I mean? And the frustrating thing is that we can do things like the warnings and stuff, but we can't teach her out of the behavior. Discipline doesn't work. Rewards don't work. She just doesn't respond to anything the way kids usually respond."

"Yeah, I know. It seems like she has wires that are misfiring or something. She just can't seem to get the 'If I..., then I...' connection. I've mentioned to a few people that something seems a little off with Emily, but I tend to get the same reaction, no matter who I talk to: 'Oh, you're just hypersensitive because you have one handicapped kid, so you're overanalyzing your other kid, too.' It's either that they blame her 'acting out' on her having a special needs sister and a broken home. But I really don't think Hannah bothers her. Emily barely responds to either Hannah's presence or absence. And yeah, I'm sure the divorce is having an effect on her, but divorce wouldn't cause these behaviors. You and I both came from divorced families, and it wasn't like this with us—or anyone else I know. But don't worry about anyone at Toddle Town judging you. They've actually mentioned that they're noticing some differences with her, too. When Debra Davis, the woman from Early Intervention, was here the other day for Hannah, she said they could evaluate her. I think they were going to do some observations at Toddle Town. I haven't heard when yet. I should call her about that." *Ugh. One more thing on my to-do list that I had forgotten about.*

Daniel continued. "Have you noticed that Emily doesn't really play?"

"I've noticed that she still parallel plays. She seems to have an interest in other kids around her, but she doesn't seem to know what to do when they're there."

"Even when I'm playing with her, she doesn't interact the way other kids do. You can tell she wants to interact with you, but she has no clue how to go about it. It makes it so difficult to play with her. I mean...I still play with her, of course, but it's frustrating. You just don't get back what you would expect to get back from a kid."

Oh no, please don't say that. If Emily's hard to be with, and Hannah is painful to be with, and I'm worrisome to be with, then it's just a matter of time before you'll get burned out and give up. "Maybe Debra will be able to find something with her evaluation. But in the meantime, just remember that you can't take anything she does or doesn't do personally. She absolutely adores you, hon. She may not know how to show it yet, but the love is still there."

"Yeah, I know. I'm just venting; that's all. But you do have a lot on your plate. You're doing really well with it, but it's still a lot to try to cope with. I think the nursing will help, but if you ever feel like it's getting to be too much, like when you were in Littleton, I want you to do whatever you have to do to take care of yourself."

"I just need a little time to adjust to everything that's been going on lately. I'll be fine."

The following week fate decided to hastily prove Daniel right, once again. During Monday morning's therapy session, Kim, the occupational therapist, had a surprising offer. "Laura, you said you'd like to work at some point, didn't you?"

"Yes. Yes, I did."

"Well, we have a part-time position available that we think you'd be great for. It's through our agency, Greater Laconia Community Services. Our parent-to-parent coordinator has moved on to a job with the state. With your degree in psychology and your life experience, we feel you'd be perfect for the position."

"Oh my God, you don't even know what perfect timing this is. What exactly does a parent-to-parent coordinator do?"

"It's mainly a position of resource for parents of children with special needs. It's for parents who want information and don't know where to find it, or want to hook up with parents of children who share similar disabilities. You'd also organize various social gatherings to get parents together in an informal setting, so they can start forming bonds on their own. There's probably more to the position than that. The person you need to talk to is Mary. Here's her number; you can call her anytime for an interview."

Laura called Mary immediately after the therapy session. They set up an interview appointment for the following Wednesday. In the meantime, Laura began orienting Joy, their first nurse. She was available for full eight-hour days on Mondays, Wednesdays, and Fridays. Having her around wasn't quite as awkward as Laura had feared. Joy seemed very nice, down to earth, and easygoing. Bizarrely enough, they even discovered that Joy had a nephew with 4p- living in North Carolina.

Laura and Daniel moved Hannah's crib from their room to the living room, so Joy wouldn't feel as if she were invading anyone's privacy. A week later, Hannah made it clear that she required nursing services at night, too. Most of her seizures started in the afternoon or evening, but this time, Emily entered their room at about 6:30 a.m. and announced, "Hannah's having another seezer."

They ran into the living room where Hannah was in her crib, involved in a full-blown status seizure. They had no way of knowing when the seizure might have started. Dr. Romano had finally been able to prescribe some paraldehyde. They were only able to obtain it through the in-patient pharmacy at DHMC, which meant they had to drive to the hospital to pick it up.

Once the technician had taught them how to administer the medication, and they learned about the dangers involved with its use, Laura understood what Mark's mother had meant when she said Laura would not have forgotten about using it. The drug was sensitive to both air and light, so the opened bottle was useless

221

after twenty-four hours. If the drug worked, Laura would have to make the long drive (nearly three hours round trip) every time Hannah seized, assuming her seizures were spaced at least twenty-four hours apart. That reality caused Laura's spirits to sink. Since paraldehyde was no longer in production, the pharmacy would not dispense any extra doses, since they would likely go to waste. But the scariest part was yet to come.

The pharmacist had handed Laura a glass syringe. "Glass syringes aren't even made anymore," he said, "but we tracked one down for you, because plastic syringes can't be used with paraldehyde. The medication will eat through the plastic. Also, avoid spilling it on the floor, because it will eat through linoleum. And certainly avoid getting any on your skin."

"But this is going into Hannah."

"Yes. You'll need to mix it at a 1:1 ratio with mineral or olive oil before administering it rectally. That will protect the lining of her rectum from the acidic nature of the medication. You'll need to insert one of these red rubber tubes rectally and push the medication in, through the tube. You don't want to administer the medication directly into the rectum. The glass syringe could break and cause injury. Oh, and once you've used all that you can from the bottle, you'll need to take it to the dump to ask about toxic waste disposal. Any questions?"

Are you kidding me? You want me to all but wear a hazmat suit around this stuff, and you expect me to inject it into my daughter? "Uh...no...I guess not. Are you sure that the oil will be enough to protect my daughter's insides from this stuff?"

"Yes. The 1:1 ratio will be sufficient."

• •

In the kitchen, Laura and Daniel carefully began drawing up the medication after forbidding Emily to come within a dozen feet of them or any of the equipment. After suffering some frustrating and very time-consuming complications, they were able to successfully administer the paraldehyde. About ten minutes later, the seizure activity stopped. Since a few hours had passed from the time they had originally noticed the seizure, they realized it was impossible to tell if the medication had worked or if the seizure had just stopped on its own.

When Laura was cleaning the apartment, later that morning, she was surprised that Mark's mother hadn't warned her about the odor. It smelled as if a train carrying vats of turpentine had just plowed into a factory that manufactures nail-polish remover. Laura opened the windows, in an attempt to introduce some oxygen to the toxic air. As they tried to put the apartment back together, Laura focused on the lightest aspect of the morning.

"What did Emily call it? A seezer?" she asked with a chuckle.

"Yeah, that's what it was," said Daniel. "Ah, that's our little girl—Seizer the Great."

"Yeah, she's quite the seizing expert now. Somehow when parents tell their kids to develop their talents, I don't think they have something like this in mind."

"I know. She could go pro at this point. She's made a real art form out of it."

On Monday, Laura explained the steps for mixing and administering the paraldehyde to Joy. "Don't worry, though," she said. "We've decided it's a two-person job, so your first step will be calling one of us home. Plus, we're out of it until I pick up a bottle at the hospital after Thursday's doctor appointment."

On Tuesday afternoon, Laura and Daniel noticed that Hannah was fussier than usual and had a slight fever. Dr. Wheeler had an opening late Wednesday morning. Laura called Joy, and she said she would walk to the hospital with Hannah for the appointment while Laura went to her job interview.

The meeting with Mary went extremely well. Every aspect of the job excited Laura. It sounded like fun, stimulating, and interesting work. Furthermore, not only were the twenty hours per week flexible, but the pay was more than twelve dollars per hour–the most Laura had ever been paid.

Laura pushed the elevator button on the way out of the office, imagining how she would tell Daniel the good news. Her daydreams were interrupted by the first-ever beep from her pager. She had purchased it after arranging for home nursing care. Joy had been instructed to page her with any questions, no matter how minor, and she was to page 911 in an emergency. This was a 911 call.

Laura ran to the nearest phone. Daniel had just gotten home from class, and Hannah was seizing. He went on to say something about seizing in the doctor's office and having to go home, but Laura couldn't comprehend the details. She just wanted to get home.

The drive from the office of Laura's new job in Laconia to her home in Plymouth took approximately forty-five minutes. She wondered how many more rides home she'd be making in a panic during the coming months.

Once home, Laura sprinted up the back stairs and ran into the apartment through the kitchen. Hannah was still seizing hard in the living room. Daniel was holding her while Joy and Daniel's friend, John, were by his side.

"So how long has it been?" Laura asked.

"Just under an hour," said Joy. "I was in the waiting room at the doctor's office when I noticed that her mouth was starting to twitch, and she had her head turned to the side. I wasn't alarmed, because she does that quite often, but it wasn't stopping. Then her right arm and leg began to jerk, and then her left. Within a minute or two, the nurse called us into Dr. Wheeler's office. He knew she was seizing. I told him when and how it had started. I also told him that we suspected an ear infection. He didn't seem phased at all by Hannah's seizing. He just went about checking her ears; it was the right ear that was infected, by the way. The prescription for the amoxicillin is on the table. Then he said we could check back in about a week, to be sure the infection was gone. That was it. He was done! He just sent us back home. I tried to tell him that you didn't have any more emergency medicine at home to stop the seizure, but he just said to go on home, anyway. It was the most bizarre thing I've ever faced as a nurse. I didn't know what else to do, so I walked her home. Daniel and John were here when I got back."

Laura immediately called Dr. Romano. He was dumbfounded. "You mean he refused care for Hannah?" he asked.

"Yeah, I guess you could say that. I mean...it couldn't get much more obvious that she was seizing, and Joy swears that she told him we have no rescue meds. He's made suggestions in the past that I not take Hannah to the ER for seizures, too."

"Well, I definitely disagree with that line of thinking. What you'll have to do is take her to the ER and have him order ambulance transportation here, so I can manage her care."

At the ER, Dr. Wheeler refused to authorize the ambulance, saying there was no need for it, and that if Laura wanted to take Hannah to Dartmouth, she should just drive over there herself. Laura relayed the message to Dr. Romano. He was furious.

"Unfortunately, the order for an ambulance has to come from the point of origin. Do you feel comfortable driving her?"

"Well, it's not like I have any choice. Yeah, I'll drive, and if she turns too blue, I guess I'll just pull over and call 911."

Hannah's seizure subsided about halfway to the hospital, two hours after it had started. Dr. Romano assessed Hannah upon their arrival, ordered them another bottle of paraldehyde, adjusted her daily seizure medications, and suggested that they may want to change pediatricians. Laura agreed wholeheartedly.

Chapter XVII

The Nature of Things

October was chaotic and went by in a flash. At the beginning of the month, Hannah had surgery for ear tubes. Emily was scheduled for surgery in November to replace her left ear tube. Hannah's chronic ear infections were inducing seizure activity, and Emily had developed allergies to four different antibiotics. Unfortunately, Hannah's surgery offered her no relief from the seizures. One week after the procedure, she suffered a two-hour seizure. Two days later (just nine days after her ear surgery), she developed an ear infection and another status seizure.

Then they were slammed with a third seizure—a three-hour status seizure, just three short days later. After three big seizures in one week, Hannah had her fourth grand mal seizure, two days later, and Dr. Romano admitted her to the PICU, hoping to get them under control.

Medications are generally a first line of defense against seizures, but Dr. Romano wanted to explore other options. In order to do so, he needed more medical details. First, he performed a 48-hour video EEG. The results weren't encouraging.

"What we've found," he said, "is that Hannah is having sub-clinical seizure activity nearly all of the time, both when she is awake and asleep. Even when we're not seeing active seizures, she still has some activity present. We also found that she has just about every type of seizure a person can have. We saw evidence of absence seizures—otherwise known as petite mal seizures—partial, partial complex, and of course, what you have been seeing more of lately, her generalized tonic-clonic—or grand mal—seizures. We also learned some valuable information about Hannah's focal points—where her seizures originate. If there is just a single focal point, it may be possible to remove the problem area of the brain and cure the epilepsy. If there are multiple focal points that only occur on one side—or hemisphere—of the brain, we can surgically cut the connection between the two hemispheres, so the seizure can't travel across the entire brain and lead to the more damaging generalized seizures. Unfortunately, we saw that Hannah has multiple focal points in at least three of the four lobes of the brain, which makes surgery not an option for us."

"So does that mean that there's no hope? There's nothing we can do?" asked Laura.

"We still have her medications to work with. With some patients, however, we have to understand that a goal of zero seizures may not be within the realm of possibility. Right now, I'll be looking to reduce Hannah's seizure activity, but I don't expect to completely stop it."

Hannah was discharged five days later, at which time she was only having a couple of small seizures per day. Laura felt bad about missing work so soon after being hired. But she also felt fortunate that the people she worked for could certainly understand her circumstances.

During the following week, Laura and Daniel grew increasingly frustrated with Hannah's lack of improvement, despite their investment of the five-day hospital stay. While her status seizures had slowed down, she was still irritable, continued to have problems with digestion and diarrhea, and was still having a lot of partial and petite-mal seizure activity. Furthermore, she began to have some slight cold symptoms and a low-grade fever almost immediately after she had finished her antibiotics. After a few days, she developed a sharp increase in seizure activity and was extremely irritable. Laura and Daniel desperately tried to manage the seizures from home, but soon Hannah was having near continuous seizure activity and had become lethargic. Dr. Romano wanted her back in the PICU.

Laura updated the nurse in the PICU. "She's had some low-grade fevers over the past few days. Tylenol and Motrin have helped, though. It's the seizures that are out of hand. I counted at least fifty between 7:30 and 9:00 this morning." Hannah was seizing as she spoke.

Hannah stayed in the PICU for two days, and then stayed on the pediatric floor for two more days. Dr. Romano reluctantly prescribed Lamictal, a new seizure medication that hadn't yet been used extensively for children. Since he had already tried every other approved pediatric medication, he felt he had no choice but to take the risk.

When they left the hospital, Hannah's seizure activity had been reduced to anywhere between thirty and fifty episodes per day, which Laura was comfortable with, but mostly, she was just anxious to get home. Having started her job less than two months earlier, she had already missed more than two weeks of work. Laura realized that even the most patient and understanding employers had their limits, but she also knew her time away from work was unpaid. She worried how she would pay for the following week of Emily's preschool, the December rent, and the bills piling up on the kitchen table. She longed to settle in and get her life back under control. However, Laura was soon reminded that the power of control was a luxury she didn't have.

Just minutes after Laura had signed the discharge papers, Hannah's diarrhea returned in full force, along with an increase in seizure activity while driving back to the apartment. Laura felt she might be able to manage the diarrhea at home, and she convinced herself that the stress of the car trip was triggering more seizures. But that night, Hannah experienced a status seizure from about 9:00 until 11:00 p.m. When the seizure stopped, she vomited a considerable amount of blood. After a short quiet period, close to twenty small-to-medium seizures continued overnight.

In the morning, Hannah vomited again. Laura and Joy took her to get scheduled blood levels drawn at the regional hospital in Laconia. Laura feared the hospital would not release Hannah after the lab work was completed. Sure enough, Hannah began seizing when they arrived at the lab. They were immediately directed to the emergency room for the lab work. The ER staff (miraculously) placed an IV, started IV seizure medications, and loaded them into an ambulance headed back to DHMC–where they had departed, less than twenty-four hours earlier.

The prolonged seizure activity had paused a few times during the ambulance ride between hospitals, but Hannah was seizing once again when Dr. Romano assessed her at the PICU. Laura felt several different emotions at once. She was embarrassed, feeling like a squeaky-wheel parent who wouldn't leave poor Dr. Romano alone. If she wasn't in the hospital complaining about seizures or side effects, she was on the phone, asking him for advice. She also felt helpless. When Hannah had experienced heart failure, at least the whole process made sense. Her heart was full of holes and needed to be repaired. Hannah would need to be stronger, and to become stronger, she would need to gain weight. In order to gain weight, they needed to feed her. Simple. The situation was easy enough to understand, so Laura could determine if Hannah was making progress, and gauge her probability of success.

But this neurological mess was anything but straightforward. Laura hated not having a way to measure their progress. She also hated feeling that her life remained on hold while Hannah's seizures continued. She would have felt better if Hannah was improving, but that wasn't happening. On the night she was admitted, Hannah had another hour-long status seizure. Later on, she had another seizure that lasted more than twenty minutes, but stopped spontaneously. After that seizure, she vomited blood again.

An upper endoscopy (a procedure in which a small camera inserted through the nose is dropped down to the upper GI tract) showed that Hannah had esophagitis, or swelling and irritation of the esophagus due to acid reflux. The doctor adjusted her medications to reduce the acid buildup and allow for the esophagus to heal. However, many of the medications for seizures increase stomach acidity, and many of the medications for reducing acidity also reduce the effectiveness of the seizure medications.

Frustrations like that led to Laura's most overwhelming feeling—simple and utter sorrow for her baby girl. No matter what the hospital team did to help Hannah, she still suffered. Laura wondered how much good they were actually doing for her.

Once again, Hannah was discharged four days after admission. Her seizures were down to a dozen or so per day. She was tolerating feedings and having wet diapers with no diarrhea. While driving home, Laura felt exhausted and overwhelmed. She was wondering, with considerable doubt, if they'd arrive back home and finally be able to stay there.

Hannah was stable enough to stay home this time, but her condition was far from improving. Although the diarrhea had stopped, she was now vomiting much more frequently. She was still having a considerable number of seizures, and the list of medication side effects they were battling continued to grow.

While Laura and Daniel struggled to cope with the situation, Laura observed how people around them responded to Hannah's condition. The person who most surprised Laura with her inability to cope was Hannah's physical therapist, Amanda. Soon after they returned from the hospital, Amanda and the occupational therapist, Kim, arrived for what Laura thought was a routine therapy session. But Amanda began the session with a confession.

"As a pediatric physical therapist, I see a lot of kids. I see some kids who are relatively happy and healthy and other kids who are more sick and going through rougher times. As I'm sure you can imagine, some cases are more difficult for me, as a human being, to deal with emotionally. In fact, some cases are just too difficult to work on at all. I can work with sick children when I feel the child has a good chance at recovery and happiness at the other end." At this point, Amanda's eyes welled up with tears. "But sometimes, when it looks like the child ...isn't...well...I just can't shut my emotions off, and it becomes too difficult on me in my personal life. Your Hannah is such a precious little girl...and I hope and pray that she can recover from all of this." Amanda was crying and trying desperately to hold herself together. "But in my heart of hearts, I...I just don't think she...and, um...and I need to step away professionally, because it's affecting me too much privately." Amanda then took a deep breath and began to compose herself. "Kim will continue to work with you, and...and I can continue to consult from the office. But I won't be coming here to work with Hannah anymore. I apologize and I hope you understand."

Laura had harbored all kinds of doubts about Hannah's future, but that admission came as a complete surprise to her. Laura saw Amanda as a knowledgeable professional. She presumably had much more experience than Laura in dealing with a situation like Hannah's. Yet, she was confirming everything Laura was feeling and fearing. Laura gave Amanda a hug, told her she certainly held nothing against her, and thanked her for all she had done in the few months she had worked with Hannah.

During the next few days, Amanda's words echoed in the back of Laura's mind. Laura and Daniel began to talk more seriously about their situation. Hannah was not improving, and Laura knew another trip to DHMC was not the answer. She and Hannah had spent two of the last four weeks in the hospital, and they were no better off than they were a month ago.

One afternoon, shortly before Thanksgiving, Laura and Daniel took Hannah to her new pediatrician, Dr. Kelley. They had been extremely happy with him, since they had switched from Dr. Wheeler. He was an intelligent, soft-spoken, caring man who had a young family of his own. Laura felt that he could relate well to them, and she found him easy to talk to. Laura and Daniel would be putting that relationship to the test. The conversation that they anticipated having would be extremely difficult.

"Dr. Kelley," Laura said, "I don't know if I told you this before, but the day Hannah got her 4p- diagnosis was also the day she was scheduled for heart surgery at Boston Children's. The thought of such a serious surgery and heavy diagnosis were pretty overwhelming. And the fact that the two situations were colliding on the same day made it nearly impossible to sort out all of the emotion—especially when I was already an emotional mess."

"Of course. I understand," the doctor replied.

Laura continued. "Both my family and the medical community made it very clear to me from the beginning that I had the right to choose against surgery. Life or death; it was my decision. That's a choice that no parent wants, but that was the choice I was faced with. So, in the few short days I had to contemplate it—with the few working brain cells I had left and with the miniscule amount of information about 4p- that I could get my hands on—I prepared to make my decision."

The doctor nodded. "Mm hmm."

Laura took a breath. "You know...when you're going through life as a typical person and you have nothing but typical people surrounding you, you don't really give much thought to the quality-of-life issue. To me, it had something to do with the job you could get, the house you could live in, how happy your family life was, how well you fit into society, and what you could offer back to that society. But, Hannah forced me to totally reevaluate its meaning. By necessity, 'quality of life' was quickly watered down to 'a life that holds more good times than bad, more healthy moments than sick, and more pleasure than suffering.' With that in mind, my life-or-death decision was based on whether or not I felt Hannah would have a life of pain and suffering if she lived, or a life of contentment—although probably a relatively unproductive life of contentment."

"I see what you mean," said the doctor.

"I agreed to the heart surgeries, Dr. Kelley, because I felt I had no right to take away Hannah's chance at happiness—her chance at a life of quality. And she made such a beautiful recovery after her open-heart surgery. I thought we had seen and survived the worst of the bad times. She even laughed for the first time."

"That's wonderful." Dr. Kelley continued to give Laura his full attention.

"So...her birthday was in August. Hannah had made it through a whole year! Probably more than most, her birthday really meant something. It was a real accomplishment. She had suffered many, if not most of those 365 days, but she had persevered. I was so proud of her for being so strong. But it was around her birthday when her seizures began to go from bad to worse, and her days began to decline from some bad, to mostly bad, to all bad. Then I started to really have second thoughts about my decision for her heart surgery."

"Oh. I see," said the doctor.

"You know...Emily was a colicky baby. She would cry and cry, and I'd cry along with her, because I couldn't stand seeing her so distressed when I wasn't able to help her. But even though it was painful and frustrating and stressful at the time, it was bearable, overall, because I knew it was going to end soon. I knew she wouldn't be entering kindergarten colicky. We just had to survive a few tough weeks or months, in order to enjoy happiness at the other end." Laura's eyes filled with tears, and she tried desperately to choke back the sobs that fought to escape. "But... with Hannah...I don't think, anymore, that she has happiness at the other end. Her seizures aren't like colic. They don't magically disappear after a month or two. Medication is the only weapon we have against them, and they're not doing her any good—even the experimental ones. As a matter of fact, they're only making things worse. Not only is she seizing all the time, but she's also not sleeping, she's vomiting blood, she's having migraines, and diarrhea and..." Laura began to cry, but she continued to fight through the tears to finish what she wanted to say. Daniel held her hand tightly, while fighting back his own tears. "She's even lost her laugh. I haven't heard her laugh or even seen her smile, in months. Dr. Kelley, I tried to play God, so that I might give my little girl a chance at a happy life. Well, I SUCKED at it! I tried and I failed...miserably." Laura continued to sob. "I have done nothing but sentence my baby to a life of pain and agony. And now...now I don't know what to do. It's not like she's on some machine that we can just unplug. If we were to stop her seizure meds, she wouldn't gracefully pass on; she'd just have more seizures. And Dr. Romano says seizure activity creates more seizure activity. So, if we take her off the meds, she suffers. And if we leave her on the meds, she suffers."

Dr. Kelley nodded while silently expressing compassion and concern.

"What it comes down to is this. We've watched her go through this horrendously painful life for too long now and...and it has just become unbearable for us to stand by any longer. We see now that God gave Hannah fatal heart defects for a reason—so she wouldn't have to endure lifelong pain. Now that I've messed it up for her, what do we do? I mean...we could stop her G-tube feeds, but I don't want to watch her starve to death. I don't want to see her in that pain. That's the whole point! We just can't watch her suffer any longer! And please, Dr. Kelley, please don't think I'm bringing up the subject of euthanasia because we're just tired of Hannah or that –"

The doctor interrupted her. "No, no; it's very clear that everything you've said to me is out of complete love for your little girl. I understand how heart wrenching the decision for surgery must have been for you. You're right. No parent should ever have to make that choice. But I think you made it with solid reasoning. Unfortunately, we can't go back. We can't take away what has been given. So we need to move forward from here. Now, I know things are pretty rough right now. And I know it must be very difficult for you—to watch someone you love, as much as you clearly love Hannah—struggle through these dark days. But as bleak as it all feels to you now, I think there's still a good chance that things will turn around for Hannah. And in the meantime, things may not be as they appear. For children who are neurologically involved, such as Hannah, cries don't often necessarily mean they are in pain. You know...I have a lot of admiration for you both. You're doing so well with Hannah, in such a difficult situation. I think, for now, you just need to try to be patient."

Laura and Daniel thanked Dr. Kelley for his time and left his office feeling emotionally drained. They respected the doctor and understood that they had put him in a difficult position. Deep down, Laura knew that she couldn't have expected him to respond with a comment such as, "Oh, okay; let's sit down and have a serious discussion about euthanasia."

As they walked across the parking lot toward the street, Laura simmered in a sense of hatred for everyone in the medical community. She hated them for placing her in the position where she had to make a horrible decision; for not warning her about what actually lied ahead of that decision; and for not admitting to what she absolutely believed—that Hannah was, indeed, a child in pain. This was a child who was suffering. This was a child who had no quality of life. And the best that this doctor could come up with was, "She may not be in pain at all; it may just seem like she's in pain."

Laura didn't blame Dr. Kelley, personally. She blamed the whole world. Life had become too cruel. Daniel wrapped his arm around her, and they slowly walked home—both of them wondering where they'd find the strength to just "try to be patient" as Dr. Kelley had suggested.

Chapter XVIII

Separate Paths

On Thanksgiving night Laura and Daniel reflected on the past year and the incredible bond they had discovered one year ago. Laura was lying in her favorite position with Daniel—in his arms while feeling his heartbeat on the side of her face. "It's been a big year."

"Yeah, and a whole lotta stuff was packed into those 365 days. Ya know, in some ways, it seems like time has just flown right by. It's hard to believe that our Thanksgiving was a whole year ago," said Daniel.

"I know what you mean. On one hand, it feels like we've lived a lifetime together; I mean, I can hardly remember life before we got together. But on the other hand, it seems like yesterday when we were in the Cow Room at David's House."

Daniel smirked. "Ahhhh...the Cow Room. I still can't believe you crept over to my bed. Man, what were you thinking?"

"What do you mean what was I thinking? How could I resist? Do you regret my moonlit journey across the room that night?" *Oh no...with all that has gone on this year, there may be a little regret rolling around in his head...maybe even a lot of regret.*

"Well, the year has certainly left its scars."

Oh, God. "You mean all of the hard times with the girls and stuff?" *Brace yourself. This may be a difficult conversation.*

"No. Actual scars." Daniel lifted his leg above the covers. "I think I still have a mark on my thigh. Yep...there it is. I guess I'm gonna have it for life."

Laura burst out laughing, in relief. He was referring to a mark on his leg, which had appeared the previous spring. One afternoon at Steve and Janet's house, Hannah was sleeping, and Emily was watching a movie with Daniel's sister, Wendy.

Wendy had agreed to watch the girls for a little while, so Laura and Daniel could go for a walk. Once outside, they attempted to find a secluded area close-by. They were excited to find a loft in an old, deserted barn nearby. For years the barn had been used for storage, and piles of old blankets remained in the loft—perfect!

They eagerly climbed the old ladder and swiftly scanned the area for the most comfortable spot. Quickly settling in, they passionately embraced and began to hastily disrobe. Then Laura felt a pinch on her hip. Soon the sense of pinching or jabbing progressed to a much more uncomfortable stinging sensation. As Laura pulled away from Daniel to investigate her hip, he was simultaneously pulling away from her to investigate his thigh. In their hasty search for privacy, they had ended up less alone than they would have preferred. The spot they had chosen concealed a disrupted nest of very angry hornets.

Looking at each other in panic, the couple jumped up, threw their clothes back on, and fled down the ladder at top speed. They finally stopped running, about a hundred feet away from the barn. Laura had been stung twice on her hip, while Daniel had endured two stings on his thigh and one on his knee. Hand in hand, they walked back to the house laughing about it.

Laura began searching for baking soda in the kitchen, so she could apply some to their swelling sting sites. "I can't believe we did that! What were we thinking?"

"Well, it sounded romantic at the time. You always see those scenes in the movies where the couple runs off to the hayloft in the barn. It's usually a pleasurable experience for them—unless the father, armed with a shotgun, finds them first. Steve doesn't own a shotgun, so I figured we were in the clear. Hollywood seems to glaze over the part where the couple is attacked by killer insects, so that scenario caught me a little off guard."

Laura smiled. "The next time we try to be spontaneous, we'll have to plan a little better."

Over the course of the year, they had gone from stealing moments together, to being banned from one another, to seeing each other on weekends and the occasional weekday afternoon, to finally living together. As Laura snuggled closer to Daniel, she thought about how thankful she was. She had never felt more at home than in the home she shared with Daniel. However, she felt almost equally thankful for the struggles they had faced. The difficult times had made their current situation all the sweeter and gave them such colorful memories. She thought what a pity it would have been, if they hadn't had the loft memory to look back on.

The holiday season blessed them with a slightly quieter period concerning Hannah. Her seizures slowed down, but their home routine remained exhausting. Hannah was irritable the majority of the time. She was consolable, but barely. Laura and Daniel devised a variety of efforts to calm her. They called it the "Hannah shuffle." Interventions—such as feeding her, walking her, driving her, or putting her in her swing—would often work, but only for ten-to-fifteen minute stretches.

Hannah was nowhere near sleeping through the night; on average she was up every two hours. Unlike most babies, who wake up to be fed, Hannah just woke up crying—and continued for up to an hour or more. Once Laura and Daniel finally soothed her back to sleep, they were soon awakened again for another round of the same routine.

The nights were grueling, but Laura and Daniel had two important allies. First, they had gotten their nursing hours increased from forty to fifty-six hours per week, which allowed for some night nursing hours. Four nights a week, a nurse came from 11:00 p.m. until 3:00 a.m., which gave Laura and Daniel a few core hours of sleep.

The other saving grace was Hannah's swing. The back-and-forth motion almost always calmed her down. However, they owned the manual crank-up kind (until Christmas arrived). Every half hour or so, it would slow to a stop, Hannah would start crying, and the swing would have to be wound up again. During the day and on the nights they had nurses, it wasn't an issue. But during the nights without nursing assistance, that additional task was wearing.

Daniel took on most of the workload. Even if he had classes the next day, he put himself in charge of night duty–for three reasons. First, his classes generally began later than Laura's job–and didn't last throughout the entire day–so he could generally nap if he needed to. Secondly, Daniel was concerned that Laura was slipping back into a state of depression. He was doing all he could to help keep her healthy and shield her from as much stress as possible. The third reason (and possibly the biggest incentive for taking the night shift), involved their nearly permanent residents, John and Drew. They were Daniel's good friends and ex-roommates from college the previous year. Technically, the two guys shared an apartment a few blocks away, but they spent so much time with Laura and Daniel, that John had even moved his cat, Chloe, to their place.

All three guys kept late nights and were huge fans of the Nintendo 64. Since the guys were all up, anyway, having a bunch of laughs playing Super Mario World or Mortal Kombat, tending to Hannah was no problem. When she finally calmed down for the night (usually between 3:00 and 4:00 a.m.) that became their cue to shut off the TV and go to bed.

Although Laura loved John and Drew, she still had mixed feelings about them essentially living with her. She could not have asked for two nicer, more supportive, more loyal, or more understanding guys to be Daniel's friends–and also hers–during such difficult times. But, they were living in a tiny two-bedroom, one-bathroom apartment. The place was already full with just Laura, Daniel, and the girls, so adding two more guys, a nurse, and a cat made the situation overwhelming. And clutter was an issue. John and Drew were wonderful guys, but neat freaks they definitely were not. With an ever-growing housekeeping workload, Laura found it easy to blame the guys.

Laura's stress regarding the housekeeping was further fueled by Hannah's home nursing care. She felt the ever-judging eyes of nurses surveying her home for forty to fifty-six hours per week. After many exhausting and miserable weeks attempting to display a perfectly clean apartment at all times, Laura relinquished control and allowed others to witness that sometimes she left dishes in the sink, junk mail on the kitchen table, and dirty clothes on the floor. Begrudgingly, she admitted to the world that she couldn't always clean the toilet weekly, much less dust weekly, and sometimes had trash overflowing from the trashcan before she could get to the dumpster.

In fact, Laura's entire life was on display for the nurses. Luckily, she and Daniel weren't particularly private people. Other men might have resented no longer being able to walk freely around the house in their boxers, but Daniel wasn't fazed in the least; he didn't care who saw him in his underwear. Some women take issue with being seen without makeup, but Laura didn't wear any. And some couples would have concerns about fighting in front of the nurses, but Laura and Daniel never fought.

What they did find difficult was parenting in front of an audience. All parents have moments they wish they could erase, such as not attending to the runny nose you should have wiped immediately. Add to that all the times you sat your child down in front of Barney, so you could focus on getting dinner ready. A daily audience, taking note of every parenting decision, was unnerving—especially when Emily's issues were becoming more and more of a concern. Laura and Daniel had learned they could not use regular parenting tactics with her; they just didn't work. And Laura imagined the nurses thinking judgmental thoughts, beginning with the phrase, "I don't see why they don't just..."

But Laura was thankful for the nursing hours, so she could work and earn enough money to pay the rent and put food on the table. She was grateful for the hours of sleep that night nursing allowed. And she loved John and Drew for their support and friendship.

Sometimes, however, she lost sight of the blessings in her life, as she struggled to adjust to the downsides.

• •

The new year offered closure to a nagging issue of the past. Laura and Kevin went to court at the end of January to finalize their divorce. Although Laura had looked forward to that day, she was still saddened and ashamed that the final document was testament to a colossal mistake she had made in her past. They had married for all the wrong reasons, at a time when they were both too young, and they were now walking away on separate paths headed in opposite directions.

Kevin excitedly threw his arms in the air, as they descended the courthouse steps on their way to the parking lot. "Finally fuckin' free!"

Laura agreed in a much quieter and more reserved fashion. "Yep." *That's funny. I don't feel as celebratory as he does. I'm definitely happy to be done with the marriage. So why am I not feeling his level of excitement?* Laura tried to distract attention away from her more solemn appearance. "So what are you going to do now—with all of your freedom?"

"Hell, I'm on my way to a bar, and I'm gonna get fuckin' wasted!"

Right...of course. What else would you do? Wait...that's what's bothering me. I'm jealous. I don't want to go to a bar, but I want some of that freedom he's rubbing in my face. He's headed off to get drunk, and I'm rushing off to Dartmouth where Hannah and her nurse will meet me for an important doctor's appointment. Then I'll have to speed back to Plymouth, in time to pick up Emily from Toddle Town. This is such bullshit! These kids are both of ours, yet he gets to pick and choose when and how he'll be a father. I mean, wouldn't it be nice if he took both girls on the weekends when he wants visitation? Don't be ridiculous, Laura. Do you actually want Kevin to have anything to do with

Hannah? You know how difficult it can be to keep your cool when you're struggling with the Hannah shuffle. Heck, Emily comes back from Kevin's place overtired and an emotional wreck. Can you imagine the shape Hannah would be in? Be careful what you wish for, chicky-poo. There's no room for jealousy here. The best interest of the girls needs to come first.

"So where are you headed now?" asked Kevin.

"Actually I'm in a bit of a hurry. Hannah has a doctor's appointment in Hanover."

"Ha. Sucks to be you! Later!" He triumphantly walked to his car.

Yep. Life isn't fair. Not even a little bit.

Laura slogged her way through the doctor's appointment and the drive back to Plymouth. Then Emily had one of her traumatic transitions that day. Since Laura hadn't been able to call ahead, so the teacher could "warn" Emily of Laura's impending arrival, Emily was taken by surprise and burst into full meltdown mode. Emily's teacher, Sophia, commented on how she was noticing these episodes more frequently.

"They don't seem to be temper tantrums. They seem to be much more...random."

"Daniel and I were discussing this the other night. I was a live-in babysitter for my cousins when I was a teen," said Laura. "My cousin Paul could throw a humdinger of a temper tantrum back then. But the difference I see, between what Paul did and what Emily does, is that Paul always had a purpose to the tantrum. It was thrown to achieve a certain goal, like maybe he wanted to watch TV, and I wasn't letting him. With Emily, they seem to be a response to something—like today's unexpected transition. But sometimes we can't even figure out what they're in response to, so they do just seem random."

Sophia agreed. "I think you're right. They can be really unpredictable. Just the other day, she went from playing with the other kids to suddenly hitting her head repeatedly against the cement floor. After the incident was over, we remembered that she had asked for some space away from the other kids, right before hurting herself. I can only assume her classmates didn't immediately comply with her request, so I guess she reached her tolerance level and acted out accordingly. But usually, we would expect a child to show more signs of irritation and complaint before such drastic behavior. Are you moving forward with her developmental evaluations?"

"Yes. I just talked with Debra the other day. Someone should be coming in soon to observe Emily for speech, and then Debra will be in to observe for other areas of learning a few days later. She'll be in touch to schedule it all with you."

"Oh, good. I've definitely noticed questionable areas of speech and language, here at school. Emily has a really hard time with multi-step directions. The other day I said, 'Emily, go put your plate and cup in the kitchen when you're done with your lunch, and then come back and sit down.' She stopped eating, walked into the kitchen with her plate and cup, stood there for a second, and then sat down on the kitchen floor and resumed eating. I don't know if she's even hearing all of the instructions. It's like she's just picking up parts of it—usually just the beginning, and maybe the end. The problem is that if she is then corrected—especially by someone other than the person giving the initial instruction—she gets upset and sometimes has a meltdown, because she thinks she's doing what she has been told to do. I'm sure these communication challenges are contributing to her level of frustration."

While driving home, Laura thought about the extreme need for patience with Emily. She worried about what that meant for Daniel and her. Understanding and patience were becoming more and more challenging to maintain when they were increasingly sleep deprived and frustrated with Hannah's constant, unrelenting, and unbearable crying. She wondered how much longer all of this would go on—and how much longer they could all go on, this way.

Chapter XIX

Dangerous Mind

Tension in the apartment intensified throughout the winter. Hannah's constant cries were affecting all of them. Unlike the bellows of a typical infant, her wails were different, yet just as intense, if not more. Laura compared Hannah's excruciating cries to a dentist's drill or a steaming teakettle, and listening to them continuously for days, weeks, and then months, was torture.

Hannah had become less tolerant of bottle feedings, car rides, and others holding her. Car rides were especially agonizing. Hannah endured the movement of the car, but any stops would send her into a rage that did not subside for miles. Laura dreaded driving through the town's gauntlet of traffic lights, stop signs and crosswalks. The only possible benefit was Hannah teaching the family better eating habits by absolutely refusing to tolerate drive-throughs.

As Hannah's behavior deteriorated, Laura and Daniel grew more distressed. Their conversation about euthanasia with Dr. Kelley was behind them, but nothing had been resolved. Watching such an innocent child in the throes of a living hell was killing them. Seeing Hannah in heart failure had been difficult, but she had slept during much of that time. Therefore, it had been easier to discount her level of suffering. Watching her seize uncontrollably was grueling, too. But even though the seizures looked horrifying, Laura still had hope that Hannah was completely unaware at those times and felt no discomfort. At this point, though, Hannah had become the epitome of a pitiful sight and the visual definition of misery, due to her inability to sleep and relentless crying.

Dr. Romano systematically tweaked Hannah's seizure medications, attempting to minimize neurological side effects that may have been contributing to her irritability and insomnia, but nothing helped. Meanwhile, he added sleep medications to Hannah's bedtime cocktail. He prescribed Ativan, then added melatonin, and then Valium, hydroxyzine, Klonopin, chloral hydrate, and amitriptyline. Some of them helped a little bit for a few nights, but nothing lasted. Laura and Daniel jokingly referred to Hannah as *the Borg* (a Star Trek reference), because she would quickly assimilate to anything they gave her, and resistance was futile.

Meanwhile, Laura was receiving evaluation results for Emily from speech therapists, occupational therapists, and (because she would be going to kindergarten the following fall) the school district. These reports included excerpts such as: *Emily covers her ears when she hears noises, has to calm herself by immersing her hands in very warm water, has a very high pain threshold, and is easily irritated and upset if touched unexpectedly. She has to have directions repeated at times, doesn't always find her chair in the room and needs to be directed, gets distracted easily, needs a strong routine, and interacts only minimally with others. It is felt Emily has trouble concentrating. She has difficulty with multi-step directions. She has short-term memory issues and poor retrieval of information. She needs information presented more slowly and needs structured questions. She needed to be cued verbally to wash her hands before snack, even when she was at the end of the line and all the other children had done so. Emily had a book and a puzzle; the teacher gave the direction to Emily: "Emily, put the book down and do your puzzle." Emily put down the puzzle and looked at the book, with an obvious effort to do as she was directed.*

Laura was exhausted from the physical strain of keeping up with her busy schedule (including Emily's weekly speech and occupational therapies, as well as her dance class; plus Hannah's weekly speech, occupational and physical therapies; routine appointments with the nutritionist; and nearly daily doctor appointments). Laura and Daniel's level of stress sometimes blinded them from seeing that their attempt to do it all was beyond their capacity. Times of incredible stress had become normal for them.

One example of the extent of their stress occurred in November. Hannah had been hospitalized for five days in early November for seizures and then bounced back less than twenty-four hours later for another five days. After Hannah's first release, they hadn't gone straight home from the hospital. Instead, Daniel and Emily had met Laura and Hannah in the surgical center for Emily's scheduled ear-tube replacement. Emily was (appropriately) scared and stressed out, Hannah was very sick, Laura was worried about losing her job, and Daniel was skipping classes to be there to help. Acknowledging the level of stress in such a situation was hard, because they were lost in a sea of turmoil, with no time for reflection. In this case, they were already on their way to the next crisis–Hannah's readmission to the hospital.

• •

The first hints of spring found Laura and Daniel feeling like shells of their former selves. Punches continued to fly at them, and they were losing the ability to fight back. Little things dug at them, such as the long haul up an icy hill and three flights of stairs every week with laundry. Irritating things pounded at them, such as expensive repairs on an aging car. Heartbreaking things stabbed them, such as Emily burning her hand or accidentally slamming it in a dresser drawer, nearly oblivious to the pain, yet acting terrified when they reached out to comfort her. And frustrating things slapped at them. When Emily asked who Hannah's daddy was, they had a tough time getting her to believe the answer.

"No," Emily insisted, "Hannah doesn't go to Daddy Kevin's house, so he can't be her daddy."

Daily stressors beat them down relentlessly, but Hannah's sleep disorder was the mother of all stressors. Sleep logs showed she was sleeping as few as three hours in as long as twenty-eight-hour stretches, and she was sleeping no longer than twenty to thirty minutes at a time. Laura and Daniel continued feeling sleep-deprived, frustrated, scared, angry, sad, and overwhelmed. They had no fight left.

Just after Easter, came another big blow; Laura lost her job. She had felt guilty about routinely calling in sick due to medical appointments, having to stay home with a sick child (or children), hospitalizations, evaluation appointments, therapy appointments, lack of nursing coverage, etc. Laura understood when Mary explained, in a gentle and understanding way, that she needed someone more reliable. They both agreed that Laura's personal life made it impossible for her to hold down a job. Laura had no idea what to do. She tried talking to Kevin about him going back to work to support the girls.

His response was quite predictable. "You should be happy with the $155 a month I'm giving you now; the state only requires that I give you $50," he said.

Laura tried calling state legal services to see if Kevin could be forced to go back to work. Mary had said she would be willing to testify that Laura could not work, despite her best effort. Laura was told that the laws were not written for families with their unique circumstances. Kevin was only legally obligated to pay child support according to what his income was–not what it could be or should be.

As Laura began looking into homeless shelters, life started to feel more and more surreal. She called every agency she could find that helped women in similar situations, but that only acted as a grim reminder that no other women were in her particular situation. The homeless shelters for women and children could not even come close to accommodating her children. Federal housing programs, such as Section 8, could help with rent, but the application process involved a long wait (unless you were already in a homeless shelter, but that had already been deemed unsafe and inappropriate for Emily and Hannah). Seasoned health and human service professionals were completely stumped, not knowing where to send Laura, what to tell her, or how to help her.

Once again, Laura found herself spinning down the drain of depression. Months earlier she had stopped taking her antidepressant, because she felt she was stable enough to face life on her own—a critical error. She recognized the depressed thoughts and feelings that had crept back in, but she was too ashamed to address them, and her reasoning was distorted. Now that she had a solid, established relationship with Daniel, who was a devoted and loving partner, she felt she had no excuse to fall victim to depression. She didn't want to put him through the worry and frustration of helping her deal with it again. She worried that he was already on the verge of saying goodbye and leaving. She felt that she just had to suck it up, shake it off, and move on.

Laura resorted to cutting her arms to try to drown out the fear and pain that were dominating her life. But, as the noose tightened (Emily acting out, Hannah not sleeping, and no money to pay bills), Laura eventually succumbed to her despair with more disturbing intensity than ever before. She had just hung up from a call with an agency, during which her last-ditch effort went poorly.

I can't do this anymore. I'm too tired. I just...I can't; I can't do it. I'm done. I've failed. I don't have it in me. Even with Daniel by my side, I can't get this right. I'm not doing anybody any good here; I just need to stop. But, what about Daniel? If you do this, you'll hurt him. Well, not nearly as much as I'm hurting him now! You know he wants to walk away. Guilt is the only thing holding him here; what else could he possibly be staying for? He needs to move on and find someone he can be happy with— someone without all the chaos. But the girls...where would that leave them? I can't stand watching Hannah suffer anymore, and I'm just gonna go rest and leave her here to somehow try to endure? But she deserves rest just as much as you do, Laura. She deserves it even more than you; look at what she has gone through...what she continues to go through. You're right. I can't just go alone. Hannah needs to come with me. But then, what about Emily? Not only would she have to go to Kevin—who is showing less and less patience for her delays and challenges— but she'd have the painful memories and confusion about why she no longer has a mother and sister. I can't do that to her. No, but something has to change. I'm spent. Through. Done. Since I can't leave Emily behind, maybe it would be better for her to go, too. We have enough seizure and sleep medication in the other room to put an entire herd of elephants down. It would be quiet, painless, and peaceful. Yeah...peaceful.

Laura sat dreamily for a few moments, basking in the peace and serenity she imagined for her and her daughters. Then, after catching her breath, she broke out in a horrified sweat. *Oh my God...I just thought about killing my girls! I actually had an action plan for killing two of the most important people in my life! What kind of MONSTER am I!* With trembling fingers, she called her doctor. She couldn't believe the words coming out of her mouth.

"I need to see the doctor. I'm having suicidal...and homicidal thoughts." She was told he could see her right away.

On the way to the doctor's office, Laura panicked, realizing that the admission she had just made could result in the girls being taken away from her. *I can't worry about that now; I'm sick in the head. If they get taken away, they'll be better off somewhere else, anyway.*

Laura was relieved when she received compassion, in place of the tongue-lashing she had expected. After discussing what had led up to her disturbing thoughts, the doctor wrote a prescription for a new antidepressant and immediately sent Laura to see a psychologist located in an office upstairs.

Laura did her best to provide the new therapist with an explanation of why she was there. He asked how Laura felt about getting some rest in the hospital. *Wow...a quiet hospital room? Meals served to me? As much sleep as I want? It sounds heavenly, except for visions of Daniel trying to hold it all together while I'm on my little vacation. I can't do that to him!* Laura convinced the psychologist that the scary thoughts had passed, made another appointment for later in the week, promised to get her prescription filled right away, and made a plan to follow if the thoughts were to return. The doctor then allowed her to go home.

Feeling extremely ashamed, Laura later discussed the matter with Daniel. He was completely supportive, and worried he had somehow not been doing enough to help her. He shuddered at the thought of having a life without Laura and pleaded with her to confide in him sooner, if she began feeling like that again. Then Daniel tearfully admitted to some dark thoughts of his own. On more than one occasion, he had fought the urge to place a pillow over Hannah's head as he struggled to get her to sleep. He wasn't angry with her or tired of her (although hints of those feelings had surfaced more, as the weeks and months of sleep deprivation had worn on). He was simply desperate to stop her suffering and felt he couldn't continue watching her in such abject misery.

Daniel suggested that Laura take a vacation and have a little time to herself. She argued against it for three reasons. One, they had just established that he was struggling as much as her. Laura certainly didn't want to drive Daniel over the edge by leaving him to deal with everything while she went away. Two, if she walked away from the situation, she feared she may never have the courage to come back. Three, they simply didn't have the money; that fact was part of the whole problem. They were dirt poor. Dead broke. But, in true Daniel fashion, he completely disregarded the issue of money.

"Look, you need to get away," said Daniel. "If you're uncomfortable with leaving us here, we'll all go. We can all go to your mom's place in Kentucky. It might not be the perfect solution, because you'll still have the stress of the girls there, but you won't be worried about being away from us, and you'll have your mom's support and a complete change of scenery with a slower pace."

"That sounds good, but where are we going to find the money?" asked Laura.

"Don't worry about the money, Laura. That'll work out. Like... we have the tax refund coming back any day now, right?"

"Then what are we going to pay the rent with! We still have next month's rent to pay here, and then our lease ends. And we'll need to move somewhere else, because there's no way we'll get this apartment again, at the rent we're paying now. Wherever we end up going, we're gonna need the first and last month's rent, a security deposit…" She began to get ramped up with the thought of their financial nightmare.

Daniel spoke firmly, yet lovingly. "Laura, let me worry about that. You make the travel arrangements; I'll figure the finances out. Trust me on this."

Laura was slowly learning to trust in Daniel's unique approach to finances, because his theory had proven true on so many occasions. The last instance had occurred the week before. Their bank account was absolutely empty, and Laura owed the daycare her weekly check. For the first time ever, she didn't have the money. Her mind raced as she agonized over what she could possibly say to the director when she picked up Emily that Friday afternoon.

To her absolute shock, the director approached Laura before Laura had a chance to seek her out. "You know what? You have been with us for some time now, and you've been such a good customer…no charge this week. This one's on the house," said the director.

WHAT? Who does that! I hadn't even mentioned our money woes to anyone here! Laura tearfully hugged the daycare director, thanked her repeatedly, and thought, *Dammit, hon, you're freakin' right again!*

The plan was to fly to Kentucky for a weeklong visit, after Daniel's final exams. Daniel had been searching for a summer job, and right before their trip, he was offered a job at True Colors, a print shop/copy center on Main Street. They were elated. Laura wondered if she would have made it through the vacation without the security of an impending income upon their return home.

The trip to Carol and Frank's 250-acre farm, just outside of Louisville, was exactly what they had needed. After a few days of fresh air, hearty meals, and beautiful sunsets over the rolling hills of the farm, Laura and Daniel felt somewhat refreshed. However, by the end of the trip, they were exhausted due to the never-ending sleep-deprivation problem with Hannah and lack of nursing assistance. Emily probably got the most out of the trip. She groomed and rode Carol's miniature pony each day and was lit up like a Christmas tree for the entire stay.

Upon their return home, Laura scrambled to pack for the move while still searching for new housing. With the promise of regular income from Daniel's new full-time job, they dared to dream of finding a place with three bedrooms. But packing and house hunting had to be put on hold. Just a few days after their arrival, Hannah had an hour-and-a-half seizure that required a trip to Dartmouth. A few of the PICU nurses were soon greeting their "frequent-flyer" patient.

"Hannah! You're back; it's been so long! Have you been a good girl? Wow, look how big you are now!"

However, the mood changed as they took Hannah's temperature. The thermometer was climbing. When it got to 38.5°C, one of the nurses remarked that Hannah was running a bit of a fever. Then, as it climbed to 40°C, followed by 40.5°C, the two bedside nurses shot each other a look of concern that got Laura's attention.

The thermometer had come to rest at 41.1°C, which Laura later learned was 106°F. They applied cooling blankets and went into PICU mode, trying to stabilize Hannah. Blood cultures later showed she had parainfluenza. Luckily, she bounced back rather quickly and was able to return home after just two days. The timing was good, because Daniel was beginning his new job, and Emily was suffering from a bad asthma attack.

Another distraction from the move was a regional Wolf-Hirschhorn syndrome conference, taking place in Connecticut. Daniel couldn't go because of his new job, but Alice, one of their regular nurses at the time, said she could accompany Laura to help out with Hannah. Laura was anxious to see the other kids again, but she was desperate to quiz other families about sleep disorders—to see if anyone else was experiencing them, and if so, what they were doing about it.

Thirteen families attended. Laura thought the conference was fascinating, but disappointing, because nobody reported suffering even remotely similar struggles with sleep. Meanwhile, Hannah's behavior continued to deteriorate. She was still almost constantly inconsolable, but she now communicated her frustration by continuously beating herself in the head with her right fist. Laura felt jealous, looking around at the other 4p- kids, whom were either sitting happily in their wheelchairs or, for the higher-functioning kids, playing calmly in the room. Even among the population where she believed she belonged, she felt different and isolated.

· ·

Laura was excited to have found a new home—a three-bedroom doublewide trailer on a half-acre of land in Plymouth's neighboring town of Campton. At a whopping $650 per month, Laura and Daniel could barely afford it, but the allure of a third bedroom for Hannah proved too tempting to refuse. Laura had concerns upon learning that the property was for sale, because they would have to vacate within sixty days if it sold during the time of their lease. However, the real estate agent/owner assured Laura that it had been on the market for more than a year, and she didn't anticipate it selling.

Moving was exhausting, but Laura's life soon took on a new feeling of belonging. Feeling like a family was so much easier in a home that could house everyone comfortably. Unfortunately, Hannah's struggles with sleep and seizures continued, Emily was still...Emily, and Daniel's near-minimum-wage job certainly didn't leave them feeling financially comfortable. But the summer months in the trailer left Laura with some positive memories: being able to grill dinner outside, meals at the dining room table together, hanging clothes on the line with Emily, enjoying alone-time with Daniel on the couch after the girls had gone to bed (without Hannah's crib next to them)—real home memories. Their new life gave them a renewed energy and enthusiasm as a family, which seemed so rare during those days.

Chapter XX

Curve Ball

In a proactive attempt to resolve Hannah's sleep issues, Laura wrote to numerous pediatric sleep centers throughout the country that spring, begging for help. Unanimously, the advice she received suggested contacting Dr. Richard Ferber. At that time, he was the leading pediatric sleep specialist who practiced out of Boston Children's Hospital. Dr. Ferber had an opening in his schedule during July, and Laura was feeling eager and hopeful.

Once in his office, she and Daniel attempted to explain the situation in great detail, including examples from sleep logs and a list of sedatives that had been tried. At the conclusion of their talk, Laura held her breath, in anticipation of some golden words of wisdom. She was dumbfounded by the doctor's response. He said they didn't have Hannah on a proper schedule, they should continue with the sedatives they were using, and they should just let her cry. Laura left the appointment in tears.

Laura and Daniel made every attempt to adhere to Dr. Ferber's advice and followed his sleep schedules. Meanwhile, Dr. Romano continued striving to find a pharmacological "cocktail" that would help Hannah sleep. The medications sedated her to the point of paralyzation; yet Hannah continued to whimper miserably while immobilized in her bed. She was unable to open her eyes, due to heavy doses of powerful drugs, yet she was still in a wakeful state. Later that summer, Laura contacted Dr. Ferber to let him know his recommendations had not changed the situation.

"Well, she's two years old," he said. "Of course she doesn't want to sleep; she's a toddler!"

Laura was livid. Hannah wasn't a two-year-old trying to manipulate her parents into reading her a second bedtime story! She was a child who couldn't sleep—despite being literally paralyzed with sedatives—and also happened to be two years old.

Laura never contacted Dr. Ferber again. Years later, Dr. Ferber issued a public apology for giving poor advice about sleep, both in his office and in his books. But Laura felt it was a small consolation.

After viewing some moving video footage of Hannah struggling to sleep, Dr. Romano suggested taking her to Dartmouth for one last try at finding an answer. During her weeklong stay, they adjusted Hannah's medications, resulting in a two-and-a-half-hour seizure and countless smaller seizures, but her sleep did not improve.

Some brighter areas in their lives helped counteract the effects from lack of sleep. Fall arrived with much anticipation. Emily started kindergarten, and Daniel headed back to school for his senior year. Laura and Daniel threw a big party for Emily's fifth birthday and surprised her with the best gift they could think of—horseback-riding lessons. Emily was more excited than ever before, and her smile made the financial risk worthwhile.

In addition, Laura made a decision that summer that significantly helped reduce her stress load. She was worn out and overwhelmed by the weekly therapy schedule. Between Hannah's and Emily's therapies, a bare minimum of six sessions per week had been scheduled. The most stressful aspect of the therapies was the list of exercises or actions for Laura to engage in. Individually, none of the directions were demanding, but collectively, they were just too much for Laura. She didn't have the time or energy to keep up with the orders, such as: Move Hannah's legs like this, three to four times per day. Try to bottle feed Hannah in this position, with your fingers held here under her chin, three or four times per day. Play with Hannah on this sensory blanket, two or three times per day. Have Emily draw letters in shaving cream once a day. Perform these specific direction-following exercises every day with Emily. Brush Emily with this sensory-integration brush, six to eight times per day, then have her jump up and down ten times, and then pull on each of her finger joints.

Laura constantly felt guilty for not living up to all of the various requests, so she finally decided to take a new approach. *Enough. I will be the mom. They can be the therapists. I will be a better mom if I'm not also trying to be six different therapists.* That decision made all the difference.

Meanwhile (playing the part of the resident pharmacist) Laura tweaked Hannah's medications, which resulted in a little glimmer of success. Her seizure activity increased slightly, and Hannah still had major issues with sleep and relaxation, but they were getting through nights with only moderate extra effort. Hannah had begun sleeping for as long as three to four hours at a time.

Unfortunately, whenever success appeared in one area of their lives, an upheaval always occurred in a few other areas. First, and probably least surprising, a developmental psychologist had tested Emily, who concluded she was technically within the normal range cognitively, but (in his expert opinion) she was learning disabled and needed assistance. On the surface these were positive results, but in reality, they worked against Emily. The test results had to be within a certain range of disability in order for her to qualify for assistive services.

For instance, in the area of speech, Emily's vocabulary was in the seventy-fifth percentile, but her receptive speech (understanding what was said and following age-appropriate multi-step instructions) was in the second percentile. She clearly needed help with receptive speech, which was important for her academic success. Unfortunately, the scores aren't viewed independently. Average scores for the different aspects of speech are determined, and then used to develop an overall score. Emily's overall score was in the high thirties, which was much lower than average (in the fiftieth percentile). However, is was not low enough to warrant assistance (two standard deviations below the mean—a phrase Laura was becoming all too familiar with).

Meanwhile, some surprising news came from the landlord. She had sold the property, and they had sixty days to vacate. Then, in the midst of the sudden scramble to pack and find new housing, they faced a new unsettling situation. Laura and Daniel had noticed Alice, one of Hannah's nurses, becoming more impatient and rough with Hannah. Laura called the nursing agency and requested that Alice's name be removed from the nurses who were available for their case.

The agency representative gave a quick response. "Well, we'll just give Alice a break—maybe a week on another assignment—and then we'll have her return to you," she said.

"No, I don't think that will work. We'd rather not have Alice come back, if possible."

The representative was insistent. "But it's best to keep a level of continuity with her care. I think you'll be pleasantly surprised at how refreshed Alice will be, after just a little break from caring for Hannah."

Does this woman really think I'd rather have another stranger walk into my house, who will require more hours of orientation? Doesn't she understand the seriousness of my request? Feeling irritated, Laura threw diplomacy out the window and leveled with the woman bluntly and honestly.

"Look," she said, "Alice is nice enough, but Daniel and I have both clearly seen that she has really gotten rough with Hannah. We don't even want to imagine what she must be doing to her when we're not here. Furthermore, Alice used to ask us if we'd mind if she left fifteen or twenty minutes early to get to a doctor's appointment or something. That was fine, because it generally wasn't a problem for us. But now, it's gotten to the point where she's outright announcing that she'll be leaving early—even hours early—yet, when I'm signing her time card, she's still documenting that she's working until the end of her shift. Well, we'd really like to use those hours elsewhere, if she's not going to work them. But I feel uncomfortable confronting her because, quite frankly, she's bigger than me, and I definitely wouldn't put it past her to get physical."

The agency representative asked a few more questions, and finally agreed to Laura's wishes. Laura breathed a sigh of relief, assuming the uncomfortable situation was over, but it had only just begun. Alice wasn't simply assigned to another case, as Laura had intended; she was fired—and lost her nursing license due to evidence of Medicaid fraud. The issue of Alice documenting worked time, that wasn't actually worked, was not just a nuisance for Laura. The government did not take it lightly.

Laura felt bad; she hadn't meant for Alice to get into trouble. However, she and Daniel soon discovered evidence of other actions that could have just as easily gotten Alice fired. For instance, Alice had stolen nearly a full bottle of Valium for Laura's depression and anxiety. Laura had taken only one dose and didn't like the way it made her feel. When they were packing to move, Daniel discovered that the bottle contained just one pill. Alice was the only other person who knew about the Valium, and she had even joked once (on a particularly stressful day) that she needed it.

Alice didn't go away quietly, either. First, she called Kevin and told him that Laura was neglecting the girls. Laura had to convince her ex-husband—with whom she was barely on speaking terms—that she was a good mother. That required a particularly difficult gulp of swallowed pride. As she was pleading her case, she was simmering with disgust, because she knew she was one thousand times the parent he was. Yet, there she was—throwing herself upon his mercy.

Alice had also called the fuel assistance agency and said Laura and Daniel were defrauding them. The agency had helped Laura and Daniel the previous winter with heating costs, and they had applied for assistance during the coming winter, as well. But Alice's call had put the entire process on hold. Laura had to provide all of her financial documentation again, and the process took three times longer, because her records were studied with extreme scrutiny.

Meanwhile, the housing situation was growing more worrisome because of so few rentals available in November. They eventually found a rustic, three-bedroom A-frame cabin in the woods. It was a little far out of town, with questionable dirt road access. Even worse, it was another home that was up for sale. But with no other options, Laura and Daniel agreed to move in.

With all of the challenges they had worked through, since the beginning of their relationship, tensions between Laura and Daniel were now at their highest. Life was a big ball of stress. They were moving during the holidays. Emily had gone from jumping onto the bus with a smile to crying and begging them not to make her go because "the kids hurt my ears." Hannah still wasn't sleeping through the night and was having a fair amount of seizure activity. Daniel's hours had been shortened at the print shop, money was extremely tight, reliable nursing help was hard to find, etc., etc. And everything felt worse than it probably was, because they were extremely battle-weary.

Laura and Daniel had an underlying disagreement that added another level of tension. The difference of opinion involved a suggestion that Dr. Romano had made when Hannah had gone to DHMC to (unsuccessfully) work on her sleep issues. The doctor had said they should seriously consider placing Hannah in a pediatric nursing facility, since her behaviors were no longer "conducive to living in a family setting." Daniel agreed with Dr. Romano. Laura had to agree that life was certainly not working out with Hannah in the house, but she just couldn't accept the idea of sending her away—for a number of reasons. The simplest was that the only pediatric nursing facility in the state was hours away, near Keene, New Hampshire. They were tied to Plymouth, because Daniel had to finish his final year at Plymouth State. Laura couldn't bear the thought of being that far away from Hannah—or Daniel.

Daniel being nearly finished with school also raised a certain amount of unspoken tension. Before long, Daniel would be moving on to a career, which, most likely, would be situated out of state. That would leave Laura in a tentative spot. She couldn't imagine herself moving away with him. Hannah, alone, had a team of more than thirty members, and both girls were receiving state services that not all states offered. Laura didn't know what to do with her conflicting emotions. She certainly didn't want to hold Daniel back, but she was afraid of moving on.

Luckily, many beautiful moments in the cabin countered the many stressors they faced. Deer in the back yard was a relatively routine sight. One day they woke to find three moose in the front yard. Another morning Emily announced (as casually as she would have reported that it was raining outside), "There's a bear on the porch." On many quiet nights, Laura and Daniel would gaze out the huge, oversized windows at the beautifully falling snow, thrilling thunderstorms, or a brilliantly displayed moon.

As the situation at school worsened for Emily, Laura began meeting with Emily's teacher and special education team. Every team member agreed that Emily clearly had issues and challenges requiring services, but due to her frustrating test results, the school district could not act upon them. They couldn't help Emily until she "got worse."

Laura set out to find another solution. She refused to force Emily to go to school. Soon Laura found what appeared to be a perfect solution. A tiny little one-room school, called Maple Cottage School, was situated further up the road. The school offered classes for kindergarten through grade three, and the maximum enrollment was eight students. Susanne, the owner and teacher, was kind, soft-spoken and appeared to be a very patient woman—just what Emily needed.

The fee was reasonably priced for a private school at $3,000 per year, set up over a ten-month payment cycle. Since Kevin agreed to pay half, Laura would only have to contribute $150 per month. Although she had no idea where she'd get the money, she registered Emily anyway and hoped to figure out the finances during the summer. Daniel would soon be graduating and working full-time, so Laura anticipated that their financial situation would greatly improve. In addition, they were saving money, which they had previously spent on activities for the girls. After becoming frustrated with trying to keep up with her peers, Emily had quit her dance class. Hannah, who had been receiving hippotherapy (therapeutic horseback riding) while Emily took her riding lessons, had grown bored with it. Emily still loved riding, but the instructor had become impatient with her slow progress, which frustrated and depressed Emily, who was giving her best effort. Both horse-related activities were soon discontinued.

Meanwhile, some other areas of life were improving. Hannah's sleep was slightly better. Daniel had graduated from college, but he decided to work for at least a year. He wanted to save money for his dream to come true—being able to attend DigiPen, a highly specialized video-game school in the state of Washington. With Emily signed up for the Maple Cottage School in the fall and spring blooming beautifully at their cozy little cabin home, for the time being, life was finally wonderful.

However, their good life began to unravel when Emily brought home a stomach virus from school. The illness made its way through the family, and Daniel was the final victim. But he didn't improve like the others. After a few days, he was still unable to hold down any solid food. After three weeks of continuous vomiting, Daniel began visiting various doctors, looking for a diagnosis and, more importantly, a remedy. He was losing weight rapidly. He had been thin to begin with (at 6'1", he weighed about 155-160 pounds), but he had plummeted to somewhere in the 140s. Most tests came back inconclusive, but a 24-hour pH probe showed that Daniel was producing ten times more stomach acid than he should have been. He was placed on a prescription-strength antacid, but it only provided minimal relief. After two months of living like this, they were becoming extremely concerned.

Unfortunately, every doctor Daniel saw ended the appointment the same way. "Are you under some sort of extreme stress? You need to make every effort to reduce your stress load."

Daniel had three big stresses in his life—Laura, Emily, and Hannah. Laura and Daniel couldn't imagine life apart, but apparently, Daniel was struggling to survive with their living arrangement. Laura tried her best to make him as comfortable as she could, hoping the problem would miraculously disappear.

They had adopted a Lab-mix puppy (and named him Chew-Barker or Chewy, for short), with the hope of him becoming a seizure-alert dog for Hannah. Daniel loved taking him out for walks in the woods, and Laura thought the dog might help him relax. She also adjusted her cooking, took over getting up with Hannah at night, and tried to keep Emily as calm as possible. But her efforts went unrewarded. Daniel's condition steadily worsened; he dropped down to 135 pounds.

Life was not cooperating with Laura's efforts to keep Daniel as stress-free as possible, either. Emily soon got chicken pox, and Hannah screamed in pain for an excruciating three weeks, before they finally figured out that she had a urinary tract infection. Then, worst of all, the cabin was sold, and once again, they had to vacate their home within sixty days.

Laura was scared. She was afraid of losing Daniel, but she was also afraid of having him stay. She and her daughters were literally killing the man she loved. He clearly needed to go away, but Laura was petrified of facing life without him. *Can I handle single parenthood? What will I do for housing? Money? Forget all that—how will I ever live without him—without my hon?*

Laura was angry, too, because the only part of her life she had been able to count on was her relationship with Daniel. What had felt solid and comforting was suddenly crumbling in front of her. Then she was livid with herself for finding any place in her heart that could possibly be angry with Daniel for being ill. Denial was interspersed with her anger. She tried to believe that Daniel was just exaggerating his nausea. She would think, *Daniel and I are meant to be together. We can't be apart; that's crazy. Daniel will get better, and our real lives will start back up any day now.* But, as the vomiting worsened and his weight loss grew more extreme, she was forced to face the truth.

All of these mixed emotions finally led to Laura's newest and most unfamiliar feeling—loss of faith. She hadn't had much faith in anything, before she and Daniel had gotten involved. Any little bit of faith she had in God was chewed up and spit out by Hannah's first hospitalization. She had some faith in people, but had been hurt enough, in the past, to build extensive walls. However, as she and Daniel had spent more time together, she grew to have complete and utter faith in Daniel, in them, and in the belief that everything will eventually work out in the end. Her mind reeled as she considered the likely possibility of breaking away from Daniel. *I don't understand why this is happening. Being with Daniel feels absolutely right. No matter what was happening, I've always had my hon to turn to, lean on, and share with— whether we were sharing smiles or tears. Has this sweet and wonderful journey of love, faith, and family come to an end?*

Somehow, I don't feel like the end is here. Why would two people, who love each other so completely, have to break apart? That's not the way it's supposed to happen; yet...here we are.

As Laura struggled through her various emotional responses to decisions about Hannah and a long-term-care facility, the prospect of Daniel moving out of state, and his sudden and completely unexpected illness, she withdrew further into herself–creating a painfully uncomfortable distance and silence between the two of them.

With their eviction date looming in August, Laura decided that a conversation with Daniel concerning their inevitable break-up was overdue. She didn't want to say the words, because that would make the situation too real; but even worse than that, she couldn't bear to hear Daniel speak them. That would hurt too much. The words had to come from her. Besides, Daniel didn't deserve the guilt from asking to walk away, in addition to the illness that was responsible for his having to leave. Silence prevailed as Laura struggled with the dilemma.

One Sunday morning, Laura stood in the hallway, agonizing, as she listened to Daniel retching in the bathroom. She knew something had to change. Daniel weakly crawled back into bed, and Laura sat down next to him, holding his hand. She tried desperately to hide any evidence of the tears in her eyes, the churning of her stomach, and the breaking of her heart.

"Hon...I think we need to...to look for separate housing when we leave here. You just can't go on like this. Maybe with a few months of rest, we'll be able to slowly work back to being together again...but for now, I just don't see how it can happen." She choked on every word, still wishing that somehow this wasn't actually happening.

After little discussion, Daniel agreed. He was as resistant to the idea of a separation as Laura was, but neither could deny that this was how it would have to be for now. With their eviction date growing closer, they packed their belongings, placing them in two individual piles. On moving day, they made a final, silent farewell sweep through the cabin. Then they slowly shut the door behind them and hugged one last time, before heading their own ways. Laura's chest burned with the ripping of her heart, as she turned and walked away from the only man she knew she would ever love.

Chapter XXI

With a Little Help from My Friends

With the logistical nightmare resulting from the scramble of splitting up the household, Laura had no time to wallow in despair over her bizarre and heartbreaking split. Daniel had settled into an apartment in Plymouth with John and another friend, Seth. Laura found a three-bedroom apartment, also in Plymouth, within walking distance from the hospital, downtown, and Daniel's place. Her new location made living apart feel not quite so distant or final, but she was actively trying to keep her distance from Daniel. Being in relationship limbo had proven to be too painful and difficult to sort out, and she had to choose a direction. Going back together wasn't possible, so she tried to focus on her independence.

Laura's rent was $650 per month, which the SSI and child-support money covered, but little was left over, so employment was a necessity. After a long, frustrating search Laura finally landed a part-time parking-enforcement job with flexible hours. Then she took a second position as a stocking-crew member at a small department store. Her days were long and tiring. Unloading the trucks and stocking shelves began at 5:00 a.m., so she had to get up at 4:30 a.m. Luckily, Olivia (one of Hannah's nurses) was an early riser, so she took the early shift with the girls. After work, Laura rushed off to any scheduled therapy or doctor appointments and then changed her clothes for her job with the police department. The day finally ended with administering the last dose of Hannah's medications at 11:00 p.m., followed by a few trips downstairs to tend to Hannah's crying.

Right after the move, school started for Emily. As Laura had hoped, Emily loved Maple Cottage School. Laura had called Susanne during the move, sadly explaining she could no longer afford the tuition, even with Kevin's contribution. Days later, Laura was shocked when Susanne told her she had found an anonymous donor to cover Laura's half of the tuition. Laura vowed that somehow, someday she'd pay back the donor.

Hannah continued to keep Laura busy with her medical needs. Her urinary tract infections had become chronic, so a maintenance antibiotic was added to her medication regime. In addition, she had swallow studies performed, which showed evidence of little-to-no peristalsis (muscle contractions that allow for swallowing). This finding suggested that oral eating put Hannah at high risk for aspiration (liquid entering her lungs, instead of her stomach). She would need to be fed exclusively by G-tube.

Laura was ready to make the change, anyway. During the previous few months, Hannah had appeared to be overstimulated by close human contact—especially eye contact—making it nearly impossible to feed her by bottle. Laura discovered that the best course of action was to walk away when Hannah would begin fussing. She even joked with the nurses about putting a No Loitering sign on Hannah's bedroom door. Laura felt like a neglectful and disgraceful parent when she explained this tactic to Hannah's new nurses. However, watching Hannah relentlessly pound herself in the head, when overstimulated, quickly helped the nurses to understand and support the unorthodox approach.

Although Laura was managing to live as a single parent with the girls, life with Emily and Hannah was anything but smooth, no matter who was living in the home. For example, soon after the move, on a beautiful, sunny day, Laura decided to take the girls for a walk. She had been missing Daniel terribly and needed a distraction. Also, Hannah had been particularly fussy, and walks generally helped. They headed out, with Laura pushing Hannah and Emily walking Chewy.

About a half mile into their walk, Emily tripped. Laura whipped around when she heard the horrifying sound of Emily's fall behind her. Laura's sudden movement nearly toppled over Hannah's wheelchair. The slight pause after Emily's fall–the one during which all parents hold their breath hoping for the "I'm-scared-but-okay" look, while fearing just about anything else–heightened Laura's anxiety. Emily rose to a sitting position, as she held her hands over her mouth. Her silent, "I'm-in-incredible-pain" kind of cry–accompanied by a rapidly reddening face–was the type that would have a parent begging the child to take that first breath before unleashing the bellow of a sob.

Emily had dropped Chewy's leash, who was then trotting around the area, so the scene included a child in a wheelchair who might be injured, a loose puppy dangerously close to heavy traffic, and an injured child (possibly severely) sitting on the sidewalk, bawling. Laura grabbed Chewy's leash, quickly scanned Hannah's body for bleeding or seizing, and then directed her attention back to Emily. By that time, blood was pouring out between Emily's fingers. Laura scooped her up. *Now what? Home? The hospital is closer than home. But what if it's just a loosened or knocked out tooth? Would taking her to the ER be overkill*? Laura desperately looked around, standing with her still screaming and bleeding six-year-old in her arms. She wrapped Chewy's leash around the handle of the wheelchair and awkwardly started pushing Hannah, one-handed, back toward the hospital and home. The street was a busy one; yet no one stopped to investigate or offer help.

Feeling uncertain whether her decision to stop at the hospital was out of necessity for Emily or due to her own utter exhaustion, Laura arrived at the triage counter–dog and all. The ER staff quickly assessed Emily's injury and discovered that her chin needed four stitches.

Laura's first instinct was to call Daniel. She had been trying to make a clean break from him; plus he needed to stay far away from this type of situation, since that was the reason they were no longer together. Still, she couldn't fight the urge, and called him. He wasn't home, so Laura reasoned that was probably for the best.

Once settled at home, Laura struggled with constant thoughts of Daniel. With her busy schedule and the company of various nurses, weekdays proved to be easier than weekends. Family members added to her already heavy stress load. Laura avoided them whenever possible. She dreaded the "I-told-you-so" looks she knew they would have. When Laura had told her father about the split, he didn't hide his feelings at all. He said, "Well, we all knew that was coming; it was just a matter of when!" Laura hadn't bothered explaining that her parting with Daniel wasn't like a traditional breakup. She couldn't see the point of trying to clarify the situation.

A few months after the move, Laura became truly angry with Daniel for the first time. He had said he wanted to try to be there for Emily whenever he could. On Halloween, Laura assumed that Daniel would walk Emily around the neighborhood. That was something they always had fun doing together, and it was something Laura couldn't do, because she had to stay home with Hannah. But Daniel didn't offer to take Emily trick-or-treating. Instead, he went to Salem, Massachusetts with John and Drew to enjoy the Halloween festivities. Laura reminded herself that it wasn't Daniel's responsibility to spend his holiday with them. She tried to reason that he had every right to spend Halloween however he wanted. But reasoning didn't help. She felt as though Daniel only wanted to be involved when it was convenient. *Well, of course he only wants to be around when it's convenient for him. That's the whole point of splitting up. Get used to it, Laura. You have set him free. There's no reason for him to stick around, and there's every reason for him to have fun with his friends. You'd better expect this, from now on. You're alone. Any time he spends with you and the girls is just an extra bonus—not something to count on or expect.*

Laura's anger subsided, and the awkward nature of her relationship with Daniel continued. Unable to stay apart, they tried going on a date. Laura attempted to approach the incident as if she were going to the movies with a friend. But she didn't even know what to call him. After exclusively calling him hon for years, Daniel sounded too foreign and weird. The movie was enjoyable, but the uncomfortable silence was obvious when Laura dropped Daniel off. They tried kissing goodnight, but it was just too awkward.

Celebrating Christmas was strange, too. Since they were part of the same extended family, they spent it together, but Laura was uncomfortable with the amount of thinking required. *Should I sit next to Daniel? Or avoid sitting next to him? What's appropriate? What's not? What is everyone thinking about us right now?*

One evening in January, soon after Laura's meter-maid shift, she and Emily were driving home from Emily's friend's house. Laura was lost in thought about what to make for dinner, what laundry needed washing, and what her work schedule was for the next day. As they entered an intersection, someone driving a pick-up truck had run a red light and slammed into Emily's side of the car. Emily bawled as Laura tried her best to check them both for injuries. Thankfully, Emily appeared to be all right and was just shaken up.

Emily was still crying. "Why did that car hit us?"

Laura consoled her. "He just forgot to stop when he was supposed to, but we're fine, so it's okay."

Then Laura jumped out of the car and yelled over to the truck, asking if everyone was all right. A man had been driving, and a teenage boy was with him.

Before he could even answer, Emily jumped out and yelled (while still sobbing), "WHY DIDN'T YOU STOP! YOU WERE SUPPOSED TO STOP!" Laura felt bad for the poor man when she noticed all the color had drained from his face. He had just hit a car, and the people jumping out of that car were a woman in a police uniform and a crying, six-year-old girl. She imagined the panic he must have felt.

Trying to keep her shaky voice as steady as possible, Laura called in the accident on her radio. As they waited for aid to arrive, reality began to sink in. She now had a totaled car that was worth next to nothing before the accident, so she could expect virtually no insurance money. She had no other means of transportation. *What am I going to do now? How will I get Emily to school, get to work, and do shopping? How will we even get home right now?*

Laura tried to shake off her worrisome thinking as an ambulance arrived. After ensuring that nobody needed a transport to the hospital, the paramedics offered Laura and Emily a ride into town and said they would have their dispatcher call someone for them. Daniel was the only person Laura could think of. When Daniel arrived, he was full of emotion. While hugging Laura, he said, "Oh, to think I could have lost you tonight!"

Facing the prospect of never being together again changed the distance between them. They began spending more time together. Laura liked it best when Daniel went to her place, because it felt like her family was back to normal—even if it was only temporary.

Meanwhile, Laura scurried to resolve her transportation issues. She would need to upgrade to a larger vehicle, since Hannah's wheelchair and equipment had grown larger and less collapsible. Laura decided a minivan would work best. But she wondered how she would ever be able to handle the payments.

Dr. Kelley had recently mentioned to Laura that he was a board member of a charity called The Starlight Foundation, which was a local version of the Make-A-Wish Foundation. He had told her that the foundation might be able to help if she specifically needed something for Hannah. Laura approached him by phone, soon after the accident.

"Dr. Kelley, I have a request regarding the Starlight Foundation, but it's rather unorthodox, so if it isn't something that can be done, that's totally fine. My car recently got totaled. I need a new one, and I'm going to need a larger vehicle. I was wondering if there are any bank executives on your board who would consider offering me a loan with better interest rates that might help reduce the payments. I have great credit, so it wouldn't be a big risk. It could even mean some advertising for them. We could do a write-up in the newspaper or something."

Dr. Kelley agreed it was certainly a unique request, but he promised to look into it. Days later, he contacted Laura, saying it wasn't possible to offer her better interest rates, but the board would be presenting her with a rather large check as a down payment on a vehicle.

Laura couldn't thank him enough. "Wow, this is such an incredible gift! I'll gladly talk to the newspaper about how generous you people have been."

"No," he said, "the gifts are all confidential. Just use this and enjoy."

Laura was soon on her way to the car dealership where she purchased a used Ford Windstar that fit both her needs and her budget (although she was stretching it somewhat).

When she brought home the vehicle, Emily had to have her say. "Mommy, I don't think that's a Minnie van. It has to be a Micky van. It's red; it isn't even pink, so it can't be a Minnie van."

Laura chuckled. But the issue that arose just a few days later, when Laura received a phone call from Dr. Kelley, was no laughing matter.

"Remember when I mentioned that the gifts provided by the Starlight Foundation are confidential? Well, I meant just that; they are to remain confidential. That means we don't advertise how we help families, and families don't talk about the gifts, either."

Laura was confused. "But I didn't."

"You must have told someone, because I got a call from a person who suggested that we shouldn't give you the check, because you had no need for a minivan and had no business buying one."

Laura went from confused to shocked. She had told only three people about the check—Daniel and Hannah's two main nurses. She was positive Daniel hadn't made the call. Even though Laura thought of the nurses as family (and never would have imagined either of them saying anything) she instantly knew which nurse it was, because she was sure which nurse it wasn't. But Laura was saddened that the woman (a) was clearly against the idea of the minivan, and (b) felt the need to try to sabotage Laura's purchase.

Laura apologized to Dr. Kelley, explaining she had never even considered that telling the nurses might be a breach in confidentiality, and she would definitely not say another word about it to anyone. The ordeal did not sit well with Laura. She had already found it difficult to accept charity, so the experience just further fueled her uncomfortable feelings of humiliation. In fact, the incident happened soon after Laura had accepted another charitable donation. Steve and Janet had offered to help with her living expenses if she decided to pursue a degree in nursing. They knew she had an interest in the field, and they encouraged her to pursue a profession that would enable her to support herself and the girls.

Classes started in February, but, in order to attend school, she had to quit her department-store job, due to an overbooked schedule. She hadn't been making much money there, but any little bit helped, especially since adding the van payments to her bills. Quitting the store job did relieve another problem, though—her constant search for early-morning sitters for Emily. Hannah's nurse, Olivia, had started providing Emily's morning care when Laura had gotten the retail job. However, within a few weeks, Olivia said she had to discontinue, because she didn't have the required patience. Laura conceded that Emily was definitely a challenge. At age six and a half, along with her behavior issues, she was still routinely having potty accidents—both bowel and bladder. She also continued to have chronic ear infections and frequent asthma attacks.

Nobody blamed Emily for the ear infections and asthma attacks, but various individuals had all sorts of opinions and commentary, regarding the accidents. Kevin's girlfriend, Stacy, attempted to keep a journal going back and forth with Laura to facilitate communication surrounding Emily's weekend visits with her father. In late February, Stacy wrote:

> *Linda took Emily sledding on Friday. Seemed like they had fun, but you know Linda; she refused to ask Emily if she needed to go potty, do the scheduled potty,*

or do the scheduled questioning, so needless to say, Emily had an accident. Linda is being a jerk about the entire thing. We tried to talk to her about why this is important and why we needed to log this stuff down. She thinks this is all "bullshit" and refuses to help out in any of the processes that we are doing.

By then, Emily's psychologist had diagnosed her with high-functioning autism. Upon receiving the news, Laura was disappointed; she had dared to hope that Emily might someday outgrow her challenges. She was also sad, scared, and maybe even a little angry. Trying to accept the reality that she was a single mother of two special-needs children was enough to send her into a panic about her future. However, Laura wasn't surprised by the diagnosis, which finally explained why Emily struggled with communication, socialization, sensory integration, learning, and the understanding of abstract concepts, such as the passage of time and the value of money. But Laura felt frustrated that people who now knew Emily was autistic—from Olivia (Hannah's nurse) to Emily's own grandmother—appeared to have no respect for the diagnosis, or the protocols and management methods in place to help Emily.

• •

Spring featured a manageable routine for everyone. School was going well for both Laura and Emily, Hannah was relatively stable with fewer seizures, and Laura and Daniel were spending more and more time together. In general, they continued to limit their time together by going out on dates, but Daniel also joined Laura on many of her drives back and forth to Concord, New Hampshire, where she was taking her classes at New Hampshire Technical Institute. Those trips often involved Daniel helping her memorize medical terms with the use of anatomy and physiology flash cards, since she had little other time to study. The trips back home were much more relaxed, and the two of them could be chattier. The relationship wasn't what Laura would have preferred, but she was happy with any amount of time she could spend with Daniel.

Daniel's health problems persisted despite the split, so he continued exploring the issue with his doctors. Although Laura didn't want Daniel to suffer from any illness or pain, part of her was still relieved that he hadn't experienced a miraculous recovery, once he moved out. But even if she and the girls weren't the direct cause of Daniel's illness, Laura knew other factors would make a future with him unlikely.

She learned that Daniel, John, and Drew were planning a cross-country trip. Daniel was still determined to attend DigiPen (the video-game school located outside of Seattle) and Andrew was intending to join him. Once accepted, they planned to pack their belongings and head west in Drew's old pick-up truck. Laura wondered if their plan was realistic, but she eventually realized her doubts had more to do with wishful thinking than with lack of faith. She wanted Daniel to succeed—to move on to the great accomplishments she knew he was capable of—but she didn't want him to go.

Money matters were changing in all directions. Laura's job with the police department came to an abrupt and unexpected end that summer when she got laid off. Hours after that blow, however, Laura received word that her name was at the top of the Section 8 waiting list. Instantly, her monthly rent shrank from $650 to only $35. Furthermore, Emily's scholarship to the Maple Cottage School had run out, and just when Laura was fretting over how she could possibly arrange for Emily to return in the fall, she received a letter from the Social Security office. Emily's diagnosis of high-functioning autism made her eligible for SSI, like her sister. That additional income provided what Laura needed to pay for Emily's tuition. Once again, Daniel's theory about money proved to be right.

As the summer wore on, the reality of not having a future with Daniel was hitting Laura harder than ever. Both Daniel and Drew had been accepted to DigiPen, and they were packed and ready to go. With each passing day, Laura struggled to avoid seeing Daniel, because it hurt too much. She knew their time together was ending, and she just wanted to get past it. She didn't want to have to face the goodbye, knowing it would likely be their last. As various family members happily reminded her, Daniel would soon be on the other side of the country.

The day Daniel left, he and Drew pulled up in front of Laura's house in Drew's little pick-up truck, crammed with their belongings. Laura hugged Daniel goodbye, hating that she had to do it, while feeling an ache in her chest that she feared would never go away. Then he was gone. Laura stood in her quiet living room, watching them drive away through the picture window. When they were out of sight, she sat on the front steps of the house. It was a beautiful late August day. The air had that particular "school-is-about-to-start" feel to it. Laura tried desperately to distract herself with thoughts of her upcoming nursing classes, Emily going back to school, and what she would make for dinner, but it was pointless. Thoughts echoed in the hollow that was now her shell. She was so empty—so alone. She had said, in the past, if her relationship with Daniel didn't work out, she was done. *Well, this is it. It's over now. We are done.*

Chapter XXII

In the Name of Love

Laura and Emily thrived as students at their respective schools. Maple Cottage continued to be a blessing for Emily, and Laura felt she had made the right decision to attend nursing school. Emily continued to visit Kevin almost every other weekend—whenever it was convenient for him. Laura was concerned with Kevin's growing irritation regarding Emily's challenges.

Kevin kept berating and insulting Emily, and she often returned home in such an emotional state that getting her to calm down would take an entire week. Laura was privy to one such incident regarding Kevin's cruel criticisms. Emily had expressed an interest in soccer, but Laura was reluctant to let her play. She anticipated Emily would struggle to keep up with the fast pace of the game and feared she would be picked on by the other kids. Emily was insistent, though, so Laura finally relented and signed her up for the sport with the town's parks and recreations program.

Laura was pleasantly surprised by how much fun Emily ended up having. Despite Emily's difficulties in keeping up with the pace of the practice, her teammates genuinely accepted her as part of the team. The situation was working out nicely—until Kevin and Stacy decided to attend one of Emily's games. Laura and Stacy became horrified when Kevin quickly grew irritated with his daughter's lack of performance.

Pacing along the sideline as the game progressed, he yelled, "Emily! Come on! What's your problem! Your team is counting on you!"

Laura hoped and prayed that Emily was too far away on the field (and too engrossed in the game) to have heard him.

• •

Daniel kept Laura updated on all of his travel adventures. They had made it to Washington, had found an apartment, and he was busy with managing a heavy load of classes. Laura was happy with the updates, but the sales pitch became uncomfortable.

"Boy, Laura, I think you'd really love it out here! We're in the city, but it's incredible. The city, itself, is really green, and just a few blocks away, you're in the countryside, and you'd never guess that you're near a city."

"That sounds really nice, but you know I can't go out there. I can't just up and move three thousand miles away with the girls," said Laura. She wished her situation was different, but she knew she had no choice.

"People move with kids every day."

"Not these kids! I can't just throw Emily into any school and pick any pediatrician for Hannah. Then there's the matter of state benefits. If Washington doesn't offer the services that New Hampshire does, we'd be out of luck."

"Well, I'm sure there's a way to move special-needs kids, too, and I'm sure that other special-needs families in Washington are somehow able to get by. They might not have the same programs as New Hampshire, but they must make it work somehow. If you want to come out here and join me, just say the word. I'll make it work, one way or another."

"But, don't you remember why we split up to begin with? You couldn't live with the girls. I can't trek out there, only to discover after six or eight months that the stress is still too much for you, and then just pack up and head back East. After we've left New Hampshire the state won't say, 'Oh, moving away didn't work out? Welcome home! Here, let's give you back all of the services you had to wait years to receive, the first time around.' I...I just can't see that working out." *Man, I can't believe I'm about to say this.* "What you need is to find someone out there. I'm sure there's somebody great out there—someone who doesn't...literally make you sick."

"Say what you want; I know it would work. And I don't even want to hear this nonsense about me being with someone else. There's nobody else for me. Besides, all there are at DigiPen are a bunch of pasty-white, nerdy guys, like me, so there are no worries of me finding someone else, anyway. Look, all you have to do is agree to it, and I'll get you here. Just trust me."

It wouldn't work—no matter how much I desperately want it to. "Well, we both have two years of school to get through right now, anyway."

Laura and Daniel continued having that conversation practically every week. Laura was so torn. She absolutely wanted to run away to Washington and be with Daniel. If no hindrances existed, she would have followed him anywhere, but she saw too many barriers to a future with Daniel. Laura's emotional pain grew with each attempt he made at convincing her to move. Feeling desperate to clarify the end of their relationship, so she could move on, Laura contacted Daniel's father and asked him to persuade his son to find someone else nearby. Laura just wanted Daniel to be happy, and she figured he had a much better chance of finding happiness with someone else.

While trying to convince herself that they were better off apart, Laura arranged a dinner date with a guy she had met online, named Pete. The evening turned out to be an awkward disaster. Pete was nice enough, but he was no Daniel, and Daniel was all Laura could think about. For her, the dinner couldn't end fast enough.

If Laura's plan was to push Daniel away, it failed miserably. A few weeks later, she was stunned to find him standing at her front door. He had decided to fly home and spend his three-day Columbus Day weekend making a final plea to work out whatever obstacles were keeping them from being together. He greeted her with a kiss that reawakened her, heated by months of built-up passion. Then Daniel made it clear why he was there.

"Laura, what we have, we're not going to find anywhere else with anybody else. We have something special, and it's worth fighting for...and it's strong enough to withstand whatever life might throw at us. I know what you're thinking: 'If that were the case, then why did we have to split up before?' Well, I think we were wrong. We've been living apart for some time now, and my stomach is really no better, so the problem couldn't have been you and the girls. Laura, I just don't know what I'd do without you. We have to make this work. If we just have faith in our love, everything else will work out. And, when it comes to the girls, we'll make that work, too. If there aren't enough services out there, then I'll just make sure I'm making enough money to pay for what they need, myself. We can do this; just look at all that we've gotten through in the past. We can do this!"

Laura's defenses melted away. *Well, how can I possibly say no to that! I mean, who does this! Who hops on a six-hour, ridiculously expensive, cross-country flight to ask for another chance at love? If I didn't already love him so much, this act alone would have me smitten.*

When Daniel came home for Christmas, he was still thin and pale, but Laura was so happy to see him again that she hardly noticed. Everyone enjoyed a wonderful holiday break. Frank and Carol had traveled from Kentucky to be with the family, so the house was especially full and festive.

Carol's side of the family decided to celebrate Christmas on the twenty-sixth that year. Daniel and Laura drove to Whitefield to spend the afternoon with them. Daniel had dropped off Laura and the girls at Laura's grandfather's house and then ran out for a quick trip to a convenience store. After awhile, Laura wondered why Daniel hadn't returned yet. The kids were getting restless and wanted to open their gifts. Then she began to hear music–bagpipe music.

She turned to find Daniel's former roommate, Seth, walking in. He was clad in a kilt and playing the pipes. She couldn't understand why on earth Seth was at her grandfather's house, but then she saw Daniel walking behind him, also fully dressed in Scottish garb.

Daniel approached Laura and bent down on one knee. He said, "Hon, I'm never happier than when I'm with you, and I would be honored if you would agree to spend the rest of your life with me. Will you marry me?"

Laura was so taken aback by the whole scene, and so overwhelmed with happiness, that she nearly forgot to speak. She replied as quickly as she could get the words out. "Of course!"

Laura thought how fitting (and hilarious) it was that Daniel had chosen McHaggis–Laura's favorite of all Daniel's alter personalities–to propose to her. She loved his thoughtful presentation and appreciated him more than ever. Everyone was clapping, and Carol was even wiping away tears. She had revealed the secret proposal to the extended family, after Daniel had called her and Steve weeks earlier to ask their permission. Carol had always been fond of Daniel, and unlike Daniel's side of the family, she had fully supported his relationship with Laura.

Daniel had to head back to Washington soon after the holiday, and Laura's life grew even busier. Nursing school was becoming more of a challenge, Emily was back in school and needing daily help with homework, Kevin was still annoying her, and Hannah continued to present a variety of unusual medical situations. She had been fussing regularly again. Her ear infections were, once more, out of control, and she was continuing to have considerable trouble with urinary retention. Both problems required frequent trips to the doctor or ER. Laura decided to take charge by obtaining an otoscope and supplies for catheterization at home, but her plan had its obstacles. Hannah's ear canals were small, so her eardrums weren't easily visualized. Trying to catheterize Hannah was also difficult. Her small size and slightly abnormal anatomy made entrance into her bladder a challenge. Laura would joke with her classmates and Hannah's nurses that she was learning more nursing skills at home than she was at school.

Luckily, Chewy had become quite helpful, by alerting Laura to one of Hannah's medical needs. Laura noticed occasions when he spent considerable time sniffing one side of Hannah's head. Before long, she realized he had become an ear-infection alert dog. He would routinely anticipate an ear infection two-to-three days before the inflammation from the illness could be detected with the scope. Chewy's help proved to be extremely useful, as it enabled Hannah get on medications right away, before her pain could get out of control.

Trying to communicate with her ex-husband continued to be an unpleasant chore for Laura. At one point, she told him about her intentions to move to Washington—and braced for the impact. Surprisingly, he received the news rather calmly—that day. However, at other times, he was so angry about it that Laura felt as if she were dealing with an entirely different person. Laura was often frustrated with Kevin's generally unpredictable nature regarding the subject of visitation. Occasionally he demanded a visit, but he frequently made excuses to skip them. One time, Kevin called just before he was supposed to pick up Emily.

"Is Emily sick?" he asked.

Laura was confused. "Uh...no," she said.

"Damn!"

"Excuse me?" Laura asked. She was further confused, and now angry.

"Well, I'm sick."

"Yeah...?" *And your point being...? I'm not gonna let you out of this one. You asked for Emily this weekend. What if I had made other plans? For Christ's sake, you've gotta suck it up and be a parent. It's not an optional title; it's a full-time gig.*

"I didn't know if she was sick, too," he said.

Laura continued to stand her ground. "Nope, she's healthy."

"Damn! I don't want her to catch what I have."

"We get sick here all the time, and *we* still take care of the girls; just wash your hands."

"Well, I don't do that."

Are you fucking kidding me? Laura expelled an exasperated sigh and spoke in utter disbelief. "Well, I guess she'll stay here for the weekend, then. Take care of yourself."

In late March, Laura invited Kevin to lunch, so they could have a serious discussion about the girls–which they had never actually done during the five years they had been apart. In the past, Kevin had complained about feeling "left out," so Laura wanted to give him the opportunity to ask questions. When they met, she told him she had just had a parent-teacher meeting with Susanne, but he wasn't interested in hearing the details. In regard to Hannah, he had no questions at all. Laura asked him, candidly, how he felt about Hannah.

He said, "It's not that I don't want to have anything to do with her. I know you say I can learn about her, but I don't have the time. I mean...it's up to you. To give you child support, I have to work. Now, if you don't mind me not giving you the money, I'll take the time to learn about her, but I can't be expected to do both, right?"

Making every effort to ignore his ridiculous reasoning, Laura told Kevin that Daniel had, once again, expressed an interest in adopting Hannah, and wondered if he would agree to relinquish his rights.

"But, before, you said it was all or nothing–that I would have to give up rights to both girls if I wanted to give up Hannah," Kevin said.

"Well, back then I was concerned about Emily feeling left out or confused, if Hannah and I both had a different last name than her. Now I'm more concerned about Hannah's well-being, in the event that I pass away during her childhood. I think Hannah deserves a dad who loves her and is involved with her. And now I'm more confident that Emily won't be bothered by different last names."

"You say that with a resentful tone."

"Of course I'm resentful. I've been to hell and back with Hannah—more times than I can count. It's nothing that anybody likes to go through, but I had to; I'm her parent. Yeah, I'm resentful that you're her parent, too, because you seem to be exempt from that responsibility."

Silence followed.

Laura continued, after she took a calming breath. "The only thing I'd like to make sure of, is that we have a written visitation agreement prepared, so if I die before Emily is eighteen, she and Hannah will have legal visitation in place."

Kevin remarked that he didn't want to rush into it. He said he'd talk to some people and get back to her. When discussing Laura's move to Washington, Kevin said he would expect to have Emily with him for the entire summer.

"I understand your position, but I have two main concerns. One is that she's falling further behind in her schooling, despite the wonderful work Susanne is doing with her. Going to summer school is almost a guarantee for many years."

"Okay—then, for a month every summer."

"Well, that brings me to concern number two. Emily tells me that Stacy says she is desperate to marry you."

"Yeah, she probably is."

"Do the two of you plan on getting married?"

"I don't ever plan on marrying anyone again or having more kids. I told Stacy that on our first date."

"You do realize that that means nothing, right?"

Kevin raised his eyebrows.

The previous fall, Stacy had told Laura she was pregnant and was elated by the news. Later, as Stacy was packing to move, she realized she was miscarrying. Panicked and heartbroken, she called Kevin to come home from work. He had said, "I've gotta work. You deal with it." Then he hung up. Stacy was devastated—by both the loss of her child and Kevin's response.

"You're talking about a girl in her early twenties; she still thinks she can change you, and one of two things will happen. Either you'll screw up and get her pregnant again, and she won't lose the baby this time, so you'll resent her, or she'll eventually realize she can't change you, and she'll resent you for denying her the life she really wants."

"Yeah, she probably will resent me."

"Well, that really isn't any of my business, other than having human concern about a nice young girl who is likely to be very upset in the future. But here's how it relates to my concern. You have very little patience when it comes to Emily's challenges."

Kevin nodded emphatically in agreement.

"Right now, that doesn't worry me too much, because I know Stacy has the patience to deal with it."

"She has more patience than me, but she gets pretty fucking frustrated, too."

"That's the concern. What are you gonna do with Emily for an entire month, if Stacy isn't agreeing to help with those frustrations? I mean, if you get too frustrated to handle a weekend, how will you handle a month?"

"Well, as she gets older, we won't have to worry about it as much, because she'll be growing out of a lot of it."

"What do you mean? You don't grow out of autism. Look at your mom. We agree that she's probably in the autistic spectrum, and she's what—in her sixties? She never outgrew it."

"Yeah, but that was before there were treatments for it. They're coming up with stuff all the time–medications and stuff–not that I'm saying we should medicate Em, but you know what I mean."

"No, Kevin. That's the problem with autism. There are no medications or anything; it takes parents and teachers, who constantly work with these kids, to help them reach their highest potential. It isn't something that goes away, and you certainly don't grow out of it."

Laura walked away from the meeting with more trepidation than when she had walked in. Laura viewed Kevin's clear denial of Emily's condition and his apparent lack of concern about dealing with future challenges as two potentially disastrous ingredients.

Later on, Kevin ended up filing for termination of his parental rights to Hannah. Laura mentioned the plan to her father during the week they were due in court for the legalities. "Why!" asked Steve.

"Because we're worried that Kevin would throw Hannah into some nursing home and just walk away, if I were to die during her childhood. Without custody, Daniel would have no say concerning who takes care of Hannah."

"Laura, that's ridiculous. If Daniel stepped up and said, 'Hey, Kevin, I know you don't want Hannah. Here, let me take her off your hands,' Kevin would jump at the chance! Let the bastard pay! He hasn't stepped up in any other way; make him pay the child support!"

After some thought, Laura cancelled the court date. Kevin was livid. "You just want my money," he said.

Laura told him he was absolutely right.

• •

By the end of the school year, Laura was missing Daniel intensely. He had secured an internship at Nintendo of America, so whether or not he'd be able to come home that summer was unclear. They were both elated when Daniel was able to fly home for the month of August, after the game he had been working on was completed early. For a few fabulous weeks, it felt like old times—with Laura's family comfortably back together.

However, before long, they were all back in school. Daniel had returned to DigiPen. Emily started her final year at Maple Cottage. Laura's senior year in nursing school had begun, and Hannah was receiving therapies in kindergarten.

Laura's workload was increasing—both in the classroom and in the clinical setting. She worked harder during those months than any other time in her life. Her schedule had jumped from having two clinical shifts to three per week. Heading out for four hours of class time was especially challenging—considering the additional schedules of Emily, Hannah, the therapists and the nurses to juggle. Heading out for eight hours of clinical time was decidedly more difficult. What made it nearly impossible was the travel time involved for completing the clinical requirements in different areas of nursing. In addition to her eight-hour shifts, Laura had commutes, which were often longer than two hours, to the various hospitals selected by her school. The stress from shuffling arrangements for the girls to allow for a twelve-to-thirteen-hour absence (three times per week) was intense.

Fatigue was a problem, as well. With hospital shifts beginning at 7:00 a.m., Laura had to be up very early in the morning—which would have been infinitely easier if Hannah had been sleeping through most of the night. Right before school had started, Laura discovered that one of Hannah's sleep medications was responsible for her urinary retention, so she had stopped using it. When Hannah's sleep difficulties subsequently worsened, Dr. Romano began the dreaded medication shuffle again. Every night Laura went to bed hoping and praying that the modifications made that night would result in a restful sleep for Hannah. With failed attempt after failed attempt, Dr. Romano talked some more about the possibility of Hannah needing care from a nursing facility.

The fatigue was amplified by the work related to preassigned patients. Before arriving at the hospital, Laura was required to complete a patient profile, which typically totaled two to four pages per patient. In her first year, she only had one patient per shift. However, as a current senior, she had two to four patients, resulting in up to twelve profiles to write per week.

When Laura wasn't tending to the girls or dealing with school, she was planning her wedding and trying to prepare for the move. Wedding planning was fun, but planning the out-of-state move was complex. Along with looking into housing and employment, Laura was researching other necessities, such as state benefits, doctors, schools, therapists, etc.

Just before Christmas, Daniel called Laura with some thrilling news. Nintendo had hired him, and furthermore, they would allow him a holiday visit back home, before getting started. By that point, they were all in need of a break together. Not only had the weeks and months leading up to Christmas been physically and emotionally exhausting for Laura and Daniel, but Emily had clearly been under an incredible amount of stress, too. One night in mid-December, as Laura was hurrying Emily along to get ready for a Girl Scout meeting, Emily stopped at the stairs, burst into tears, and yelled, "I'm so stupid! I should just kill myself!"

Laura spun around, desperately hoping she had heard wrong. "What!"

"I should just get a big stick and stab myself with it until I'm dead!"

Laura's heart sank, and she felt sick. She held Emily in her arms, telling her she was so sorry she felt that way, that she would be devastated without her, and that she certainly was not stupid. After talking about it for a few minutes, Laura asked Emily if she had ever felt that way before.

"Yes," she said, "when people yell at me when I do things wrong."

Laura made an appointment for Emily to see her psychologist, Dr. Stevenson, as soon as possible. After her appointment, the doctor reported that Emily most often felt suicidal "at Daddy Kevin's house, because he yells at me a lot."

Laura called Kevin to inform him that he had a suicidal daughter, and he said, "She's just doing it for attention. Hey, if you've got the balls to off yourself, I say go for it. If you're that stupid, you deserve it. I'm not putting up with that shit."

At that point, Laura had no words for the disgust she felt toward her ex-husband. No words at all.

With the end of Christmas break, they were saying goodbye to Daniel again—but not for long, this time. Laura and Emily saw him again, just a few weeks later. Laura had wanted to take a trip to Washington to scout out an apartment and more importantly, to have a meeting with someone in the Department of Developmental Disabilities (DDD), Washington's state agency in charge of servicing children like Emily and Hannah. While they were gone, Hannah stayed at New Hampshire's only pediatric nursing facility, Crotched Mountain, in Greenfield.

Emily had a great time in Washington, so Laura felt encouraged that the transition of the move planned for June wouldn't be too hard on her. Also, Laura's mind was set at ease when she met with a DDD representative, who assured her Washington services would be adequate and available for both girls.

The final semester of nursing school was absolute hell. About a month into it, Laura decided that the most important thing she had learned from nursing school was why a nursing shortage existed in the country—surely because no one in his or her right mind would ever want to be a nurse. The clinical work was the most bothersome. Laura couldn't stand the feeling of the instructors constantly watching over her shoulder, quizzing her on every move she made.

"You're patient is in pain, and there are orders for Tylenol and Motrin. Why are you choosing the Tylenol?"

...*Uh...because it's the first one listed on the med list?* "Hmmm...I guess I don't know."

"Well, these are the things you're going to have to know as a nurse! Why wouldn't you give the Motrin to this patient? It's because this patient is also on Coumadin, so you would be putting

288

the patient at risk for internal bleeding, if you gave the Motrin. These are things a senior nursing student should know! I can't believe you ladies don't know this by now!"

That tongue-lashing left Laura asking herself, *If it would be dangerous to give the patient Motrin, then why the hell did the doctor prescribe it*? Laura was slowly going out of her mind. Even when she felt she was having a shining moment as a nursing student, she was reprimanded. For example, she had been caring for a disabled child on her pediatric rotation. The mother mentioned how stressed out she was with all of the expenses. Laura had shared information with her about how she could get diapers paid for through Medicaid, because her son was older than three years. The mother was elated and Laura beamed; finally she felt as if she were really helping. But Laura was chastised, hours later, for "stepping on the toes of fellow staff members" because that information was supposed to be provided by the patient's social worker, not a nurse. With her ego deflated and head hung low, Laura headed home.

For the next several weeks, Laura felt as if all forces in the universe were preventing her from getting that God-forsaken nursing degree. Her responsibilities had begun to feel like too much for one person to handle. She was going to class and doing most of the homework. She was also writing up reams and reams of patient profiles, helping Emily with her homework, making their meals, and cleaning the house. In addition, she was scheduling nurses, therapy sessions, doctors' appointments and babysitters, and packing for the upcoming move. Plus, she was making the table decorations for the wedding by hand (because she couldn't afford to buy them), and she was up every few hours at night with Hannah. Even the weather seemed to be working against her. After tending to Hannah at night, Laura would then head outside to shovel the driveway, because record amounts of snow had fallen that winter, and she couldn't afford to pay anyone to plow.

A few weeks before graduation, Laura reached the breaking point. She nearly flunked out of nursing school. She had been working a clinical shift that included caring for a patient who had diabetes. Laura was supposed to obtain a blood-sugar reading before the patient had lunch, so she delegated the finger poke to a nursing assistant. She failed to track down that nursing assistant to get the results, and totally forgot about it until later in the afternoon when it was almost time to leave.

Laura thought, *Oh, that should be fine; if his blood sugar had been off, surely she would have reported that back to me.*

Laura was mistaken. The reading had been slightly high, and the patient had required a small dose of insulin at lunchtime, which Laura failed to administer. Laura took the patient's vital signs and another blood-sugar reading, which had returned to the acceptable range.

Laura understood she had made a mistake, felt horrible about it, and had learned from the experience. But the instructor insisted Laura should remain there, at the end of the shift, to report the error to the doctor. When the doctor didn't respond to multiple pages, Laura asked the instructor if the oncoming nurse could take the doctor's impending call. The instructor interpreted Laura's request as an anxiety problem related to talking to the doctor. Then the instructor began a strong-worded lecture about Laura needing to take responsibility for her actions. The instructor emphasized that, as a nurse, Laura will have the lives of patients in her hands, and she can't be intimidated by the thought of talking to a doctor.

Laura lost control; she completely blew up. With a red face and stamping feet, she yelled, "You think I'm nervous about talking to some doctor! I talk to doctors every day! And, believe me, I am FAR from being intimidated by them. Way too many times when I've talked to them, I've known they have no idea what they're talking about. I'm not intimidated by talking to some doctor! The patient is fine. I know I did something wrong, but no significant harm was done. I'm simply saying I have to get home to relieve a nurse who is now late getting to her next client!"

The doctor called moments later. He said, "That's fine. Just continue his current plan of care."

What a genius! Boy...I certainly am glad I stuck around for those brilliant words!

Because of her outburst, Laura learned she had to face the nursing-school board. The members of the board were shocked by Laura's behavior, and expressed that her actions were most unexpected from her. Laura apologized, explaining she was under an incredible amount of stress. They decided they would allow Laura to stay in the program, only because she was doing so well in the classes and had demonstrated great talent and skill during previous shifts. With bated breath, Laura squeaked her way through the final few weeks of school.

Graduating from nursing school meant more to Laura than any other milestone she had reached before. She walked out knowing she had put her heart and soul into it. She had pushed herself harder than ever before, and it all paid off in the end. She wasn't even sure if she would use the degree (she still had feelings of lingering discontentment regarding nursing), but those feelings didn't detract from her excitement at the moment she received her diploma.

Laura then focused on the much-more-exciting matters of the wedding and move. She wanted to make the most of the new beginning she was facing by basking in her pleasure. She was so incredibly happy and excited that the entire experience was night-and-day different from her first marriage ceremony. Every aspect of the planning, and every thought about the celebration, came from an entirely new direction and had a completely dissimilar and far-superior touch. While the wedding was budgeted modestly, Laura allowed herself some important splurges. She got the dress she had dreamed of and the cake she had always imagined. She even planned a spa day with Carol and her maid of honor, Faith—her closest companion, confidant, and source of support during many of Laura's most challenging times. Faith had been a fantastic nurse for Hannah, but an even better friend.

On the morning of the wedding, Laura awoke to beautiful sunshine. She breathed a huge sigh of relief, since she had planned an outdoor ceremony. The reception would take place at the same location—a quaint bed-and-breakfast in the picturesque town of Franconia.

Laura could hardly contain herself as she waited for the ceremony to begin. She was exceedingly overjoyed at having the opportunity to say "I do," and time couldn't pass fast enough for her to join Daniel—or rather, reunite with Daniel again. She hadn't seen him since January. After five long months, she missed him terribly.

Then she got the word she had been waiting for; it was time to go. Laura had vastly underestimated the flood of emotion she was consumed by—as she emerged from the house and first caught sight of her family and friends sitting in their seats—all eyes upon her. Emily was walking ahead of Laura, and Will, the best man, was pushing Hannah in her wheelchair—both girls adorned in their beautiful matching flower-girl dresses. Emily was tossing flower petals daintily along the path to the altar. The wedding party was in place and—and there he stood—the man she couldn't wait to spend the rest of her life with. She loved him more than she ever imagined having the capacity to love someone. She clutched her father's arm tighter, trying desperately (but rather unsuccessfully) to hold back tears. Laura had wanted to look her best for Daniel—and not have mascara running down her cheeks when the minister told him to kiss the bride!

Before that day, Laura hadn't ever felt or even understood the sentiment of such a ceremony. A wedding ceremony had always been some formal hodge-podge you had to endure to get to the festivities that followed. The graduation Laura had recently enjoyed served as a small precursor to what she was experiencing here. For the first time, she was experiencing a wedding ceremony that wasn't just a formality; it actually meant something. Now was the time to reflect upon love, as the graduation had been a time to reflect upon accomplishment. She was walking down this path toward her husband-to-be as an entirely different woman from the time they had met. She had learned so much from loving Daniel, Emily, and Hannah. She was now stronger and more courageous because of that love. She loved herself more than ever before, and she had found faith. She didn't think she ever would have guessed before—or even had the ability to understand—how key those ingredients are in a successful relationship. The truth was that she and Daniel had beaten the odds so many times throughout the years. Statistically, they never should have made it as a couple. But not only luck had led them to this moment; their love had guided them there.

The ceremony actually offered some comic relief to Laura's overwhelming sense of emotion. She attempted to soak in every word of the vows that had become so meaningful to her. However, when she and Daniel had to repeat "in sickness and in health," and "for richer or poorer," both Laura and Daniel chuckled softly. Laura quietly murmured, "Health? Richer?" They'd been so happy together, during times of unrelenting sickness and poverty, that she couldn't imagine the bliss they could experience with good health and prosperity.

Laura and Daniel felt the entire day and evening were perfect in every way. They danced. They laughed. They never left each other's sight. Late that night, Laura cuddled into her favorite spot on Daniel's chest as he slept. She smiled as she recalled memories of her time thus far with Daniel. She nearly giggled out loud, thinking back to the Cow Room—the unorthodox starting point of their relationship—and how he had thoughtfully offered her the stuffed cow with angel's wings for Hannah. Now, after so many twists and turns, struggles, and triumphs, he was offering Laura every part of himself for the rest of his days on earth, and she thought how incredibly lucky she was.

Thank you so much for taking the time to read our story. Please remember there are chapter pictures, an epilogue, and much more at http://www.withangelswings.net